THE
POETICAL WORKS OF
RICHARD SAVAGE

The Poetical Works of

RICHARD SAVAGE

EDITED WITH NOTES AND

COMMENTARIES

BY

CLARENCE TRACY

Professor of English in the University of
Saskatchewan

CAMBRIDGE

AT THE UNIVERSITY PRESS

1962

PUBLISHED BY

THE SYNDICS OF THE CAMBRIDGE UNIVERSITY PRESS

Bentley House, 200 Euston Road, London, N.W. 1
American Branch: 32 East 57th Street, New York 22, N.Y.
West African Office: P.O. Box 33, Ibadan, Nigeria

©

CAMBRIDGE UNIVERSITY PRESS

1962

Printed in Great Britain at the University Press, Cambridge
(Brooke Crutchley, University Printer)

CONTENTS

v

vi

ACKNOWLEDGMENTS

FOR advice and assistance on many occasions I am grateful to Professor Allen Hazen, Professor Gwyn Jones, Professor Nicholas Joost, Professor A. D. McKillop, Professor George Sherburn, Mr Michael Shugrue, Professor Ralph Williams, Professor Hermann Tracy, and the late Mr Norman Ault.

Microfilms and photostats have been kindly furnished by the following libraries: The Public Record Office, The British Museum, The Bodleian Library, The Huntington Library, The Folger Library, The Library of the University of Texas, The Newberry Library, Harvard College Library, and Yale University Library. Rare editions have been lent me by the Library of the University of Chicago and Professor Gwyn Jones.

Preparation of the manuscript was made easier by research grants given me at various times by the Universities of Alberta and Saskatchewan, and publication has been generously assisted by the Humanities Research Council, using funds provided by the Canada Council.

C. T.

ABBREVIATIONS

AB	Clarence Tracy, *The Artificial Bastard, a Biography of Richard Savage* (Toronto, 1953).
Account	Samuel Johnson, *An Account of the Life of Mr Richard Savage* (1744), contained in his *Lives of the English Poets*, ed. G. B. Hill (Oxford: Clarendon, 1905), vol. II.
Boswell	Boswell's *Life of Johnson*, ed. G. B. Hill and rev. L. F. Powell (Oxford: Clarendon, 1934), 6 volumes.
GM	*The Gentleman's Magazine*. (Reference is made to issues of this magazine belonging to the eighteenth century in this way: *GM*, 53, 491 means page 491 of the volume of the magazine for 1753.)
Hist. Reg.	*The Historical Register*.
LM	*The London Magazine* (Reference is made in a manner similar to that used for *GM*.)
MP	*Miscellaneous Poems and Translations*, by Savage *et al.* 1726.
OED	*Oxford English Dictionary*.
RS	Richard Savage.

NOTE: The place of publication of all books referred to is London unless a different place is mentioned. Additional bibliographical information is given in the Index.

INTRODUCTION

EIGHTEENTH-CENTURY readers thought highly of Savage as a writer, laying his shortcomings to the charge of his upbringing, his education, and his misfortunes. As a mere boy, known only as the author of some 'treasonable and seditious pamphlets', he was already recognized in Grub Street and employed in correcting the work of a less talented writer of Jacobite propaganda. A few years later, when he had emerged from the underworld, Aaron Hill spoke of his 'genius', painstakingly criticized his work, and helped him get it into print. Pope read *The Wanderer* three times through, liking it better with each reading.[1] And Samuel Johnson, his greatest admirer, described him shortly after his death in 1743 as 'a man whose writings entitle him to an eminent rank in the classes of learning',[2] and bestowed special praise on *The Wanderer*, *The Bastard*, *The Triumph of Health and Mirth*, and the last of the *Volunteer Laureats*. To meet the public demand for his *Account of the Life of Mr Richard Savage*, in which these opinions were expressed, it was reprinted six times before 1781. Meanwhile a selection from Savage's poems appeared, a splendidly printed two-volume collection of his works went through two editions, and his tragedy, *Sir Thomas Overbury*, was successfully produced at Covent Garden with the approval and assistance of the brightest lights of the London stage. In 1781 Johnson incorporated his by now well-known *Account* in his *Prefaces* to the *Works of the English Poets*, allowing it to stand as he had at first written it, where its warm tones contrast with the bleakly judicial judgments passed there on Milton and the Metaphysicals. If Savage had been an early enthusiasm, it was one that he did not grow ashamed of and that he shared with many of his contemporaries.

---

[1] *Account*, pp. 364–5.   [2] *Ibid.* p. 322.

Today the literary world thinks otherwise. Mr T. S. Eliot remarks that his obstacle in reading Johnson's *Lives of the Poets* is that he has not read and cannot be induced to read most of the poets that Johnson wrote about.[1] Consequently for us the *Lives* are apt to be rather a biographical record of the states of Johnson's critical mind than works of criticism. Similarly, Savage is read today, when he is read at all, for the light he throws on Johnson and on the taste of the first half of the eighteenth century. Time has a habit of bringing about such revolutions, and it is unlikely that anybody will read Savage again for sheer poetical pleasure. Yet his historical interest is strong; he is a sensitive weather-vane in the winds of eighteenth-century taste. And it is no small thing to have meant so much as he meant to so perennially interesting a man as Johnson was. Who can say that he understands Johnson who has not read and in his imagination responded to the poetry of Savage? Admittedly, a great deal of it is rubbish, as eighteenth-century readers themselves recognized, but scattered about in his work are evidences of a feeling for language and genuine poetical power. Read altogether, his poetry is the expression of an eager, audacious, and strangely fascinating mind.

One of his earliest admirers called him 'tow'ring *Savage*'.[2] The epithet must have stuck in his memory, for he used it in his own writing with reference both to himself and to his concept of the poet as bard, which has seldom been so unequivocally stated as in the third canto of *The Wanderer*:

> There sits the sapient *BARD* in museful Mood,
> And glows impassion'd for his Country's Good!
> All the bright *Spirits* of the *Just*, combin'd,
> Inform, refine, and prompt his tow'ring Mind!
> He takes his *gifted Quill* from *Hands divine*,
> Around his Temples Rays refulgent shine!   (ll. 191–6)

This is the familiar stereotype of the mad poet whose eye rolls in a fine frenzy. He is an enthusiast: he receives special revelations from heaven (canto IV) and at his death (canto V)

---

[1] *On Poetry and Poets* (1957), p. 163.   [2] 'Clio.' See *MP*, p. 250.

he is instantly transformed into a beautiful seraph clad in regal vestments. In spite of the formlessness and incoherence of the poem, the theme of *The Wanderer* stands out clearly; it is a defence of a concept of the poet that we have grown accustomed to call romantic. The poet is a teacher and prophet, in close touch with the heavenly powers, and inspired by a burning love of his fellow men.

Such a poet is a law to himself. In 'the *Muse*'s airy Clime', writes Savage,

> In measur'd Rounds Imagination swims,
> And the Brain whirls with new, surprizing Whims![1]

Savage himself was much given to 'new, surprizing Whims'. Even his warmest admirers were aware of the weaknesses in form shown in his longer poems; Aaron Hill described one of them, now lost, as 'a wilderness of wit' that needed much pruning and transplanting. He attributed the fault to the exuberance of Savage's imagination. 'Your genius is so greatly indebted to *Nature*', he went on to say, 'that, having heaped all her bounties on you, she will never forgive you the extravagance of spending all her stock, when, by a commerce with *Art*, you may so vastly encrease it.'[2] Certainly, Savage was exuberant. He experimented with metrical forms (tetrameters, ballad stanzas, and other stanza forms, including the Pindaric *à la* Cowley), and tried his hand at various poetical styles, such as those of Young, Pope, Thomson, and even Ambrose Philips. He wrote satires, occasional lyrics, verse essays, character-sketches, erotica, epistles, and long reflective and didactic poems. Admittedly, he failed to develop to perfection any poetical manner of his own, but there is no denying that he was versatile.

Savage's bard is one of 'God's spies', an omniscient being able to see through walls in order to report on the doings of

---

[1] *The Authors of the Town*, ll. 97–8.
[2] Letter to Savage, 3 April 1721. *European Magazine*, VI (1784), 191. The printed text reads 'on her stock', but I have altered it here to read 'all her stock'.

men. Johnson valued Savage accordingly as a 'critick on human life'.[1] The range of his knowledge is impressive; he constantly drops in his verses the names of writers of the past, and quotes from their works—Bacon, Locke, Newton, Spenser, Buchanan, Virgil, Cicero, to name only a few—and he has picked up a great deal of miscellaneous and out-of-the-way information. In particular he had an intimate acquaintance with all ranks of society, from the lowest haunts of the indigent up to the drawing-room of Lord Tyrconnel. The modern reader may not see much in Savage's pictures of upper-class life except reflections of the poet's longing to be accepted in that level of society, but he will associate the best of Savage's pictures of low life with those given in the works of Vanbrugh and Smollett, and perhaps Hogarth and Morland. These occur almost invariably in his satires, which, when not inspired by personal pique, have a rude vigour and unmistakable air of authenticity. The prose *Author to be Let* (1729) is witty and vivid, and exhibits a true picture of Grub Street. Of the verse satires the best is *The Progress of a Divine*. Johnson and many others in the eighteenth century thought it immoral, and it is by no means evenly sustained, but the modern reader is likely to be not so much shocked by it as struck by its earthy vividness.

Even before Savage wrote *The Wanderer*, he, like his 'sapient *BARD*', glowed 'impassion'd for his Country's Good'. His 'Jacobite Poems' were a youthful prelude to his statement in *The Picture* that the ambition of his life was to be fulfilled not in poetry but in action:

> Think not light Poetry, my Life's chief Care,
> The Muse's Mansion is at best but Air!
> Not sounding *Verse* can give great Souls their Aim,
> *Action* alone commands substantial Fame.
> Though with clip'd Wings I still lie flutt'ring here,
> I'd soar sublime and strike the Topmost Sphere.

By action, of course, he meant political action, and he fancied himself in this poem an all-powerful aristocratic minister of

---

[1] *Account, passim.* E.g. pp. 371 and 430.

state ruling his country wisely for its own good. These six lines represent the pinnacle of his arrogance, so far as it was expressed in poetry, but, although he subsequently grew more humble in his language, cancelling in a later edition the last four of the six lines just quoted and throwing in his lot with the Whig panegyrists,[1] his ideal of the public-spirited citizen remained aristocratic. Derived perhaps from the Duke of Rutland and other blue-blooded friends and patrons, it was expressed in haughty terms in sketches like those of Horatius, in *To a Young Gentleman*, *A Painter*, and the three rebel lords who die in the fifth canto of *The Wanderer*, in the third of whom the tragic flaw was excessive love of his country. The ideal dominating his Whig poems, like *Religion and Liberty* and *Of Public Spirit in Regard to Public Works*, in spite of his praise of political liberty and commerce, is that of a prince who builds palaces and founds colleges, who digs canals and opens up harbours, and who actively disseminates civilizing influences from the top down. The nearest Savage got to participation in public life was the writing of these poems, for neither Walpole nor the Prince of Wales, to whom they were dedicated, deigned to acknowledge them or employ their author. Nevertheless, they reveal what is to most readers the best side of his character: his hatred of slavery, his respect for learning, his intelligent interest in planned colonization, his love of peace, and his general concern for public welfare.

Finally, Johnson also commended Savage several times for his originality and power of imagination, speaking of his 'effervescence of invention', praising him for the 'gaiety of ideas' in *The Triumph of Health and Mirth*, and drawing attention to the 'solemn scenes' in *The Wanderer*—particularly the speech of Suicide, which he thought 'terrifick'. Undoubtedly there was vigour and audacity in his imagination, whether he wrote in the major or minor modes, and it is most apparent to the modern reader when his inspiration was

---

[1] Cf. C. A. Moore, 'Whig Panegyric Verse, 1700–1760', *PMLA*, XLI (1926), 362–401.

autobiographical. The macabre episodes in *The Wanderer*, for example, must have been a reflection of his recent dreadful experience in prison awaiting execution, the irrelevance with which the three doomed lords obtrude themselves suggesting in particular that Savage must have been the prey of some sort of compulsion. In fact, his best verse nearly always came from the depth of his egoistic soul. He parades his bleeding heart before his readers' eyes with considerable flair and often with considerable effectiveness. *The Bastard* is one of the most self-centred poems ever written, and it has, both in its 'gayer' beginning and its soberer ending, the vigour and audacity of which I have been writing. The opening lines have often been praised:

> Blest be the *Bastard*'s birth! through wond'rous ways,
> He shines eccentric like a Comet's blaze.
> No sickly fruit of faint compliance he;
> He! stampt in nature's mint of extasy!
> He lives to build, not boast, a gen'rous race:
> No tenth transmitter of a foolish face.
> His daring hope, no sire's example bounds;
> His first-born lights, no prejudice confounds.
> He, kindling from within, requires no flame;
> He glories in a *Bastard*'s glowing name.

* * *

This edition of Savage is a belated fulfilment of a promise made in his lifetime but never kept.[1] In 1734 he printed a proposal for a subscription edition of his works, but Johnson informs us that he was never able to send his copy to the printer and that he spent the money as he received it. But he kept his proposal in circulation, occasionally freshening up its date. In 1737 he reprinted it in the *Gentleman's Magazine* for February, describing the projected collection as his 'Works in Prose and Verse', and promising to include in it 'several Pieces..., humorous, serious, moral and divine, never printed before'. The price was set at half a guinea,

---

[1] For Savage's biography see Clarence Tracy, *The Artificial Bastard, a Biography of Richard Savage* (Toronto, 1953).

and delivery was promised by Michaelmas-Day next. Michaelmas-Day next came and also the Michaelmas-Day following without seeing the publication of the book. But even in 1739, after he had left London for ever, he continued to advertise his subscription wherever he wandered.

He told Johnson that in this edition he would reprint neither *The Progress of a Divine*, which had given offence, nor some of the *Volunteer Laureats*, of which he had a low opinion,[1] and he would also, no doubt, have suppressed the 'Jacobite Poems' and *The Convocation* for political reasons. On the other hand, during the 1730's, he had revised several of his other poems probably in order to fit them for this collection. The first of these revisions, that of *To a Young Gentleman, a Painter*, was done in 1730, and the others during the next six years, viz.: *The Picture*, *The Friend*, *On the Recovery of...the Dutchess of Rutland*, *The Bastard*, *The Triumph of Health and Mirth*, and *The Genius of Liberty*. In revising them, Savage removed the marks of their occasional character and brought up to date the opinions he had expressed in them. In addition to these, he had on hand at least one unpublished poem. Several times he refers to his 'Epistles upon Authors', which he tried in vain to have published in *The Gentleman's Magazine*—rejected most likely because it was too satirical. The previously published but anonymous *Authors of the Town* may have been the nucleus of this poem, and his later poem, *On False Historians*, was almost certainly at one time a part of it. The manuscript, however, has disappeared and along with it all record of what else it contained. As for new prose, he would have had to write it, unless he had written works now unknown —such as a second part to *An Author to be Let* (which he not only promised but advertised) or the projected essay on tragedy mentioned in the preface to *Sir Thomas Overbury*—or unless he meant to include some hitherto unacknowledged anonymous essays published in periodicals like the *Plain*

---

[1] *Account*, pp. 384, 390.

Dealer[1] and the *Grub-street Journal*.[2] The proposal did not promise any plays, and it is unlikely that he would have included his revised version of *Sir Thomas Overbury* before it had been produced on the stage. But no doubt he would have included all his other published pieces.

When Savage died in prison in Bristol in 1743 there must have been some manuscripts among his effects, but, with one possible exception, they do not seem to have been available at first, perhaps because they had been impounded by his creditors. Mary Cooper, the bookseller who beat Johnson into print with an edition of Savage's last poem, *London and Bristol Delineated*, may have got her manuscript of it from Bristol, but Johnson, who must have received a considerable quantity of his biographical materials from Bristol, was able to print no new poems or even to quote from revised texts of old ones. The variant readings which occur in his copious quotations appear to have resulted from lapses of memory.[3] It was not until 1749 that Cave, his publisher, was able to lay his hands on the one manuscript which we know for certain to have existed in Savage's

---

[1] Nos. 101 and 116. Cf. A. D. McKillop, 'Letters from Aaron Hill to Richard Savage', *Notes and Queries*, n.s. 1 (1954), 388–91.

[2] In his dedication to *A Collection of Pieces...on the Dunciad* he denied that he had ever been connected with any journal, and Johnson noted (*Account*, p. 360, n. 2) that he had declined an invitation to join the staff of the *Grub-street Journal*. The initials 'R.S.' often appear in the pages of that journal, but it would be difficult to prove they were intended to designate Savage, who made several contributions under his full name, presumably as a free-lance.

[3] Variants in the quotations in *Account*: p. 48, l. 2. Grows] Shews; l. 11 or] and; p. 59, l. 2 excel] instruct; l. 3 thee] whom; l. 16 charms] sooths; p. 89, l. 6 of] with; p. 91, l. 72 *thou*] then; p. 95, ll. 13–14 Goodness, the Generosity of which] Goodness and Generosity, which; p. 96, l. 26 on] upon; l. 33 into] to; p. 97, l. 9 When] While; l. 13 She flies] I fly; p. 124, l. 123 those] these; l. 124 shall] should; p. 128, l. 265 Happiness] Fortitude; l. 271 low Arts] mean Acts; p. 149, l. 426 Rod] Road; p. 151, l. 484 though] and; p. 152, l. 535 Darkling] Darking; p. 161, l. 14 Wit, Love, Music] Wit, and Music; l. 27 life's the life] life's the Source; p. 162, l. 47 There oft] There of; l. 48 gale] Breath; p. 172, l. 59 whilst] while; p. 227, l. 81 Doors] Gates; p. 241, l. 65 feign'd] fam'd; p. 244, l. 14 *Cases*] Causes; p. 262, l. 25 by] with; l. 32 Grace, and Force] Force and Grace; p. 263, l. 22 the] *omitted*; l. 27 on] *upon*; p. 264, l. 36 came] am; p. 265, ll. 63–4 By means of which natural Defect,] *omitted*; l. 83 (page 59)] *omitted*; p. 266, l. 94 grow] be; l. 111 'em] them; l. 112 but] *omitted*; l. 117 have had me] have me.

effects, that of his play, *Sir Thomas Overbury*. No other manuscripts have since come to light.[1]

Having secured his manuscript, Cave planned to exploit the interest aroused in Savage by Johnson's *Account* (1744) by publishing a volume of his works. In 1753 he published in the *Gentleman's Magazine* a digest of Johnson's biography, intended, as Professor Sherbo has suggested, for advertising, stating in a footnote that he would publish the collection later that year.[2] But he died before he could keep his promise.

In 1761 another bookseller, J. Turner, brought out a badly printed little volume called *Various Poems...By the late Richard Savage, Esq.* which contained only three of the poems—*The Wanderer*, *The Triumph of Health and Mirth*, and *The Bastard*. These were the ones most highly praised by Johnson and the preface to the volume was made up almost entirely of cribbings from Johnson's life. It is very unlikely, however, that Johnson had anything to do with the publication. The editor, whoever he was, was careless: he misquoted on the title-page the title of the second of Savage's poems, though in the preface, where he was plagiarizing Johnson, he managed to get it right. And in the heading to the poem itself, he used still a third variation. Moreover, though he took his text of this poem from the first edition of it, he made changes in order to incorporate some, but not all, of Savage's revisions. Still stranger, he added one variant that seems to

---

[1] Johnson got most of his materials from Edward Cave, who most likely employed an agent in Bristol. In 1749 he received the manuscript of *Sir Thomas Overbury* from Tho. Cadell, a Bristol bookseller, whose name is listed in the Bristol Poll Books at intervals from 1739 to 1781 as bookseller and stationer, and whose account was credited by Cave with five guineas on account of this transaction. John Nichols, *Literary Anecdotes of the Eighteenth Century* (1812), VIII, 415. Frank Baker, 'Thomas Cadell', *Proceedings of the Wesley Historical Society*, XXII (1939–40), 164–8. Cadell had possibly been Cave's agent also in 1743. Perhaps the two-month delay that occurred in the publication of Johnson's *Account*, which was finished in December 1743, was due to Cave's hope of securing other new materials, to compensate for his disappointment over *London and Bristol Delineated*, which had long before been advertised as a particular feature of the forthcoming biography. *General Evening Post*, 25, 27 August 1743.

[2] *Notes and Queries*, CXCVII (1952), 51–4.

have been his own invention: he altered the name of the heroine, called by Savage either 'Tyrconnel' or 'Belinda', to 'Saphira'. This name had appeared in no printed text during Savage's life.

This little anthology is only an unfortunate episode in the process which eventually produced the first complete edition in 1775. Its editor and publisher was Thomas Evans, who dedicated it to Thomas Harris, Esq., in a letter signed 'The Editor', and added an explanatory note signed 'E.' He reprinted Johnson's life, cutting out almost all the quotations from Savage's works, no doubt on the reasonable grounds that they were redundant in a publication in which all of his works were to be included later on. Most important of all, he collected the works which were to be included, missing only a very few pieces now known, such as *The Convocation* and some anonymous ones. The first volume contained Savage's plays, and the second his poems. Evans began by reprinting the contents of *Various Poems*, consequently perpetuating 'Saphira' along with other peculiarities of that text. Next he printed the poems from Savage's separate editions, followed by the ones from *Miscellaneous Poems* and the files of the *Gentleman's Magazine*, in that order, completing the volume by copying *London and Bristol Delineated* from Johnson. Evans's methods of constituting a text were haphazard by modern standards, but not unusual in his time. Most likely it is largely what Savage himself would have done.

This is virtually the end of the bibliographical history of Savage's works, in spite of a surprisingly large number of editions produced in the fifty years after 1775. None of them, so far as I have been able to discover, has any textual importance. Even the volume devoted to Savage in *The Works of the English Poets, With Prefaces, Biographical and Critical, By Samuel Johnson* (1779) is no exception to the rule. It is a reprint of Evans's second edition (1777) with minor adjustments quite within the competence of an eighteenth-century printer. The prose works and plays were of course omitted, and *The Progress of a Divine* was suppressed, probably at Johnson's insistence.[1]

* * *

This edition is based on manuscripts and London editions published in Savage's lifetime or shortly after his death. All the texts used are listed in the headnote to each work, the one reproduced being in each case marked with an asterisk (*). Normally this is the latest text that appears to have had the author's supervision and not to have been merely a reprint, and it is reproduced as it stood. But in four cases—namely, *To a Young Gentleman, a Painter, The Picture, A Poem on the Recovery of the Dutchess of Rutland,* and *The Triumph of Health and Mirth*—I have reproduced instead the earliest text, because these poems are topical and the earliest texts have greater freshness and point. I could see no merit whatever in producing a synthetic text of Savage's poetry, being convinced that the reader has a better chance of understanding what Savage has to say when he reads a text in the form in which Savage actually produced it. However I have corrected a few obvious errors, usually silently, and have regularly expanded the contractions sometimes used by the printers to save space, as well as *tho'* and *thro'*. And I have normalized the use of the question and exclamation marks, and of the apostrophe in possessives, as well as of *ere* and *e'er*. All other emendations and all significant variants between the texts consulted are recorded in the notes.

[1] Cf. *GM*, 79, 599.

CLARENCE TRACY

THE UNIVERSITY OF SASKATCHEWAN

THE POEMS

JACOBITE POEMS

TEXT: *MS, Public Record Office, S.P. 35/7/78.

These five poems were discovered by Professor James Sutherland and described in a letter to the *Times Literary Supplement* (1 January 1938); they are now printed in full for the first time.

The government suspected RS of treasonable activities connected with the Jacobite rising of 1715, and a certain Robert Girling, evidently a spy, sent copies of these poems to the Secretary's office as incriminating evidence, alleging them to be RS's. The following covering letter is preserved with them:

Sr.

All these Maniscripts I Coppy'd from some sent me by Mr. Robert Tooke who tould me he tooke the same Coppy's from the Origanal Maniscript's of Mr. Richard Savage's own Wrighting, and some of these Coppy's I have seen my Selfe, of Mr Savage's own hand Wrighting, which I Know pᵗticulerly well, and the Said Savage was about a Year & half or two Year's ago Pardon'd for Publishing, & being the Author of Several Treasonable & Seditious Pamphlets, But since that has write a great Many More then he did before, and as he himself tould me had Corrected Several pamphlets for one Weston who was Clarke of Gray's Inn, all this I am ready to Make oath of and I beleive Mr. Took will do the Same, Wittˢ. My hand.   Robt. Girling:

The history of the text given above is circumstantial and clear: RS's MSS were copied by Tooke, whose transcript was in turn copied by Girling. But the reason for this devious descent is not easy to understand. Even if the government could not seize RS's papers, there is no apparent reason why Tooke's copies were not used. Internal evidence throws little or no additional light, for most of the peculiarities of the MS are attributable to carelessness, ignorance or the illegibility of the originals. An occasional crux may be the result of oral transmission. On the other hand the reading 'sheer'd' for 'shar'd' in l. 98 of *Britannia's Miseries* indicates careless penmanship. Consequently the text is not sacrosanct. But I have added or altered nothing without giving account of what I have done either in the notes or within brackets, except that I have silently omitted a large number of superfluous apostrophes and expanded all abbreviations. Also I have used discretion with capital letters which in the MS are often not perceptibly different from lower case ones.

Whatever may be the history of the text, there is no reason for rejecting RS as the author. In *The Convocation* and the *Prologue to Henry VI* he echoes the sentiments if not the actual words of the 'Jacobite Poems', and the allusion to Mackartney in *An other* [*Littany*] (ll. 17–18) had a peculiarly personal significance.

Girling's covering letter is dated from its reference to RS's pardon (which occurred in November 1715) as having been granted 'about a Year & half or two Year's ago'; accordingly the letter must have been written in the summer or fall of 1717. Girling's memory, however, must have played him slightly false, for as early as 6 July the government proclaimed an amnesty covering all acts of sedition performed before 6 May 1717 (*Hist. Reg.* 1717, pp. 247 ff.). The letter must have been written earlier. Internal evidence also dates three of the five poems. *Britannia's Miseries* could not have been written before 13 July 1716, for it records the deaths of John Hall and William Paul (ll. 141–6), who were executed together on that day; and it was probably written some time before the end of that year, for it speaks of the fates of many of the lesser prisoners as undecided (l. 148), whereas by 30 November only two were still awaiting trial in Newgate (*Hist. Reg.* 1716, pp. 549–50). *A Littany for the Year* must have been written at much the same time, because of the reference in ll. 11–12 to the sentences passed on the prisoners, especially Derwentwater, and probably towards the end of the year, since it is a series of prayers for the new year. *An other* [*Littany*] was probably written just afterwards, and the reference in it to the light sentence passed on General Mackartney (ll. 17–18) pins both poems down to 1716. In the two remaining poems, *An Ironical Panagerick* and *The Pretender*, there are no definite clues, but the more hopeful tone in which both were written and the obvious purpose of arousing people to action, as well as the hint in the second (ll. 5–8) that hostilities had not yet broken out, suggest that they were written before the rising in the fall of 1715, and certainly before its collapse in January 1716. Consequently they stand here as the first of RS's known works.

[1.] An Ironical panagerick on his pretended Majesty G— by the Curse of G— Userper of Great-Brittan ffrance and Ireland, Nondefender of the faith &c

GEorge looks when he the Name of King assumes,
Like Esop's Jay, drest up in borrow'd Plumes.
All gaze Surprized, to see him thus adorn'd;
By none he's envy'd, but by Princes scorn'd.
Sure with Mock-Titles Fate did him array   5

To make him Thus rediculously gay.
Plac'd on his Brow a Crown of cares and weight,
A pageant Sceptre in his Hand of State.
And what's a Riddle, that you may Explain,
Gave him a Wife, but gave him ne'er a Queen;   *10*
For Prince of Wales adopted him a Son,
Who (like the Crown he wears) is not his own;
And Churchil for his chief Support is given,
The greatest Sycaphant, that's under Heaven;
Who to all Monarchs fawning Homage pay'd   *15*
Sworn to be true to all; yet all betray'd.
O Prince did'st thou but know how thou art Used,
My Heart e'en bleeds to see the[e] thus abused;
O quick ere thou art tost about by Fate,
Recall thy Honour ere it is to[o] late,   *20*
Forsake Ambition and no more be Vain;
Thou art not young—this thirst of Power restrain.
Resign to Royal James what is his Right,
Learn to be Just; lest thou art forc'd in Fight,
Else wilt thou be Disrob'd, as was the Jay,   *25*
Strip'ed of thy Vanities, then turn'd away.
Or Heav'n will Death for thy Ambition send
For Death is Commonly Ambition's End.

9–12 RS repeated the accusation that the Prince of Wales was illegitimate in *An other* [*Littany*], l. 8, and *Britannia's Miseries*, l. 18.
10 but gave] but give *MS*.
23 Royal James. I.e. James Stuart, the Pretender.

[2.] The Pretender

TWo Kings we have, the One is true,
    The other a pretender;
To him, so call'd, is that Name due?
    Or him we call Defender?

2

Pray Justly let's decide the Cause   *5*
    With reason, not the sword;
The latter gives Userp'd Applause,
    The first does Truth afford.

3

Is't he whose Name is George[,] a Wight,
    That proves no Saint at Helm?   *10*
Isn't he that is St. George's Knight
    Our Champion of the Realm?

4

Who can the Former's Right evince?
    From Birth it does not spring:
The latter is our Native Prince,   *15*
    And Born a British King[.]

5

The one to change his Faith A[b]road,
    Pretended to the Nation,
But t'other dares prefer his God
    Before his Coronation.   *20*

6

Isn't he pretended God's anointed,
    Who, by Theft, is Crown'd?
Is he, who shou'd be such appointed,
    Less Just, because Dethron'd?

7

Is he, who makes a Breach of Trust,   *25*
    As property's Defender?
Or he who like his Claim is Just,
    The king or the pretender[?]

---

12 Cf. *Ironical Panagerick*, l. 23.
19 t'other] the t'other *MS*.

8

Can God's be In Rebellion's Voice,
   Or Traytor's Right promote [?]   *30*
If Kings are by the Nation's Choice
   Pray put it to the vote [!]

9

No longer Let us then Miſtake
   The King for the pretender.
Nor the pretender a King Make[,]   *35*
   But Right to right surrender.

[3.] Britannia's Miseries.

O Muse Britannia's Miseries rehearse,
  Whilſt inmoſt Sorrow flows in every Verse;
Mourn her Misfortunes in your pompous Lays[,]
Correct her Foes, and give her Lovers Praise.
Firſt grieve her King's a Royal Exile made,   *5*
Proscrib'd her Patriots and her Church betray'd,
Her laws corrupted, and her Land become
As sway'd by Tyrants was unhappy Rome!
In our Made-King, the Sum of those we see,
The Church her Mother, and her Nero he;   *10*
A greater Parracide, that now is rose,
Owns, to defile, and smiles upon her Foes.
The Skies in Prodigies foretell each Year

6 Proscrib'd] Prescrib'd *MS.*   *8* Rome!] Roome! *MS.*

13 Belief in prodigies and omens was far from extinct at this time. See Gay's
Trivia (1716), Swift's *A True and Faithful Narrative* (1717?), Thomson's *Summer*
(1727), Collins's *Ode on the Popular Superstitions* (1749), and Johnson's *Idler*, No. 10
(1758). Even an educated woman like Lady Hertford found a display of northern
lights disquieting. She wrote to her mother, Mrs Thynne, in 1719: 'I hope you were
not frighted by the lights in the sky. I was so happy as not to see them, but by all
accounts they were very terrible' (H. S. Hughes, *The Gentle Hertford* (New York,
1940), p. 46). The prodigies mentioned by RS are an eclipse of the sun (ll. 15–16),
the freezing over of the Thames (l. 19), a storm (ll. 37–40), a meteor (ll. 125–8), and
perhaps a shower of meteorites (ll. 131–2). Compare *The Wanderer*, III, 80–106.
But see *On False Historians*, ll. 19–28.

New Creuelties for England's Soil to bear.
The Sun at first withdrew his Beams of Light,   15
Whilst the Horn'd Moon o'er shaded us with Night.
But as the Sun exerts its Rays again,
So May the Cuckold Fall, the Monarch reign.
Our Thames foretold, in Icy Fetters bound,
Captivity, that Loyal Heros found.   20
Curst be the days in each Revolving Year[,]
Mark'd may they in the Kalender appear,
When those, who strove their Monarch to Enthrone,
For their dear Countrey's Freedom lost their own:
When Peers and Heros were processions made,   25
And bound like Slaves, in horrid Tryumphs led!
So wou'd Whigg-Wretches, if they had Power, bring
In the Same Ignominious Bonds their King:
Methinks I on the Royal Captives gaze,
And see vile Crouds affront 'em as they pass;   30
Applauding George, and with vail'd Caps prepare,
To hurl his dirty Glories in the Air.
Whilst others Mov'd (as their Concern appears)
At the sad Sight let fall their silent Tears;
But the Brave Heros by their Fates were Made   35
As Much above their Pitty, as their Aid.

15–16 '[April] 22 [1715]. This Day happen'd the most remarkable Eclipse of the
Sun that had been seen in Great Britain for above 500 Years before' (*Hist. Reg.*
1715, p. 56*).
  18 The 'Cuckold' is George I. Cf. *An Ironical Panagerick*, ll. 9–12.
  19 'The Frost, which began the latter End of *November* last, continu'd with small
Intermissions, 'till the 8th or 9th of this Month [February], with greater Severity
than had been known in the Memory of Man. The River *Thames* was quite frozen
up, and abundance of Booths were built upon it' (*Hist. Reg.* 1716, p. 115). Sutherland has pointed out that RS used a phrase from Gay's *Trivia*:

> 'When hoary *Thames*, with frosted osiers crown'd,
> Was three long moons in icy fetters bound.'   (II, 357–60)

23 ff. Cf. ll. 147–8 n.   23 strove] stroove *MS*.
  27 Whigg. The MS clearly reads 'Wigig', which must be a copyist's mistake for
'Whigg'.
  31 vail'd =doffed. Cf. 'His Hat, which never vail'd to human pride . . .' *Dunciad B*,
IV, 205.
  33 their Concern] they Conseirn *MS* (?).

20

When late fierce Winds controul'd each Swelling Wave,
Nor Waters left the Soil or Banks to Lave;
Would Heaven had then to the Userper's cost
Renew'd the Scene of Pharoah and his Host.   40
Britons[,] shall Userpation taint the Throne,
And Make the Land in sad Opp[r]ession Groan?
O think how far sad Poverty's intail'd[,]
Think how Injustice has by Wrongs prevail'd:
Think of Rebellion, how we're Wretched made   45
By Standing Armies and a ruin'd Trade;
Repent your needless, and Rebellious Cares
Of French Dragoons—Imaginary Fears;
Their now as Prophesies revers'd, for such
That's feign'd of them, is real of the Dutch.   50
For Shame, your Native Bravery resume;
Nor let the land their Province thus become.
Has the pure Church so many Martyrs cost,
E'en your King's Life, to be in Ruin lost?
Shall the dear Native Prince from that King sprung,   55
Like age accomplish'd, though in Years, but Young;
The only Relick of the Royal Race;
(Whose Angel's Nature wou'd the Scepter Grace)
Be forc'd to wander through the World forlorne,
And rue the time, He was your Monarch born?   60
O think of Charles, and give the Youth his due,
Think of that King that lost his Life for you.
Think of the Uncle and the Sire Exil'd,
Think of the Unhappy Parents and the child.
Think how the good old King, when he retir'd[,]   65
Griev'd at your Faults in Foreign Climes expir'd.

---

37 ff. Apparently RS is expressing the wish that the king had been drowned,
probably while crossing the channel on his way to Hanover on his first trip home
after his accession. The newspapers of the time, however, made a point of recording
the good weather he had for the crossing (*Daily Courant*, no. 4592, 9 July 1716).
Possibly the emphasis given to it indicates that the Jacobite underground had been
prophesying a disastrous crossing.

50 the Dutch. Whig foreign policy under Stanhope was pro-Dutch, a treaty
having been concluded between England and the States-general in February 1716.

Think of his Widd[o]w and his Orphan left
In Exile wretched, of their Rights bereft:
If e'er the Pious Ann deserv'd your Love,
If your Land's Suffering can your Valour move,   70
Rouse up once More for Royal James's Sway,
St. George in George shall the Land's Dragon slay;
A greater Curse and more tyranick Thrall,
Than Plagues to Pharoah, or to Israel Saul.
See how the Patriots of the Land become   75
Martyrs, if here, or Exiles from their Home.
Ormond[,] that once Preserver of our State,
Like Hannibal, finds Banishment his Fate;
Reduc'd to seek reliefe in Foreign Courts;
There with his Prince in distant Climes resorts.   80
To Carthage Hannibal for Refuge fled,
As Ormond now to Gallia sues for Aid.
The late (curst Sound) his Titles wou'd deface,
And blast the Honours of his Glorious Race.
But though such Heros, like the Stuert's Blood,   85
Are yet for this ungreatful Land too good;
May he at last his Noble Deeds renew,
And with our King Restor'd, our Foes subdue[.]
Great St. John, who in Youthful Glory shone[,]
Nipt in his Bloom (like Ormond) was undon[e];   90
With Mar, who sought his Monarch to restore,
Whilst all in Exile their Land's Ills deplore.
Her Derwentwater's Fate Britannia Morns,
The first and greatest of her Martyr'd Sons.
He from the Royal Martyr did proceed,   95
And in his fall a Noble Stuart Bled.
As Blood of Kings did Radclif's Veins dilate,

---

78 Fate;] Fate. *MS.*   79 seek] such *MS.*
79–80 Cf. Addison's *Cato* (1713), II, iv, 44–5:
          'Reduced like *Hannibal,* to seek relief
          From court to court....'

83 Perhaps the reading should be: 'the State (curst Sound)', the word 'state'
having unpleasant connotations for RS. Cf. Vaughan's 'darksome statesman' in
The World, l. 16.

He shar'd with that his Brave Great Grandsir's Fate.
Who cou'd behold such Noble Virtues fall,
And not (like Brutus) own the Generous Call?   *100*
He scorn'd (when Honour summon'd[)] Friendship's Bond,
And from oppression freed his Native Land.
His Friend he knew not, when a Tyrant grown,
But stab'd that Cæsar that Userp'd the Throne.
Junius Expell'd the Tarquins for a Rape,   *105*
Then shall Userping Villanes Escape?
No, let the Monster's Blood for this attone,
The Whole Mock-Royal Race, that...the Crown
And Heccatombs of those from James the Throne[.]
Be the great Vengeance righteous Ruler's Trust[,]   *110*
For what's now Creuelty, will then be Just.
O George, thy Councels are the Nation's Bane,
Vile Regicides by thy Pernitions reign,
They Murder'd Royal Charles in his great Race again.
But May Blind Fortune to the Right incline,   *115*
And Derwentwater's Fate be Justly thine.
Next Brave Kenmure the Scaffold did Assend,
Great in his Life, and Glorious in his End[.]
The Dying Hero with an Awfull grace,
Smiled on the Fate, which then he cam[e] t'embrace.   *120*
He conquer'd Death, and Bravely made him his,
Looking on Life, but what at best it is,
Given for our Countrey's Service, not our own,
And when that calls, to lay it bravely down.
What Wrath in Heaven we for this Bloodshed find,   *125*

---

98 shar'd] sheer'd *MS.*   108 that...the Crown] *hiatus in MS.*

125–8 'March 6, [1716].... The same Evening, about Eight of the Clock, was seen
a strange *Phænomenon* in the Sky. It appear'd at first like a huge Body of Light com-
pact within it self, but without Motion; but in a little Time it began to move and
separate, extending it self towards the West, where it seem'd, as it were, to dispose of
it self into Columns, or Pillars of Flame: From thence it darted South-East with
amazing Swiftness; where, after many undulatory Motions and Vibrations, there
appear'd to be a continual Fulguration, interspers'd with Green, Red, Blue, and
Yellow, Then it mov'd towards the North, from whence, in a little Time, it renew'd
its wavy Motions and Coruscations, as before, which continu'd to be seen 'till past
Three in the Morning' (*Hist. Reg.* 1716, p. 116. Cf. *ibid.* pp. 217–18). A full account
of this 'strange phænomenon' is contained in the *Philosophical Transactions,* no. 365

In fiery Vapors puffed by ev'ry Wind?
The rolling Flames Whig's Devilish Tryumph bore,
And shew'd their Fate for all this purple Gore.
Next to these Peers the Valiant Oxburgh fell,
Whose Head, o're Death does his great Tryumph tell. 130
The Sky its Glorious Monument appears,
And shews his Vertue's Epitaph in Stars.
Gascoign his copied Fate did soon perform,
An Angel's Soul deck with an Angels Form:
Hereditary Vertue in him Shone, 135
Transmited from each Father to the Son.
The Grandsir's Death for James's Grandsire was,
The Father died for his great Father's Cause.
This laſt for him disdain'd Life's perjur'd Bait,
And greatly chose Submission to his Fate. 140
Next fell Ill fated Ecclesiaſtick Paul,
Of Life too fond; exerted in his fall.
With him great Hall[,] Whig's Envy as our Pride;
Who liv'd an Hero, and a Martyr died.
We in that Noble, Loyal Patriot find 145
A Roman Soul in British Mould inshrin'd[.]
More Loyaliſts too tedious to recite,
In Preſton shar'd and here there Doom may meet.
Thus have they fell for an Userper's Sake
Who fain of Cruelty wou'd Merry make. 150
As he betray'd the Church and Nation's Laws,

(1720), article III, pp. 66–70: 'A Description of the great *Meteor* which was on the
6th of *March* 1715/6. . . .' Lady Cowper also described it and the sensation it caused
in the London streets (*Diary of Mary Countess Cowper* (1864), pp. 91–2. According to
local tradition it was long known in the north as Lord Derwentwater's Lights.
Collins mentions it in his *Ode on Popular Superstitions*, ll. 74–7, but thought it a
display of northern lights. Elsewhere it has been described as a comet. Cf. *The
Wanderer*, III, 80–106.   *129* Oxburgh] Oxbough *MS.*
    142 RS uses the word 'exerted' in the sense of 'brought to light'. 'Of life too
fond; exerted in his fall' means, 'the fact that he was too fond of life was brought to
light in his fall'. Cf. l. 17.
    148 A court martial was held in Preston after the battle, at which the prisoners
holding the king's commission were sentenced to death for desertion. The other
prisoners were taken to London for trial in civilian courts. See the trials in *Hist.
Reg.* for 1717.

24

He'd give them Life to injure there King's cause.
With the vile Bate he'd Loyalty controul,
And save the Body, but Damn the Soul.
O Mercy[,] thou art no More in England bred,   155
But with late Exiles to our Monarch Fled.
In his Sweet Nature you your Self display;
His Soul's your Temple, and your Deed his Sway.
In Royal James your Influence dwells alone,
Then with his Reign adorn the British Throne[.]   160
O Heaven[,] let here the Pious Monarch shine
By Mercy, like the Deity, Divine.
May he reſtor'd, gain Love and true renown,
And Guardian Angels hover round his Crown.
Long May his Hand the British Sceptre sway,   165
Whilſt Subjeĉts love the Monarch they Obey.
And May the Throne ne'er want[,] the Land to grace,
A Royal Offspring of the Stuart's Race.

[4.] A Littany for the Year

FRom all the Mischiefs I shall Mention here
Preserve us Heaven in this approaching Year.
From Civil Wars, and from uncivil things,
That hate the Race of all our Queens and Kings,
From those who for self ends would all betray,   5
From Saints, that Curse, and Flatter when they pray.
From those, that hold it Merit to Rebell,
In Treason, Murder and in Theft Excel.
From those new Teachers, that have diſtroy'd the old,
From those, that turn the Gospel into Gold,   10
From an high Court, and that Rebellious Crew,
That did their Hands in Royal Blood imbrue,
Defend us Heaven, and to the Throne reſtore
The Rightfull Heir and we will ask no more[.]

11–12 RS refers to the trials in London of the Jacobite prisoners taken at the battle
of Preston. Cf. *Britannia's Miseries*. One of the executed prisoners, the Earl of
Derwentwater, had 'royal blood' in his veins; see *Britannia's Miseries*, ll. 93–116 n.

25

[5.] An other [Littany]

FRom each true Sinner and pretending Saint,
From Proteſtants, that as Dissenters Cant,
From Church Defenders, that the Faith betray
And Guides, whose Doctrines lead their Flocks aſtray.
From Iron Rods in ruling Scepters Shewn,   5
From Foreign Tyrants, on the British Throne,
From Those who would the Royal Birth disgrace,
Yet own for Wales, a Prince of Spurious Race,
Against their Monarch for his Faith declare
And for the Vineyarde would deſtroy the Heir.   10
From Christians, who for Murder bid reward,
More for their King, than Jews for Heaven's high Lord[,]
Whose Moderation's by Oppression Shewn,
And Knaves, who Judge each Conscience by their own[.]
From new Invasions, like the old, whose Head   15
Not to feirce Battles, but Surrender led,
From Mercy for Mackartney's Murder found
(For Execution to the Juſt Renown'd)
And last from Whigs deliver us, who bring
Userping Rulers and Abjure their King.   20

---

8 Cf. An Ironical Panagerick, ll. 9-12 n.

THE Convocation:
OR,
A Battle of Pamphlets.

TEXT: *THE Convocation: OR, A Battle of Pamphlets. 1717.

This poem was never reprinted, and copies are now rare. 'As his Judgment ripened,' wrote RS's anonymous biographer in 1727, 'he grew himself ashamed of this Piece, and contributed all he could to suppress the Edition, so that, it having but an indifferent Sale, very few of them are in any body's Hands at present.' Samuel Johnson had not read it.

It must have been written after 29 July 1717, the date of the last of the pamphlets referred to (i.e. Whitby's *Answer to Dr Snape's Second*

26

Letter to the Bishop of Bangor), and before 25 November, when Bishop Hoadly's *Answer to the Representation* came out, a document RS would not have ignored.

The Bangorian Controversy, the occasion of this poem, grew out of the Jacobite rising of 1715–16, and particularly out of the suppression by the government shortly afterwards of the *Collected Papers* of the nonjuror, George Hickes, in which the Church of England was charged with heresy, schism, perjury, and treason. This action occasioned a series of pamphlets culminating in two sensational contributions by Benjamin Hoadly, Bishop of Bangor, leader of the low-church Whig clergy: *A Preservative against the Principles and Practices of the Non-jurors both in Church and State* (1716), and *The Nature of the Kingdom or Church of Christ, a Sermon* (1717). The outraged high-church clergy immediately seized upon these two works and instituted proceedings against their author in the lower house of Convocation, which appointed a committee of nine to bring in a report. The committee sat from 3 to 10 May and presented a strongly worded condemnation, which was adopted by the lower house. But on 17 May, before the report could be forwarded to the upper house, the government arbitrarily prorogued Convocation, and did not allow it to reassemble for synodical business. Prorogation was followed by the furious newspaper, pulpit, and pamphlet war of which RS is historian.

For thee the Prelate will his Church betray.

How's Panegyrick on K. W.

W HEN Vertue's Standard Ecclesiasticks bear,
   Their sacred Robe the noblest Minds revere.
All to its Guidance do their Thoughts submit,
But such who triumph in licentious Wit;
And nauseous Mirth as high Desert esteem,   5
When rais'd by Scorn upon Religion's Theme!
As Kings by Right Divine o'er Nations sway,
As the most worthy, their high Pow'rs obey;
Homage by all is to the Priesthood born,
And none but Fools their Heav'nly Pastors scorn.   10
      Yet censure not the Muse's Freedom here:
If urg'd by Errors, she must seem severe!

Motto: Giles Jacob, *Historical Account of the Lives of the English Poets* (1720), pp. 298–9, mentions a *Panegyrick on King William* among Howe's works, but I have not found a text of it.

Though keen her Satyr, she no Envy bears;
Though Priests she lashes, she their Function spares.
Nor for ill Members such the Clergy calls,   15
But on their Shame, and not their Glory, falls.
   Of all the Plagues with which the World is curst,
Time has still prov'd that *Priestcraft* is the worst.
By some, what Notions through the World are spread?
On Falshoods grounded, and from Int'rest bred;   20
Errour has still the giddy World perplext,
Whilst Scripture gilds it with some sacred Text.
This wild Opinions Strife and Faction brings,
The Bane of Nations, the Misrule of Kings.
Priests oft profane what they from Heav'n derive;   25
Some live by Legends, some by Murders thrive,
Some sell their Gods, and Altar-Rites deface,
With Doctrines some the Brain-sick People craze.
   The Pagan prey on slaughter'd Wretches' Fates,
The *Romish* fatten on the best Estates,   30
The *British* stain what Heav'n has right confest,
And *Sectaries* the Scriptures falsly wrest.
   Amongst the Tribe, how few are, as they ought,
Clear in their Souls, instructive in their Thought!
The Good, like Prophets, shew their Precepts pure;   35
The Ill with Craft the Heav'nly Light obscure;
False to their Trust, they lead their Flocks astray,
And with their Errors cloud the sacred Way.
   Though artless Numbers may my Verses throng,
Yet now Religion's Cause inspires my Song: 40
Undaunted then, my Muse, thy Purpose say,
And for the *Church* thy warmest Zeal display!
An *Erring Prelate* let thy Lays proclaim,
And sing the *Convocation*'s sacred Fame.
   When dire Confusion bore a dreadful Hand,   45

---

17 Compare the opening of *On False Historians*.
  43 ff. Erring *Prelate*. Bishop Hoadly. He is also the 'Learn'd Author' of line 51.
His two 'libels' are identified in the headnote. Pope criticizes him for writing exces-
sively long sentences (*Satires of Dr John Donne*, IV, 73), and so RS's remark about his
style may be ironical.

And sore Divisions shook the guilty Land;
When Schisms rent the Church, Faction the State,
And Schoolmen's Quarrels did new Broils create;
'Midst Crowds of *Libels* publish'd to enrage,
Writ to corrupt, but not t'improve the Age,   50
Forth to the World from a Learn'd Author came
Two, which bear Censures equal to their Fame:
By some admired, and by some contemn'd,
Prais'd by the Vulgar, by his Peers condemn'd.
Some pleas'd with Charms the Syren Stile may give,   55
Regard not Poysons that their Souls receive:
But the sage Brethren lurking Dangers find,
Against the Laws of God and Man design'd.

His first Essay was 'gainst *Nonjurors* wrote,
With equal Spleen and false Quotations fraught;   60
Which shews how easie 'tis in each Dispute,
T' asperse those Reasons which we can't confute.
But why such Treatment does that Clan deserve?
Must they not pray, because they almost starve?
They for their Consciences their *All* have lost;   65
Many, Preferment: Few such Zeal can boast.

59–88 RS is here summarizing Hoadly's first pamphlet, *The Preservative*, but not
very well. Hoadly defended the actions of the government in forcing the abdication
of James II, and then in depriving of their livings all clergymen who would not
take oaths of loyalty to the new king. In support of the second of these points, he
made a distinction between the spiritual authority conferred on a priest by his
sacred office, which the government could not take away, and the right to exercise
that authority in the administration of the sacraments and the performance of other
public functions, which, he asserted, was derived from the secular government.
But his argument was two-edged, for he went on to minimize the importance of dogma
and ordination, asserting that priesthood is an inner and spiritual power conferred,
not by the laying on of hands, but by the grace of God. 'Every one may find it...to
be true,' he wrote, 'that his Title to God's favour cannot depend upon his actual
being, or continuing, in any particular Method; but upon his *Real sincerity* in the
conduct of his Conscience, and of His own Actions under it' (p. 90). He did not,
however, as RS makes out, go so far as to say that Jews and heathens may be saved
merely by virtue of their sincerity. While allowing the nonjurors credit for sincerity,
as RS points out, he condemned them for laying too much emphasis on forms and
doctrines, especially the episcopal succession. Hoadly's sermon on the *Nature of the
Kingdom* is an argument in support of the characteristically dissenting doctrine of the
priesthood of all believers. Since the kingdom of Christ is not of this world, it may
be inferred that Christ did not delegate to any earthly officers or institutions the
absolute right to judge what is true in religion.

God's Fav'rites yet he calls 'em 'cause *sincere*:
A Name he makes *Jews*, *Turks* and *Christians* bear,
Persuasions true, and those which Errors throng,
Sincerely holy, and *sincerely* wrong.   70
Tyrants in Bliss, like Martyrs, shall appear,
'Cause their Ill Zeal is, like the Good, *sincere*!
    Can't the *Nonjurors* then this Favour claim?
Are they Exceptions from its gen'ral Aim?
Shall *Sect'ries*, *Jews*, nay *Heathens* thus enjoy   75
What he wou'd them of Christian Faith deny?
    Another's Conscience, none, he holds, can know;
Why then presumes he theirs to censure so?
If from *Sincerity* Faith aught can claim,
Hard *Deprivations* theirs aloud proclaim.   80
    Next, *Ordination* to explode he seems,
Orders are *Trifles*, Church-Commissions *Dreams*!
The Sense it self these Explanations own,
Which none unbyass'd, can as just disown.
    What more can Deists to the Church reply?   85
They in this wise her Sacraments deny;
Against her Canons and her Forms combine,
And with such Wretches will a Bishop joyn?
    The Topmost Sequel next, of his Essays,
The Pulpit trumpets, and the Press displays.   90
New Doctrines still advanc'd, the World alarm,
And all his Brethren with Resentment warm.
Ye Pow'rs! If Priests thus their own Craft betray,
If what they should conceal, themselves display,
Atheists may well mysterious Rights deride,   95
Nor suffer sacred Faith as Reason's Guide.
    But whilst th' Infection through the Nation flies,
A Rev'rend Author to the Work replies.
Oh *S N A P E*! what Charms thy *Genius* here bestows;

---

79 aught] ought 1717.

99 Andrew Snape's *Letter to the Bishop of Bangor* (1717) was the first important answer to Hoadly. Its tenor is indicated in this sentence: 'I solemnly profess that the whole Drift of your Argument appears, to my View, to be level'd not against any one particular Branch of our Establishment, but against the whole Frame and System

Where nervous Sense in candid Smoothness flows.   *100*
Sublime thy Thought! with no harsh Stile defil'd,
Bold in thy Charge! yet in Expressions mild:
Reason Divine in each illustrious Page,
Points out those Errors, which you here engage.

So *Henry* wrote, by Heav'n inspir'd, when he   *105*
From *Luther*'s Errors strove the Faith to free:
When that great Title in Return was born,
Which has e'er since by *British* Kings been worn.

The Gospel's Light does here such Clouds dispel,
As *Magus*'s Witchcraft by th' Apostle fell.   *110*
So wrote that Tribe in sacred Annals past,
When Nations yielded, and the Faith embrac'd.

The Clergy now in *Convocation* meet,
And in Debate on these new Doctrines sit.
No Contest in th' inferiour House arose;   *115*
But one Consent these dang'rous Errors shews.
None cou'd oppose! So plain did they appear:
Nor Doubts could rise their Innocence to clear.

He, who a Priest, a Prelate's Doctrine blam'd,
Is, now a Prelate, here himself arraign'd.   *120*
He, who did once a worthy Doctor gall,
Finds now just Judgment on his Errors fall.

The first is *Moss* appointed in this Cause;
Who the sharp Charge against this Church-man draws.

---

of it at once: Nay, not only against the Polity of the *Church of England*, but against all Ecclesiastical Polity whatever' (p. 34).

105 The *Assertio Septem Sacramentorum* (*c.* 1521) of Henry VIII was written against Luther. Leo X rewarded him with the title of *Fidei Defensor*.

110 Acts viii. 9–24.

119–22 These lines allude to two earlier controversies in which Hoadly had been involved: (1) with Francis Atterbury in 1706–8 over the interpretation of 1 Cor. xv. 19, and in 1708–10 over passive resistance (*A General Dictionary*, s.v. Atterbury); and (2) with Edmund Calamy in 1702–5 over episcopal ordination and conformity (*ibid.* s.v. Calamy).

123–54 The committee of the lower house of Convocation, under the chairmanship of Thomas Sherlock, reported that Bishop Hoadly's two works tended (1) 'To subvert all Government and Discipline in the Church of CHRIST, and to reduce his Kingdom to a State of Anarchy and Confusion', and (2) 'To impugn and impeach the royal Supremacy in Causes Ecclesiastical; and the Authority of the Legislature, to inforce Obedience in Matters of Religion, by Civil Sanctions'.

31

On his sweet Tongue learn'd Elocution dwells,   125
Which in loud Strains the World their Duty tells.
His smooth Persuasions Men from Ills entice,
Reveal the Gospel, and di[s]pel their Vice.
  Next, Learned *Sprat* in this Performance joins,
Who sprung from a late Pious Prelate's Loins: 130
His Father's Goodness did his Function grace,
And the Son's Vertues do his Footsteps trace.
  Next, Florid *Biss* the glorious Cause maintains,
Who vaſt Applause from juſt Attention gains.
Vert'ous his Soul, his Mind does Wisdom shew,   135
And wholsome Doctrines from his Learning flow.
  Sherlock's a Name that ever will survive:
For the dead Sire does in the Son revive.
Amidſt the Clan, the Son is nam'd t' oppose
The Ill that from such Innovations grows.   140
  Next in the Liſt, but not the leaſt, is *Friend*,
Worthy the Cause now chosen to defend!
Let tutour'd Youth his wondrous Learning prove,
As to the Church his Actions do his Love.
  Cannon and *Davies*, *Barrel*, *Dawson*, ſtand,   145
And act in Concert with this sacred Band.
These, to the Upper House are nam'd to give
The Charge, which there they with Consent receive.
  But ere the Aim of all this Zeal was done,
It here was vanquish'd when 'twas scarce begun.   150
As *Jove* on high *Olympus* feign'd to sway,
With Thunder parted an immortal Fray:
To end the Jarrs that in Religion fall,
GEORGE from the Throne at once prorogues 'em all.
  But thus the Parties, more incens'd with Rage,   155

---

154 Convocation was prorogued 17 May 1717.
155–85 The bibliography of the Bangorian Controversy is large and complicated.
The most complete list of the many publications is that given in the *Works* of Benjamin Hoadly (1773), II, 381–401, but it includes no more than a small number of the
newspaper notices, advertisements, poems, and other minor items. John Philips's
farce, *The Inquisition*, was published in octavo in 1717. According to Baker's *Bio-
graphia Dramatica* (1812), it was never acted, but in the *Post-Boy* (no. 4344, 1 June

Cease not the Contest; but new Conflicts wage.
In Print their Quarrels still confuse the World,
And Libels now promiscuously are hurl'd!
Their Trumpet Scandal loud Detraction sounds,
Diffuses Lies, and Reputations wounds.   160

　　　Thus Paper-Squibs wing'd from the Presses fly!
Alarm! inflame! and loud for Answers cry!
Answers pursue th' Attack! Both Parties write!
Pens are their Swords, and Papers urge the Fight!
The Chiefs with Conduct both maintain the Day;   165
Others confound; but none decide the Fray.
Those best succeed, whose Works the Curious buy,
Whilst Scrawls neglected, on the Compter lie.
But still the Press supplies each empty Brain, ⎫
No *Cyclop* Authors form the Bolts in vain,   ⎬   170
Thence they rush forth, and do the War sustain. ⎭

　　　As thus they 'ngage amidst this Clash of Arms,
Quills, I shou'd say, that thus the Town alarms!
A Minor *Phillips*,* now Romance is scarce,
Seizes Religion, as a Plot for Farce.   175
His Muse grown weary of the *Northern Climes*,
Strives here to raise dull Satyr from the Times.
The High Church now with double Rage he wounds,
Faith serves for Mirth, the Clergy for Buffoons.
Yet the wise Work to aid a *Churchman* means,   180
The aptest Hero for such low-stil'd Scenes.

　　　Demetrius† aims to copy his Design;
Jo's ridicul'd, that *Ben* again may shine.
The worthiest all, the Spleens of Wretches raise,
And Farce to deck the Lawn bestows the Bays.   185

* *The* Inquisition, *a Farce, by* J. Phillips. [RS]
† Joseph *and* Benjamin: *Or, Little* Demetrius *toss'd in a Blanket: a Farce.* [RS]

1717) it was advertised for sale 'as it was Acted at Child's Coffee-House, and the King's
Arms Tavern in S. Paul's Church-Yard...'. Philips had previously written on
'northern subjects': *Earl of Mar Marr'd* (1715) and *The Pretender's Flight* (1716).
Joseph and Banjamin, ANON., was published 13–15 June 1717 by J. Morphew, according
to the *Post-Boy* (no. 4350, 13–15 June 1717), but I have found no record of a performance. Seven answers in pamphlet form to Snape are listed in Hoadly's bibliography for May 1717, all anonymous.

3   33

Libels the *Convocation* now abuse,
Which not worth Notice, wou'd but pall the Muse:
Answers to *Snape* the World's Attention claim;
But pass unheeded, like each Author's Fame.
    B——r's chief Letter bears the great Applause;   *190*
For learning varnishes the vilest Cause;
Oft casts false Beauties, and obscures each Taint,
Makes Right look wrong, th' Offender seem the Saint;
Howe'er through Eloquence there still are view'd,
The Charge evaded, but the Guilt pursu'd.   *195*
    Now *H——dly*'s Text *Trap*'s Genius does convey;
Its Beauties here the Errors there display.
Sherlock, and He, who for the Church appear,
Snape's just Remarks from each Evasion clear.
    Next, *Law*, whose Writing does his Worth proclaim,   *200*
Answers the Doctrines which the World inflame.
His Strength of Judgment their weak Force repels;
Their Errors lashes, their Defence reveals.
    Hilliard, like *Trap*, the Soul's true Guidance shews,
All see the Poyson, and its Cure disclose.   *205*
Cockbourn's Remarks have by Church-Canons prov'd,
How from its Bounds such Heresy's remov'd,
That their own Words against such Guides prevail,
Where Errors drive 'em from its sacred Pale.
    Now from the *Tories* Pamphlets rush apace,   *210*
Answers to *Answers* thus the Contest trace.

---

190 *B——r.* I.e. Bangor (Hoadly). The chief letter is *An Answer to the Rev. Dr
Snape's Letter to the Bishop of Bangor*, published 28 May 1717 (*Daily Courant*, no. 4868).

196 Joseph Trapp's *Real Nature of the Church and Kingdom of Christ* was published
3 June 1717 (*Daily Courant*, no. 4873), but as it had been preached on 19 May, it
cannot have been a commentary, as RS suggests, on Hoadly's *Answer*.

198 *Remarks upon the Bishop of* Bangor's *Treatment of the Clergy and Convocation*, By
a Gentleman. 1717. According to the bibliography in Hoadly's *Works*, it 'is
generally agreed to be Dr Sherlock's'.

200 William Law published *The Bishop of Bangor's Late Sermon*, 13 June 1717
(*Daily Courant*, no. 4882) as well as two later contributions.

204 Samuel Hildyard published a sermon against the Bishop of Bangor, 6 June
1717 (*Daily Courant*, no. 4876, 6 June 1717; and Hoadly's *Works*, II, 381–401).
Perhaps Hilliard is the same man.

206 John Cockburn published *Answers to Queries concerning some important Points
of Religion*, 8 June 1717.

34

In vain with Slander *Whigs* the Truth wou'd foil:
For Scandals back upon themselves recoil!
The *Tories* now their former Pleas enlarge,
And in *Replies* they thus renew their Charge.   215
   By *Quæry* first they urge this strange Mistake:
Can *Ben*'s Resistance passive *Bangor* make?
What *Hoadly* preach'd, thus *Bangor* does evince,
'*Twas lawful to resist a Tyrant-Prince*!
   Here he reviles a King expell'd his Throne,   220
Who for his Conscience sacrific'd his Crown.
Swoln with Preferment thus the Wretch prophanes
The Sacred Reliques with unhallow'd Strains.
Cou'd He no other dark Evasions bring,
But to asperse a poor departed King?   225
   As Conscience-Freedom thus he grants to Slaves,
By Nature thoughtless,—he a King's enslaves.
The Rights of Kingdoms, as he here proclaims,
He those of Christian Faith at once disclaims.
What Charity can suit the Rules he owns?   230
Or Loyalty the Love he bears to Crowns?
Such partial Treatment Sov'reign Rulers braves!
Of Slaves makes Princes, and of Princes Slaves.
   All Earthly Pow'rs he in Christ's Church disowns,
Regardless of his Function, or of Crowns.   235
Why is the King its great Supreme no more?
Why is the Pow'r from God's Vicegerent tore?
   In vain false Logic thus at Truth wou'd aim,
To prove Christ's Kingdom and his Church the same;
Heathens and Devils then Church-Members are,   240

216–51 I have been unable to identify this pamphlet. Ll. 216–19 refer to Hoadly's
earlier controversy with Atterbury over passive resistance (see ll. 119–22 n.),
Quæry evidently maintaining that the Whig policy, though it originated in open
opposition to James II, was really only a passive resistance. In ll. 238–41 RS refers
to the point originally made by Hoadly in his sermon on *The Nature of the Kingdom or
Church of Christ*, and attacked by the Tories, that the Kingdom of Christ is his Church;
and in ll. 242–51 he brings out another point, for which the Tories violently attacked
Hoadly, i.e. that prayer should be a 'calm and undisturb'd Address to God' (see
Snape's *Letter to the Bishop of Bangor*, pp. 10–11 and Bishop Hoadly's *Answer to the
Rev. Dr Snape*.)

'Cause they Subjection to his Kingdom bear.
Why a *cold*, *lifeless* Motion is Pray'r made?
The World's great Saviour sweated as he pray'd.
   An eager Zeal we in the Garden find,
Which on the Cross possess'd his anxious Mind;   *245*
Exerted Transports in his Accents hung,
And flow'd with Fervour from his Heav'nly Tongue.
      When on our Knees to Heav'n's high Throne we bow,
Love, as inspir'd, shou'd purest Raptures shew.
The Soul exerted, shou'd each Wish impart,   *250*
And for its Off'ring throw a contrite Heart.
      Whilst thus these Errors Churchmen all explode,
And clear the Vapours which the Faith wou'd cloud;
Snape, who to head the Van did first appear,
With equal Conduct now commands the Rear!   *255*
His second *Answer*'s for th' Engagement chose,
Which does the Prelate's weak *Defence* expose.
      This, which his Plea does of its Force despoil,
No Pen can answer, nor Resistance foil.
When Truth thus sallies forth, Evasions all   *260*
Start from the Conflict, and confuted fall.
In vain new Pamphlets to their Rescue run,
Their Chief retreats, the Vict'ry is begun:
Those, who the Church against its Foes maintain,
Beneath its Banners thus the Glory gain.   *265*
      But still their Pride will not the Conquest yield,
Like Wasps disarm'd, they buz around the Field;
Or, from the Press, whilst envious Nonsence springs,
They hiss, like Serpents that have lost their Stings.
      Behold! They drop the Theme they can't oppose,   *270*

---

254 Snape's *Second Letter to the Lord Bishop of Bangor*, 28 June 1717 (*Daily Courant*, no. 4895).

270 ff. In his *Second Letter* Snape asserted that Hoadly had originally written his sermon in less carefully guarded language than that which appears in the printed text, and that he had consulted 'a certain Person' who persuaded him to introduce quali-fications. This charge gave rise to a long series of advertisements and letters which

And *Advertisements* their Retreat disclose.
With Aims evasive seem to swell the News,
And what shou'd Glorious be, to *Farce* reduce.
    Now the *Courant* for War is made the Plain,
Where *B—g—r* pours forth all his Force again.   *275*
Howe'er ill poſted, yet more desp'rate grown,
To guard this Breach, his Reputation's thrown!
His Pen with Fury does *Snape*'s Strength assail.
He charges!—True: But does that Charge avail?
    Carlisle here seconds *Snape*! The Plea maintains!   *280*
Whilſt baneful Discord 'twixt each Prelate reigns.
If, as *Church-Pillars* we the Mitres ſtile,
Tott'ring by Jarrs they shake the sacred Pile!
Errors ſtart up! whilſt weak the Structure ſtands,
And Factions rage, as in divided Lands!   *285*
Altars 'gainst Altars rise! Confusions spring!
And a long Train of endless Horrors bring.
    Fierce Advertisements now i' th' News are seen
From these two B——s and a trifling D——.
With zealous Warmth each in the Conteſt burns,   *290*
Whilſt from the Truth the D——n Deserter turns.
    Carlisle then quits the Plain, whilſt neither yield,
And urges *Bangor* to a nobler Field:
Nor for his Standard Advertisements rears!
But in a Stile more Glorious now appears.   *295*
Still in Retreat *Bangor* his Flag displays,
And fiercer Vollies from the News conveys.
By *Kennet* ſtrengthen'd, in Opinion high,
He does the Foe with future Deeds defie!
    When in his Hand he shall the Pencil bear,   *300*

---

appeared in the press between 28 June and 15 July 1717:—*Daily Courant, Post-Boy, The Evening Post,* and *St James Evening News.* The Bishop of Carlisle was involved as endorser of the accusation, and the Dean of Peterborough (White Kennett) as the 'certain Person' (these are the 'two B[ishop]s and a trifling D[ean]' of l. 289). The Dean, however, quarrelled with the Bishop of Carlisle, disclaiming any knowledge of the facts, and so eventually the storm blew over. 5 July 1717 the Bishop of Carlisle published *A Collection of Papers scattered lately about the Town in the* Daily Courant, etc. *with some Remarks upon them.*

The Victor's Honours in the Draught he'll wear.
How can true Colours then the Work assure,
If Him they flatter, Them in Shades obscure?
    What can these prove, but mere Evasions all?
Which quit the Contest, and on Trifles fall?   *305*
Snape's heavy Charge as yet unanswer'd stands,
And either Vict'ry or Defence demands!
    Now from a Party Clamours rise in vain
Against *Carlisle*, who does his Plea maintain,
Spite of the D——n, who in Desertion flies,   *310*
And *Peter* like, what once he own'd, denies.
    Truth is the Bulwark thus keen Envy storms!
The *Dæmon* rages deck'd in various Forms.
Here, like a Churchman, dress'd in sacred Stile,
With smooth Corruptions she'd the World beguile, *315*
And seem t'advance the Church, whilst she'd ensnare
Its Rites, its Orders, and Foundation, *Pray'r*.
    Next Politician like, she'd raise Debate,
To bring the Faith subservient to the State;
Like a false Light, their black Designs to gild,   *320*
Or Ground, on which vile Policies she'd build.
    Lastly, In Slander cloath'd, she sallies forth
To blast those Fames that bear the noblest Worth!
In this black Form the Fiend each Libel shews,
Which fiercely arm'd 'gainst *Snape* or *Carlisle* goes!   *325*
Here against *Trap*! From *Sykes* 'gainst *Sherlock* there,
Where *Bangor*'s Postscript does its Aid declare.
    'Gainst thee, O *Sherlock*! Such Efforts are vain:
They but asperse what they can never stain.
Thy Foes augment by Scandal, Crimes they'd clear,   *330*
As their black Charge thy Vertue scorns to bear!
Thy Strength of Reason stems the rapid Course,
And rowls it backwards with resistless Force.

---

326 Gilbert Burnet, *A Letter to the Rev. Mr Trap, occasioned by his Sermon* (2nd ed. 1717). Arthur Ashley Sykes, *A Second Letter to Dr Sherlock...with a Postscript to the Rev. Dr Sherlock...*by Benjamin Hoadly, 12 July 1717 (*Daily Courant*, no. 4907). There was a further pamphlet later from each of Sykes and Sherlock.

Next *Whitby* seems (as he'd *Snape*'s Worth oppose)
Weak as the Cause in which Defence he rose.   *335*
    As Frantick *Dunton* with the Tribe combines,
Th' Ecclesiaſtick with the Madman joins.
Pardon the Muse that on such Trifles dwells,
One shews his Weakness, one his Phrenzy tells!
As These, so Others, such Essays have made,   *340*
Who, like their Chief, not answer,—but *evade*.
    How can Divines here seem to give Applause,
Where Heresies support the impious Cause?
A Cause, which on the Church's Triumph frowns,
And levels Mitres, as Resiſtance crowns.   *345*
Enthusiaſts, Sect'ries, here with Aid supply,
And wing'd like Serpents, at our Altars fly!
But o'er these Fiends the Faith at length shall reign,
Which *Worthies* thus with bright Essays suſtain!
    Hear then, ye Pow'rs; on your own *Works* look
        down!   *350*
Where are your Rites, when Supplication's gone?
Who shall your Altar's Sacraments prepare,
If Pious Zeal's depriv'd of *Fervent Pray'r*?
Who at the *Throne of Grace* shall Homage pay,
If your own Prieſts their sacred Truſt betray?   *355*
Assiſt! inspire! and with a light Divine,
Now let the Faith from Clouds in Glory shine!
    Oh *Snape*! Assert! Pursue the sacred Cause!
Improve the Soul! Defend the *Church*'s Laws!
Still to thy Aid the sacred Scriptures bring,   *360*
Whilſt Brighteſt Youths from thy Tuition spring!

---

334 Daniel Whitby, *An Answer to Dr Snape's Second Letter to the Bishop of Bangor*,
published 29 July 1717 (*Daily Courant*, no. 4921). He wrote a second pamphlet in
1718.

336 John Dunton probably published anonymously *The Pulpit-Lunaticks, or a
mad answer to the m[ad Report] made by a Committee of Mad Prie[sts upon?] Benjamin,
Lord Bishop of Ba[ngor], etc.* In his *Hanover-Spy* (1718) Dunton complains that he had
not been suitably rewarded by the ungrateful government for his assistance 'at a
Time when the Spotless Honour and Veracity of the Bishop of *Bangor* was
aspers'd...' (p. 10).

They, as Examples, shall thy Worth proclaim,
And to Time's End shall consecrate thy Fame!
The *Convocation* may to joyn thee meet;
And what's so well begun, as well compleat.   *365*

A POEM ON THE Memory of Mr. KEENE.

TEXT: *MEMOIRS OF THE LIFE OF Mr. *THEOPHILUS KEENE*,
The late Eminent TRAGEDIAN. To which is added, ELEGIES,
PASTORALS, ODES, and POEMS: *By several Hands*..., 1718.

This rare volume, published 16–23 August 1718 (according to the
Original Weekly Journal), contains an anonymous life of Keene and a
number of memorial poems, one of them signed 'Richard Savage'.
The publisher of the volume, William Rufus Chetwood, who was a
friend of RS, wrote that the life was also by him (*A General History of
the Stage* (Dublin, 1749), p. 180). RS probably became acquainted with
Keene at the theatre during 1717–18, perhaps through Christopher
Bullock or Aaron Hill.

VAIN and uncertain is this mortal State,
  Life's ever subject to the Storms of Fate.
When our good Genius wou'd our Actions view,
Some envious Planet sheds its baleful Dew:
Infectious Plagues forth from *Pandora* flye!   *5*
For Life's but giv'n to learn us how to Die.
Death here an universal Tyrant Reigns,
And ev'ry Station must receive his Chains.
The Stoick's Vertue, nor the Statesman's Art,
Nor Warriour's Courage can resist his Dart;   *10*
The Fair one's Beauty, and Physician's Skill
In vain Oppose him, they his Sting must feel.
All Lives a-like are destin'd to the Grave,
The Wise, the Weak, the Monarch, and the Slave;
But Fate the Best first to Destruction calls,   *15*
And Wretches Flourish whilst true Vertue falls.
    IN such an Age *Keene*'s happier Soul is gone!
With Angel's Wings 'tis from his Bosom flown!

The Tragick Muse her Debt of Sorrow pays,
And at his Hearse attempts his Deathless Praise; *20*
He, whose juſt Action and whose skilful Tongue
So oft have Grac'd what She triumphant Sung.
Majeſtick roughness in his Form was seen,
And *Roman* Grandeur dress'd his aweful Mien!
His manly Voice the *British* Genius fir'd, *25*
And *Albion*'s Youth with glorious Thoughts inspir'd.
    Whilſt Sorrow's mournful Note his *requiem* Sings,
The chearless Muses flag their drooping Wings.
With *Cypress* Crown'd they all his Fate deplore,
Weep at his Loss, and Sigh he is no more. *30*
    OH! Why must He, who so much worth reveal'd,
Thus to blind chance his Life a Victim yield?
But Time has shew'd in a preceeding Age
The Ruins of the Fam'd *Athenian* Stage;
And Death has in a different Series view'd *35*
Roscius and *Betterton* a-like Subdu'd.
    YET ſtill my Muse *Keene*'s hapless *Exit* Mourn,
And drop a Tear upon his peaceful Urn.
The *Bays* shall rooted in his Ashes grow,
And on his Tomb a deathless Verdure show. *40*
Whilſt to his Fame the Muse shall Yearly pay
An ODE, as to her own *Cecilia*'s Day.

An EPISTLE *to Mrs.* OLDFIELD *of the* Theatre Royal.

TEXTS: (1) *MP* (1726), pp. 187–90.
    (2) FAITHFUL MEMOIRS OF THE LIFE, Amours *and* Performances, OF That justly CELEBRATED, and most Eminent ACTRESS of her Time, Mrs. *Anne Oldfield*....By WILLIAM EGERTON, Esq;... MDCCXXXI. (Evidently copied from *MP*.)

In the *Faithful Memoirs* of Mrs Oldfield the information is given that this poem was 'occasioned by' Mrs Oldfield's 'Playing CLEOPATRA in *All for Love*'. This play was revived, after a lapse of twelve years, on 3 December 1718, and was acted at least once a season afterwards for many years. Consequently, the date of the poem must be 1718.

41

WHile to your Charms unequal Verse I raise,
Aw'd, I admire, and tremble as I praise.
Here Art and Genius new Refinement need,
Lift'ning, they gaze, and, as they gaze, recede!
Can Art, or Genius, or their Pow'rs combin'd,   5
But from *corporeal Organs*, sketch the *Mind*?
When *Sound* embody'd can with *Shape* su[r]prize,
The Muse may emulate your Voice and Eyes.
      Mark rival Arts Perfection's Point pursue!
Each rivals Each, but to excel in You!   10
The *Bufte* and *Medal* bear the *meaning Face*,
And the proud *Statue* adds the *Pofture*'s Grace!
Imag'd *at length*, the bury'd *Heroine*, known,
Still seems to wound, to smile, or frown in Stone!
As Art wou'd Art, or Mettal Stone surpass;   15
Her Soul ftrikes, gleaming, through *Corinthian* Brass!
Serene, the *Saint* in smiling Silver shines,
And *Cherubs* weep in Gold o'er sainted Shrines!
If long-loft Forms from *Raphael*'s Pencil glow,
Wondrous in Warmth the mimic Colours flow!   20
Each Look, each Attitude, new Grace displays;
Your Voice and Motion Life and Music raise.
      Thus *Cleopatra* in your Charms refines;
She lives, she speaks, with Force improv'd she shines!
Fair, and more fair, you ev'ry Grace transmit;   25
Love, Learning, Beauty, Elegance, and Wit.
Cæsar, the World's unrival'd Mafter, fir'd,
In her Imperial Soul, his Own admir'd!
Philippi's Victor wore her winning Chain,
And felt not Empire's Loss in Beauty's Gain.   30
Cou'd the pale Heroes your bright Influence know,
Or catch the silver Accents as they flow,
Drawn from dark Reft by your enchanting Strain,
Each Shade were lur'd to Life and Love again.
      Say, sweet Inspirer! were each Annal known,   35
What living Greatness shines there not your Own?
If the griev'd Muse by some lov'd Empress rose,

New Strength, new Grace, It to your Influence owes!
If Pow'r by War diſtinguish'd Height reveals,
Your nobler Pride the Wounds of Fortune heals!   *40*
Then cou'd an *Empire*'s Cause demand your Care,
The Soul, that *juſtly thinks*, wou'd *greatly dare*.

    Long has *feign'd Venus* mock'd the Muse's Praise,
You dart, divine *Ophelia*! *genuine* Rays!
Warm through those Eyes enliv'ning Raptures roll!   *45*
Sweet through each ſtriking Feature ſtreams your Soul!
The *Soul*'s bright *Meanings* heighten *Beauty's Fires*:
Your Looks, your Thoughts, your Deeds, each Grace
      inspires!

    Know then, if rank'd with Monarchs, here you ſtand,
What Fate declines, you from the Muse demand!   *50*
Each Grace that shone of Old in each fam'd Fair,
Or may in Modern Dames Refinement wear;
What-e'er juſt, emulative Thoughts pursue,
Is all *confirm'd*, is all *ador'd* in *You*!
If Godlike Bosoms pant for Pow'r to bless,   *55*
If 'tis a Monarch's Glory to redress;
In conscious Majeſty you shine serene,
In Thought a Heroine, and in Act a Queen.

44–5 The meaning is that Mrs Oldfield not only has acted the role of mistress to
an emperor on the stage, but also, like Ophelia, has loved a prince in real life. Cf.
Wanderer, v, 61. The author of the *Faithful Memoirs* translated some lines from
Menander in her honour, and in them substituted the name of Ophelia for that of
Thestylis, 'not only because it runs smoother in our *English* versification; but for
another Reason which I flatter myself will be obvious to every Reader' (p. 156).

To Mrs. ELIZ. HAYWOOD,
ON HER NOVEL CALL'D *LOVE* in
EXCESS, &c.

TEXT: *LOVE in Excess; OR THE FATAL ENQUIRY, A
NOVEL. Part the Second....By Mrs. Haywood...[?1720].

The existence of this poem was pointed out by G. F. Whicher in his
Life and Romances of Mrs Eliza Haywood (New York, 1915), pp. 15–16 n.

It appears at the beginning of the second instalment of the novel. The first instalment, according to Whicher, came out towards the end of 1719, and the third was advertised as published in *Daily Post*, 26 February 1720. Consequently the second was most likely published early in 1720. RS's poem was reprinted in succeeding editions of the novel, of which there appear to have been five, in addition to collected editions of Mrs Haywood's works. RS himself did not reprint it, and it was unknown to the editors of his *Works*.

FAIN wou'd I here my vaſt Ideas raise,
To paint the Wonders of *Eliza's* praise;
But like young Artiſts where their ſtroaks decay,
I shade those Glories which I can't display.
Thy Prose in sweeter Harmony refines,   5
Than Numbers flowing through the Muse's Lines;
What Beauty ne'er cou'd melt, thy Touches fire,
And raise a Musick that can Love inspire;
Soul-thrilling Accents all our Senses wound,
And ſtrike with softness, whilſt they Charm with sound! 10
When thy COUNT pleads, what Fair his Suit can flye?
Or when thy Nymph laments, what Eyes are dry?
Ev'n Nature's self in Sympathy appears,
Yields Sigh for Sigh, and melts in equal Tears;
For such Descriptions thus at once can prove   15
The force of Language, and the sweets of Love.
    The Myrtle's Leaves with those of Fame entwine,
And all the Glories of that Wreath are thine!
As Eagles can undazzl'd view the Force
Of scorching *Phœbus* in his Noon-day Course,   20
Thy Genius to the God its Luſtre plays,
Meets his Fierce Beams, and darts him Rays for Rays!
Oh glorious ſtrength! Let each succeeding Page
Still boaſt those Charms and luminate the Age:
So shall thy beamful Fires with Light divine   25
Rise to the Spheres, and there triumphant shine.

An APOLOGY *to* Brillante,

for having long omitted writing to her in Verse.
In Imitation of a certain Mimic of Anacreon.

TEXT: *MP (1726), pp. 174–5.

The table of contents in *MP* supplies the information that the 'certain Mimic' or 'Ape' of Anacreon was Ambrose Philips, who contributed five imitations of Anacreon to the *Freethinker* in 1721. Cf. *The Authors of the Town*, l. 129. RS's poem, which was most likely written in the same year, does not appear to have been an imitation of any one poem by Philips, but it uses the seven-syllable line of which Philips was fond, and his trick of repetition.

Can I matchless Charms recite?
  Source of ever-springing Light!
Cou'd I count the vernal Flowers,
Count in endless Time the Hours;
Count the countless Stars above,   *5*
Count the captive Hearts of Love;
Paint the Torture of his Fire,
Paint the Pangs those Eyes inspire!
(Pleasing Torture, thus to shine,
Purified by Fires like Thine!)   *10*
Then I'd ſtrike the sounding String!
Then I'd thy Perfeƈtion sing.
    Myſtic World!—Thou *something More!*
Wonder of th'Almighty's Store!
Nature's Depths we oft descry,   *15*
Oft They're pierc'd by *Learning's Eye;*
Thou, if *Thought* on *Thee* wou'd gain,
Prov'ſt (like Heav'n) Enquiry vain.
Charms unequall'd we pursue!
Charms in shining Throngs we view!   *20*
Number'd then cou'd *Nature's* be,
Nature's self were *poor* to *Thee.*

To the Right Honourable BESSY Countess of ROCHFORD
(Daughter of the late Earl RIVERS)
when with Child.

TEXT: *MP (1726), pp. 282–5.

Bessy Savage, illegitimate daughter of Richard Savage, Earl Rivers, was married in 1714 at the age of fifteen to Frederick Nassau-de-Zulestein, third Earl of Rochford. She had two children, William Henry, the fourth earl (b. 1717), and Richard Savage de Zulestein, who was probably born in 1723 (G.E.C., *Complete Peerage* (1895), VI, 383, says that he was 57 when he died in 1780). RS's poem, then, must have been written in 1723, during her second pregnancy. She was most likely the sister of whom RS wrote to Aaron Hill in 1724, complaining of 'her silence and behaviour' (*European Magazine*, VI (1784), 194).

AS when the Sun walks forth in flaming Gold,
Mean Plants may smile, and humble Flow'rs unfold.
The low-laid Lark the distant Æther wings,
And, as she soars, her daring Anthem sings!
So when thy Charms cœlestial Views create,   *5*
My smiling Song surmounts my gloomy Fate!
Thy *Angel-Embryo* prompts my tow'ring Lays,
Claims my fond Wish, and fires my future Praise!
May It, if *Male*, its *Grandsire's* Image wear!
Or in its *Mother's* Charms confess the *Fair*!   *10*
At the kind Birth may each mild Planet wait!
Soft be the Pain, but prove the Blessing Great!
    Hail *Rivers*! Hallow'd Shade! descend from Rest!
Descend and smile, to see thy *Rochford* blest!
Weep not the Scenes through which my Life must run,   *15*
Though Fate, fleet-footed, scents thy languid Son!
The Bar that, dark'ning, cross'd my crested Claim,
Yields at Her Charms, and brightens in their Flame:
That Blood, which, honour'd, in thy *Rochford* reigns,
In cold, unwilling Wand'rings trac'd my Veins!   *20*
Want's wint'ry Realm froze hard around my View!
And *Scorn's* keen Blasts a Cutting Anguish blew!
To such sad Weight my gath'ring Griefs were wrought,

Life seem'd not Life, but when convuls'd with Thought!
Decreed beneath a Mother's Frown to pine,   25
Madness were Ease to Mis'ry form'd like Mine!
　　Yet my Muse waits thee through the Realms of Day,
Where lambent Light'nings, round thy Temples play!
Sure my fierce Woes, will, like those Fires, refine,
Thus lose their Torture, and thus glorious shine!   30
And now the Muse Heaven's milky Path surveys,
With thee, 'twixt pendant Worlds it wond'ring strays!
Worlds! which, unnumber'd as thy Vertues, roll
Round *Suns!*—fix'd, radiant Emblems of thy *Soul!*
Hence Lights refracted run through distant Skies,   35
Changeful on Azure Plains in quiv'ring Dies!
So thy Mind darted through its Earthly Frame,
A wide, a various, and a glitt'ring Flame.
　　Now a New Scene Enormous Lustre brings!
Now Seraphs shade thee round with Silver Wings!   40
In Angel-Forms thou see'st thy *Rochford* shine!
In each sweet Form is trac'd Her beauteous Line!
Such was her Soul, ere this selected Mold
Sprung at thy Wish, the sparkling Life t' infold!
So amidst Cherubs shone her Son refin'd,   45
Ere Infant-Flesh the new-form'd Soul enshrin'd!
So shall a sequent Race from *Rochford* rise,
The World's fair Pride—Descendants of the Skies.

VERSES *sent to* AARON HILL, *Esq;*
with the Tragedy *of* Sir Thomas Overbury, *expecting him to correct it.*

TEXT: *MP* (1726), pp. 77–8.

Sir Thomas Overbury was produced at Drury Lane Theatre on 12 June
1723 (J. Genest, *Account of the English Stage*, III, 106–9). Since this
poem is a request for help in getting the manuscript into final shape,
it must also have been written in 1723. In the 'Advertisement' to the

play RS thanked his 'Best and Dearest Friend, Mr *Aaron Hill*, for his many judicious Corrections in this Tragedy'. Hill also supplied a prologue and an epilogue.

I

A S the Soul, stript of mortal Clay,
    Grows all divinely fair,
And boundless roves the milky Way,
    And views sweet Prospects there.

II

This Hero, clogg'd with drossy Lines,   5
    By thee new Vigour tries;
As thy correcting Hand refines,
    Bright Scenes around him rise.

III

Thy Touch brings the wish'd Stone to pass,
    So sought, so long foretold;   10
It turns polluted Lead, or Brass,
    At once to purest Gold.

PROLOGUE,

Spoken at the Revival of Shakespear's King Henry *the* VIth, *at the* Theatre Royal *in* Drury-Lane.

TEXTS: (1) KING *HENRY* VI. A TRAGEDY. As it is Acted at the Theatre-Royal in *Drury-Lane*....*Altered from* SHAKESPEAR, *in the Year* 1720, By *THEOPHILUS CIBBER*.... The SECOND EDITION. ...1724.
    (2) *MP* (1726), pp. 86–7.

This play was revived on 5 July 1723, during the summer season, with RS acting the role of the Duke of York (J. Genest, *Account of the English Stage*, III, 110). The *Daily Post* for that day announced that there was a new prologue, but did not mention the poet's name. This prologue was first printed in the second edition of the play, where RS's name was again not given. Angered, no doubt, by these slights, RS, when he printed the prologue in *MP*, wrote under the title: 'Printed before the Play from a spurious Copy.'

TO Night, a patient Ear, ye *Britons* lend,
    And to your great Forefathers' *Deeds* attend.
Here cheaply warn'd, ye blest Descendants view,
What Ills on *England*, Civil Discord drew.
To wound the Heart, the martial Muse prepares;   5
While the red Scene with raging Slaughter glares.
    Here, while a Monarch's Suff'rings we relate,
Let gen'rous Grief his ruin'd Grandeur wait.
While *Second Richard*'s Blood for Vengeance calls,
Doom'd for his Grandsire's Guilt, poor *Henry* falls. 10
In Civil Jars avenging Judgment blows,
And Royal Wrongs entail a People's Woes.
Henry, unvers'd in Wiles, more Good than Great,
Drew on by Meekness his disastrous Fate.
    Thus when you see this Land by Faction tost, 15
Her Nobles slain, her Laws, her Freedom lost;
Let this Reflection from the Action flow,
We ne'er from Foreign Foes could Ruin know.
Oh let us then intestine Discord shun,
We ne'er can be, but by Ourselves, undone.   20

3-4 Cf. Addison's *Cato* (1713), v, iv, 112–13:
    'From hence, let fierce contending nations know
    What dire effects from civil discord flow.'

4 Discord] Discords *1724*.
5 martial] warring *1724*.
6 Cf. *To a Young Gentleman, a Painter*, l. 26.
11 Civil Jars] Storms of Wrath, *1724*.

18–20] That Foreign Foes could never make us bow. / While to our selves w'are true, The World must own, / *England* can never be, but by her Self, Undone. *1724*.

To Mrs ELIZA HAYWOOD,
on her NOVEL, call'd, The Rash Resolve.

TEXTS: (1) [Eliza Haywood, *The Rash Resolve*, etc., 1724 (published December 1723). Not seen.]
  (2) *Applebee's Weekly Journal*, 14 December 1723.
  (3) **MP* (1726), pp. 161–4.

DOom'd to a Fate, which damps the Poet's Flame,
A Muse, unfriended, greets thy rising Name!
Unvers'd in Envy's, or in Flatt'ry's Phrase,
Greatness she flies, yet Merit claims her Praise;
Nor will she, at her with'ring Wreath, repine,   5
But smile, if Fame and Fortune cherish thine.
  The Sciences in thy sweet Genius charm,
And, with their Strength, thy sex's Softness arm.
In thy full Figures, Painting's Force we find,
As Music fires, thy Language lifts the Mind.   10
Thy Pow'r gives Form, and touches into Life
The Passions imag'd in their bleeding Strife:
Contrasted Strokes, true Art, and Fancy, show,
And Lights, and Shades, in lively Mixture flow.
Hope attacks Fear, and Reason loves Controul,   15
Jealousy wounds, and Friendship heals the Soul:
Black Falshood wears bright Gallantry's Disguise,
And the gilt Cloud enchants the Fair-One's Eyes.
Thy Dames, in Grief, and Frailties, lovely shine,
And when most mortal, half appear divine.   20
If, when some Godlike, fav'rite Passion sways,
The willing Heart too fatally obeys,
Great Minds lament what cruel Censure blames,
And ruin'd Virtue gen'rous Pity claims.
  Eliza, still impaint Love's pow'rful Queen!   25
Let Love, soft Love! exalt each swelling Scene.

---

1 Flame] Fame *Applebee*.   7] THE Sister Sciences thy Genius warm, *Applebee*.
10 fires] charms, *Applebee*.   12 imag'd] imagin'd *Applebee*.
15] Thus Fear flies Hope, large Reason Love's Controul *Applebee*; Hope attacks Fear, and Reason Love's Controul *MP*.   17 bright *Applebee*] black *MP*.
25 impaint] impatinet *Applebee*.   26 exalt] adorn *Applebee*.

Arm'd with keen Wit, in Fame's wide Lists advance!
Spain yields in Fiction, in Politeness, *France*.
Such Orient Light, as the first Poets knew,
Flames from thy Thought, and brightens ev'ry View! 30
A strong, a glorious, a luxuriant Fire,
Which warms cold Wisdom into wild Desire!
Thy Fable glows so rich through ev'ry Page,
What Moral's Force can the fierce Heat assuage?
  And yet,—but say, if ever doom'd to prove   35
The sad, the dear Perplexities of Love!
Where seeming Transport softens ev'ry Pain,
Where fancy'd Freedom waits the winning Chain!
Varying from Pangs to visionary Joys,
Sweet is the Fate, and charms, as it destroys!   40
Say then,—if Love to sudden Rage, gives way,
Will the soft Passion not resume its Sway?
Charming, and charm'd, can Love from Love retire?
Can a cold Convent quench th'unwilling Fire?
Precept, if human, may our Thoughts refine,   45
More we admire! but cannot prove divine.

To Mr. Herbe[r]t Tryst, Esq;
on the suddain News of his Marriage with
Mrs Vernon.

TEXT: **Applebee's Weekly Journal*, 15 February 1724.

The *Historical Register* for 1724 reports that on 6 February 'Herbert
Tryst, of the City of Hereford, Esq;' was married to Mrs Vernon, a
widow. In the previous year RS had dedicated *Sir Thomas Overbury* to
him, without having asked his permission, but with 'a Sense of past
Favours'. In 1726 Tryst subscribed to *MP*.

FRom Melancholy's shade, receive a Muse,
Void of false Praise, and free from venal Views!
Silent no more, no longer she repines!
Silence were mean, when worth successful shines.
Enliven'd at your Bliss, her lays attend   5

A Bridegroom, Patron, and diſtinguiſh'd Friend!
Friendship like yours, a gen'rous Warmth reveals,
Which Gratitude alone returning feels.
      United Raptures now my Genius raise,
Wonder and Joy, and worth-attract[e]d Praise!   10
If e'er thy Youth Lov[e]'s wanton pow'r confess'd,
If e'er his random Arrows reach'd thy Breaſt;
The God, repenting, tries a nobler Art!
Deeper the Wound! and surer ſtrikes the Dart!
More ſtrong the Fire! the Passion clearer shines!   15
It purges, and exalts what It refines!
Souls, thus refin'd, exalted Blessings claim,
Wealth, Beauty, Vertue, and eternal Fame!
Beauty is Wealth, when Love and Honour grows,
And Fame will blossom sweet, where Vertue flows.   20
      Still may a thousand Graces guard your Fair!
Still may kind Planets make your Peace their Care!
Still may new Scenes of Bliss, each Hour, invite!
May smiling Infants crown the dear Delight!
The Beauteous Plants, beneath thy Godlike Hand,   25
Shall rise, shall flourish, and shall Grace the Land.
      Prove thus your Transport laſting, and refin'd!
The bright[,] th'extensive Emblem of your Mind!
Vertue shall shine in Fame, when Life decays,
And triumph o'er th'World-consuming Blaze.   30

To a Young Gentleman, a *Painter*, Advising
him to draw a Certain *Noble* and *Illuſtrious*
Person, occasioned by seeing his *Piĉure* of
the *Celebrated CLIO*.

TEXTS: (1) *The Plain Dealer*, no. 15, 11 May 1724.
   (2) *London Journal*, 23 January 1725.
   (3) MP (1726), pp. 26–30: 'To Mr. JOHN DYER, a Painter', etc.
   (4) *The Plain Dealer* (collected edition, 1730), I, 115–16: 'To a Young
Gentleman, a *Painter*: Occasioned by seeing his *Picture* of the *Celebrated
CLIO*.'

This is the first in an exchange of poems that took place between RS and John Dyer in 1723–4. Dyer is remembered today as a poet, but in 1723 he was known rather as a painter, and his portrait of Clio inspired the present poem. The development of this theme led RS to propose to Dyer as a subject for a picture the noble Horatius. His identity has not been discovered. Dr Williams has suggested the sixth Duke of Somerset, father-in-law of the Countess of Hertford, which whom Dyer was acquainted. Ralph M. Williams, *Poet, Painter, and Parson: The Life of John Dyer* (New York, *c.* 1956), pp. 45–50. RS's lines fit the 'proud Duke' strikingly in several respects, but not closely enough to make identification certain. A more likely candidate may be the Duke of Rutland, who became RS's patron in 1724 and was perhaps Clio's lover. But RS's lines are generalized, and no individual need have sat for them. In any case, RS was at least unconsciously describing his own ideal self—elevated to his proper social position as a giver rather than receiver of aristocratic partronage. Cf. Horatio in *The Wanderer*, v, 541 ff.

RS revised this poem for the 1730 edition of the *Plain Dealer*, but I have given the original version here, because it is important to preserve the exact words which Dyer read and to which he replied. In the revision RS left out a large part of the character of Horatius.

FORGIVE an Artless, an Officious Friend,
Weak, when I Judge, but willing to Commend;
Fall'n as I am, by no kind *Fortune* rais'd,
Depress'd, Obscur'd, Unpitied, and Unprais'd,
Yet, when these well-known Features I peruse,   5
Some Warmth awakes,—Some Embers of a *Muse*.
   YE *Muses, Graces*, and ye *Loves* appear!
Your Queen, your VENUS, and your *CLIO*'s here!
In such pure Fires her Rising Thoughts refine!
Her Eyes with such Commanding Sweetness shine!   10
Sure such bright Tinctures through yon Æther glow,
Stain Summer Clouds, or gild the Watry Bow:
If Life PIGMALION's Iv'ry Fav'rite fir'd,
Sure some Enamour'd *God* this Draught inspir'd!

9 Rising] real *1730*.
11] Such vivid Tinctures sure through Æther glow, *MP*; Such living Tinctures through yon Æther glow, *1730*.
13–20 *Omitted 1730*.

Or, if you rashly caught *PROMETHEAN* Flame,   *15*
Shade the sweet Theft, and mar the Beauteous Frame!
Yet if those Chearing Lights the *Proſpeƈt* fly,
Ah!—Let no pleasing View the *Loſs* supply.
Some dreary *Den*, some desart *Waſte* prepare,
Wild as my *Thoughts*, or dark as my *Deſpair*.   *20*
    BUT ſtill, my Friend, ſtill the sweet *Objeƈt* ſtays[,]
Still ſtream your Colours Rich with *CLIO*'s Rays!
Sure at each kindling Touch your Canvass glows!
Sure the full Form, inſtinct with Spirit, grows!
Let the dull Artiſt puzzling Rules explore,   *25*
Dwell on the Face, and gaze the Features o'er;
You eye the Soul—there genuine Nature find,
You, through the Meaning Muscles, ſtrike the Mind.
    NOR can one View such boundless Pow'r confine,
All Nature opens to an *Art* like thine!   *30*
Now Rural Scenes in simple Grandeur rise!
Vales, Hills, Lawns, Lakes, and Vineyards feaſt our Eyes!
Now *Halcyon Peace* a smiling Aspeƈt wears!
Now the *Red Scene* with *War* and *Ruin* glares!
Here *Britain*'s Fleets o'er *Europe*'s Seas preside!   *35*
There Long-loſt *Cities* rear their Ancient Pride!
You from the *Grave* can half redeem the Slain,
And bid *Great JULIUS* charm the *World* again:
Mark out *Pharsalia*'s, mark out *Munda*'s Fray,
And image all the Honours of the Day.   *40*
    BUT if new Glories moſt our Warmth excite,

15–20 The meaning in these lines is difficult to follow. The general sense seems to be that the painter must have stolen the fire of Prometheus to have painted so well, and that, to avoid being punished, he may have to fly to a 'dreary *Den*' in some desert.

17 Chearing *Bodleian copy of 1724*] clearing *British Museum copy of 1724*.

21–2 She smiles, she speaks—she blushes, while we gaze, / I hear your Colours and I feel their Blaze: *1730*.

23 Sure] More *1730*.   24 Sure] Till *1730*.

26] Dwell on the Lines and creep the Features o'er; *1730*.

27 there genuine Nature find,] the Source of Likeness find, *1730*.

28 You, through] And through *1730*.

39 Mark out *Pharsalia*'s] Revive *Pharsalia* *1730*.

40] And re-awaken Darkness into Day, *1730*.

If Toils untried to noblest Aims invite;
Wou'd you in Envied Pomp unrival'd reign,
Oh, let *HORATIUS* grace the Canvass Plain!
His *Form* might ev'n *Idolatry* create,   45
In *Lineage*, *Titles*, *Wealth*, and *Worth Elate*!
Empires to him might *Virgin Honours* owe,
From him *Arts*, *Arms*, and *Laws* new Influence know.
For him kind Suns on Fruits and Grain shall shine,
And future Gold lie rip'ning in the Mine: 50
For him Fine Marble in the Quarry lies,
Which, in due *Statues*, to his *Fame* shall rise.
Through those bright Features *CÆSAR*'s Spirit trace,
Each conqu'ring Sweetness, each imperial Grace,
All that is soft, or eminently great,   55
In *Love*, in *War*, in *Knowledge*, or in *State*.
　　　THUS shall your *Colours*, like his *Worth*, amaze!
Thus shall you *Charm*, enrich'd with *CLIO*'s Praise!
Clear, and more clear, your Golden Genius shines;
While my dim *Lamp* of *Life* Obscure declines: 60
Dull'd in damp Shades it wastes, unseen, away,
While yours, Triumphant, grows one Blaze of Day!

46–52] *In 1730 these seven lines are replaced by*: Serenely striking, and unproudly great.
55] All that has Softness, Terror, Wisdom, Weight, *1730*.
58] Thus shall you merit even your *CLIO*'s Praise! *1730*.
59 Golden] Sunny *1730*.
62 grows one Blaze of Day!] blazes into Day. *1730*.

The PICTURE.

To Mr. DYER, *when in the Country.*

TEXTS: (1) *MP (1726), pp. 294–8.

(2) *GM*, 36, 743: '*An* EPISTLE *to Mr* JOHN DYER, *Author of* Grongar Hill, *in Answer to his from the* Country, *to the* Son *of the late* Earl Rivers, *at* London; *written in the Month of* April.'

(3) *LM*, 36, 693.

This is the second in the exchange of poems with Dyer, who had replied to RS's *To a Young Gentleman, a Painter* in a poem entitled *To Mr Savage*,

Son of the late Earl Rivers (*MP*, pp. 291–3). Since Dyer was in Italy in April 1725, this poem must have been written in 1724.

Dyer's reply had taken a surprising form: a scolding to RS for continuing to look for social rank and position. Consequently in *The Picture* RS defends his desire for rank on the ground that it is necessary to one who aspires to win fame for himself and to do good to others, not through 'sounding *Verse*', but through '*Action*', presumably in public life. When revising his poem in 1736, however, RS changed his ground; he deleted his wish to 'soar sublime and strike the Topmost Sphere', substituting a panegyric on 'life's middle state' (i.e. the middle classes). I print the early version of this poem, for reasons similar to those mentioned in the headnote to the previous poem.

WHile various Birds in tuneful Consort sing,
    And charm the Prospect of the opening Spring;
While to thy Dreams the Nightingal complains,
Till the Lark wakes thee with its mirthful Strains;
My Thoughts all dim'd, all influenc'd by Despair,   *5*
A deep, a dire, confirm'd Distraction wear;
Till thy bright Verse and Friendship, ever kind,
Dawn a sweet Comfort o'er my dark'ning Mind.
       Oh! cou'd my Soul through Depths of Knowledge see,
Cou'd I read Nature and Mankind like Thee;   *10*
I shou'd o'ercome, or bear the Shocks of Fate,
And ev'n draw Envy to the humblest State:
But if Designs of Worth my Meaning forms,
Th' unfinish'd Fabricks fall by sudden Storms:
Yet some raise Honour from each ill Event,   *15*
From Shocks gain Vigour, and from Want Content.
       Think not light Poetry, my Life's chief Care,
The Muse's Mansion is at best but Air!
Not sounding *Verse* can give great Souls their Aim,

1] Now various birds in melting consort sing, *GM*, 36; *LM*, 36.

2 And charm the Prospect] And hail the beauty *GM*, 36.

3 While] Now *GM*, 36; *LM*, 36.

4 its mirthful] her chearful *GM*, 36; *LM*, 36.

5–8] Wakes, in thy verse and friendship ever kind, / Melodious comfort to my jarring mind. *GM*, 36; *LM*, 36.

13–15] Thou can'st raise honour from each ill event, *GM*, 36; *LM*, 36.

19–22] But, if more solid works my *meaning* forms, / Th'unfinish'd structures fall by fortune's storms. *GM*, 36; *LM*, 36 (cf. ll. 13–14).

Action alone commands sub‌stantial Fame.　　　　　*20*
Though with clip'd Wings I still lie flutt'ring here,
I'd soar sublime and ‌strike the Topmo‌st Sphere.
　　Falsly, we Those of guilty Pride accuse,
Whose God-like Souls Life's *Middle* State refuse:
Self-Love, ina‌ctive, seeks ignoble Re‌st,　　　　　*25*
Care sleeps not calm, when Millions wake unble‌st.
Mean let *Me* shrink, or spread sweet Shade o'er *All*,
Low as the Shrub, or as the Cedar *Tall*.
　　Then I'll write on—‌still I reserve my Hope,
Though envious Chance, contra‌cts my A‌ction's Scope;　*30*
Though Wealth denies what my proud Wants require,
By Wisdom, Sov'reign-like, I'd ‌still aspire;
Thus to Enquiry prompt th' imperfect Mind,
Thus clear dim'd Truth, and bid her bless Mankind.
From the pierc'd Orphan thus draw Shafts of Grief,　　*35*
Arm Want with Patience, and teach Wealth Relief.
　　Titles, when worn by Fools, I dare despise;
Yet they claim Homage, when they crown the Wise.
When high Di‌stin‌ction marks deserving Heirs,
Desert ‌still dignifies the Mark it wears.　　　　　*40*
But who to Birth *alone* wou'd Honours owe?
Honours, if True, from Seeds of *Merit* grow:
Those trees, with sweete‌st Charms, invite our Eyes,
Which from our own Engraftment fruitful rise!
Still we love be‌st what we with Labour gain,　　　　*45*
As the Child's dearer for the Mother's Pain.

23] Oft have I said we falsly those accuse, *GM*, *36*; *LM*, *36*.

25] *Self-love* (I cried) there seeks ignoble rest; *GM*, *36*; *LM*, *36*.

28] *After this line* GM, *36 and* LM, *36 insert the following couplet:* 'Twas vain! 'twas wild!—I sought the *middle* state, / And found the good, and found the truly great.

29–32] Though verse can never give my soul her aim; / Though action only claims substantial fame; / Though fate denies what my proud wants require, / Yet grant me, heav'n, by knowledge to aspire! *GM*, *36*; *LM*, *36*.

33] Thus to enquiry let me prompt the mind! *GM*, *36*; *LM*, *36*.

36] *After this line* GM, *36 and* LM, *36 insert the following:* To serve lov'd liberty inspire my breath! / Or, if my life be useless, grant me death! / For he, who useless is in life survey'd, / Burthens that world, his duty bids him aid. // Say what have honours to allure the mind, / Which he gains most, who least has serv'd mankind?

The Great, I neither envy nor deride;
Nor stoop to swell a vain *Superior*'s Pride;
Nor view an *Equal*'s Lot with jealous Eyes;
Nor crush the Wretch, *Beneath*; but mourn his Cries.   50
Where Friendships flourish, I'd no Jars create,
Nor by Another's Fall advance my State.
Nor misuse Wit, against an absent Friend:
I dare the Vertues of a Foe defend.
Through Wealth and Want true Minds preserve their
        Weight,   55
Meek, though Exalted; though Despis'd, Elate:
Refug'd, or wrong'd, They equal Precept know,
And prize the Patron, and forgive the Foe.

        Though strait my Fortune, still my Thoughts extend:
This is the *Picture* of thy absent Friend.   60
Though cruel Distance bars my *grosser* Eye,
My Soul, *clear-sighted*, draws thy Aspect *Nigh*;
Though lost to Comfort, compass'd round by Care,
Spleen in my Breast, and in my View Despair;
Through the deep Gloom thy quick'ning Merit gleams,   65
And lights up *Fortitude* with Friendship's Beams.

---

47 I neither envy] I wou'd nor envy *GM*, 36; *LM*, 36.

49 Lot] hope *GM*, 36; *LM*, 36.

50] Nor crush the wretch *beneath* who wailing lies. *GM*, 36; *LM*, 36. *After this line* GM, *36, and* LM, *36 insert the following couplet:* My sympathizing breast [soul *LM*, 36], his grief, can feel, / And my eye weep the wound, I cannot heal.

51] Ne'er among friendships let me sow debate! *GM*, 36; *LM*, 36.

54 I dare] Let me *GM*, 36; *LM*, 36.

55 Through Wealth] In Wealth *GM*, 36; *LM*, 36.
   Weight,] state, *LM*, 36.

56 Despis'd] disgrac'd *GM*, 36; depress'd *LM*, 36.

57–8] Gen'rous and grateful (wrong'd or help'd) they live; / Grateful to serve, and gen'rous to forgive. *GM*, 36; *LM*, 36.

59–60] This may they learn, who close thy life attend; / Which, dear in mem'ry, still instructs thy friend. *GM*, 36; *LM*, 36.

62 Aspect] virtue *GM*, 36; *LM*, 36.

63–4] *Omitted in* GM, *36 and* LM, *36.*

65] Through her deep woe that quick'ning Comfort gleams, *GM*, 36; *LM*, 36.

The FRIEND.

Address'd to AARON HILL, Esq;
[First Version]

TEXT: *MP (1726), pp. 126–8.
(Drastically revised in 1736, see pp. 215–18.)

In his Advertisement to *Sir Thomas Overbury* (1724), RS wrote: 'On that *worthy Gentleman* [Aaron Hill]...it will be my Pride, to offer my Sentiments, in a more distinguishing Manner hereafter.' The result was *The Friend*. It is another product of the discussion of 'true greatness' that took place in the Hill coterie in 1724. See *AB*, p. 71, and *European Magazine*, VI (1784), 278.

O Lov'd *Hillarius*, thou by Heav'n design'd
   To charm, to mend, and to excel Mankind!
To thee my Hopes, Fears, Joys, and Sorrows tend,
Thou Brother, Father, nearer yet!—Thou Friend!
Thou dearer far (Oh, what can equal thee?)   5
Than Int'rest, Kindred, Love, or Fame, to me.
   The Rich, the Great, of envious Care complain,
I, from unenvy'd Want, a Triumph gain;
Kind are my Wrongs, I thence thy Friendship own!
What State cou'd bless, were I to thee unknown?   10
Oft thy Reproof has flush'd me o'er with Shame,
From thy rich Soul I caught Ideal Flame!
While shun'd, obscur'd; or thwarted and expos'd,
By Friends abandon'd, and by Foes enclos'd,
Thy guardian Counsel softens ev'ry Care,   15
To Ease charms Anguish, and to Hope Despair.
   If meaner Views extort reluctant Lays,
I rob thy Virtues to give others Praise;
Think not to swell vain Minds my Theft's applied,
No—in thy Worth I'd paint a gen'rous Pride.   20
Fain wou'd I count thy wondrous Virtues o'er,
Aid me, ye Bards; with me the Theme explore!

---

1 *Hillarius*. Most of the members of the coterie had nicknames and used them freely in the poems printed in *MP*.
17–19 Hill had evidently criticized RS for writing dedications with mercenary views.

With me *Hillarius* sing!—the theme implies
Sweetness and Strength, A Mind serene and wise.
Mark him, ye Proud—Beneficent he lives,   25
Urges no Wrongs, is injur'd, and forgives;
Peerage he honours, when by Worth acquir'd;
Worth is by Worth in ev'ry Rank admir'd:
Peerage he scorns, when Titles Insult speak,
Proud to vain Pride, to honour'd Meekness meek.   30
In ev'ry Thought, in ev'ry Action, Great,
In Leisure active, and in Care sedate.
Nature, enobled, here delights to blend
Th'aspiring Bard and condescending Friend:
While some with cold, superior Looks, redress,   35
Relief seems Insult, and confirms Distress:
He, when he views the Soul with Wrongs besieg'd,
While warm he acts th'Obliger, seems th'Oblig'd.
That venal Bliss which others court, he flies,
That worthy Woe they shun, attracts his Eyes.   40
The humane Virtues his sweet Life compose,
The humane Frailties are alone his Foes.
  Hillarius, ever lov'd, and ever kind,
Thou just, thou gen'rous, thou exalted Mind!
Thou, clear in Cares, can'st Fortune's Smiles outshine: 45
What wou'd'st thou not, were Wealth and Greatness thine?

VERSES,

occasioned by reading Mr. AARON HILL's POEM,
call'd GIDEON.

TEXT: **MP* (1726), pp. 205–8.

Aaron Hill's biblical epic, *Gideon*, must have been written by 1722,
because in 1749 he wrote that it had lain by him 'for above three Times
the Space prescribed by *Horace*' (Preface to *Gideon* (1749)). RS probably
read it in MS in the same year in which it was completed, because in
a letter to him dated 3 November 1722, Hill wrote: 'I long…for Gideon,
as it will be a proof of your cure, as well as for his own beauties; and as
he will ever stand in my view a lasting argument, a never-to-be-

demolished monument of the unmerited favour and condescension of my most generous and ingenious benefactress [i.e. "Clio",—Mrs Martha Fowke Sansom]...' (*European Magazine* VI (1784), 190). Hill was probably asking for the return of his manuscript. What benefits had been conferred on him by Clio I do not know, and I find it hard to reconcile what he wrote about her then with a letter he wrote to her, allegedly in 1724, in which he introduced her to *Gideon* apparently for the first time (*Works* (1753), I, 25). Possibly the second letter has been misdated. RS published one lengthy section of *Gideon* in *MP*.

I

L ET other Poets poorly sing
    Their Flatt'ries to the *vulgar Great*!
Her airy Flight let wand'ring Fancy wing,
    And rival Nature's moſt luxuriant Store,
To swell some Monſter's Pride, who shames a State,   5
Or form a Wreath to crown tyrannic Power!
Thou, who inform'd'ſt this Clay with aɔtive Fire!
Do Thou, supreme of Pow'rs! my Thoughts refine,
    And with thy pureſt Heat my Soul inspire,
That with *Hillarius'* Worth my Verse may shine!   10
    As thy lov'd *Gideon* once set *Israel* free,
        So He with sweet, seraphic Lays
        "*Redeems the Use of captive Poetry*,
Which firſt was form'd to speak thy glorious Praise!

II

Moses, with an enchanting Tongue,   15
Pharaoh's juſt Overthrow sublimely sung!

N.B. *The Lines mark'd thus* " *are taken from* Gideon. [RS]

---

10 Hillarius. Cf. *The Friend*, l. 1.

13 Cf. 'So, now, all-pow'rful Guide! invig'rate *me*,
        Successful, to redeem the *Use*, of long-lost *Poetry*!' (*Gideon*, 1, stanza 1).
In his note on these lines, Hill explains that 'To *redeem* the *Use* of Poetry,...is to restore it to the *Praise* of *God*, to the Advancement of true *Virtue*, and to Animation of those noblest *Passions*, which lend Wings to human Ardour'.

15–20 Hill had also turned two poetical parts of the Old Testament into English Pindaric odes: Exodus xv. 1 21 ('I will sing unto the Lord, for he hath triumphed gloriously; the horse and his rider hath he thrown into the sea') and II Samuel i. 19–27 ('The beauty of Israel is slain upon thy high places: how are the mighty fallen!'). Though not connected with *Gideon*, they were printed in the notes to Book 1 in 1749, pp. 45–9.

When *Saul* and *Jonathan* in Death were laid,
Surviving *David* felt the *soft'[n]ing* Fire!
    And by the Great Almighty's tuneful Aid,
    Wak'd into endless Life his mournful Lire.   *20*
Their diff'rent Thoughts met in *Hillarius'* Song,
Roll in one Channel more divinely strong!
With *Pindar's* Fire his Verse's Spirit flies,
"*Wafted in charmful Musick through the Air!*
Unstop'd by *Clouds, It reaches to the Skies,*   *25*
    And join'd with Angels' Hallelujahs there,
Flows mix'd, and sweetly strikes th' Almighty's Ear!

III

Rebels shou'd blush when They his *Gideon* see!
That *Gideon*, born to set his Country free.
O, that such Heroes in each Age might rise,   *30*
Bright'ning through Vapours like the Morning Star,
Gen'rous in Triumph, and in Council wise!
Gentle in Peace, but terrible in War!

IV

When *Gideon, Oreb, Hyram, Shimron* shine
Fierce in the Blaze of War as they engage!   *35*
    Great Bard! What Energy, but Thine,
Cou'd reach the vast Description of their Rage?
    Or, when to cruel Foes betray'd,
    Sareph and *Hamar* call for Aid,

---

24   'The Voice of Gideon, sweetly loud,
        Wafted his charmful Musick to their Ear.'
                      (Book II, in *A Specimen of* GIDEON, n.d.)

28–33 Notice RS's return here to the theme of the 'Jacobite Poems', *The Convocation*
and the *Prologue to Henry VI*. Hill explained that his epic was intended to glorify
a limited monarchy, and to extol the virtues in a people of intrepidity in foreign war
and the spirit of domestic liberty.

34–7 Oreb was a Midianite prince who in Book I was captured by Gideon when
leading a raid into Hebrew territory. In Judges vii. 25, he is slain by the Ephraimites.
The names of Hyram and Shimron occur in books 7 and 6 respectively as published
in *A Specimen of* GIDEON.

38–45 Allusion is made in these lines to the episode entitled 'Sareph and Hamar',
published in *A Specimen of* GIDEON. It is entirely unbiblical. Hill's Hamar was the
daughter of a Tyrian saint.

Loſt, and bewilder'd in Despair,   *40*
How piercing are the hapless Lover's Cries?
What tender Strokes in melting Accents rise?
Oh, what a Maſter-piece of Pity's there?
Nor goodly *Joash* shows thy Sweetness less,
When, like kind Heav'n, he frees 'em from Diſtress!   *45*

V

Hail Thou, whose Verse, a living Image, shines,
In *Gideon*'s Charaĉter your own you drew!
    As there the graceful Patriot shines,
    We in that Image bright *Hillarius* view!
Let the low Crowd, who love unwholsom Fare,   *50*
When in thy Words the Breath of Angels flows,
Like gross-fed Spirits sick, in purer Air,
Their earthy Souls by their dull Taſte disclose!
    Thy dazzling Genius shines too bright!
And they, like Speĉtres, shun the Streams of Light.   *55*
But while in Shades of Ignorance they ſtray,
    Round Thee Rays of Knowledge play,
    "*And show Thee glitt'ring in abſtraĉted Day.*

---

58 Cf. *Gideon*, III, stanza XXVI:
    'And shows him, glitt'ring, in *abstracted Day*!'

To the Excellent MIRANDA
(Consort of AARON HILL, *Esq;)*
on reading her Poems.

TEXT: *MP (1726), p. 286.

Mrs Aaron Hill contributed seven short poems to *MP*.

EAch soft'ning Charm of *Clio*'s smiling Song,
  Mountague's Soul, which shines divinely ſtrong!
These blend, with Graceful Ease, to form thy Rhime,
Tender, Yet chaſt; sweet-sounding, Yet sublime!

Wisdom and Wit have made thy works their Care,   5
Each Passion glows, Refin'd by Precept, There!
To fair *Miranda*'s Form Each Grace is Kind;
The Muses and the Virtues tune thy Mind.

A POEM
on the Recovery of
her Grace the Dutchess of *RUTLAND*
from the Small-Pox.

TEXTS: (1) **MP* (1726), pp. 1–4.
   (2) *GM*, 36, 480: '*On the Recovery of a* Lady *of* Quality *from the* Small-Pox.'
   (3) *LM*, 36, 449.

The Duchess of Rutland was reported in the newspapers to be recovering from smallpox at the beginning of April 1725 (*The Weekly Journal*, no. 336, 3 April). In revising his poem in 1736, RS dropped the names of the Duke and Duchess, the connection between them and him having been broken in the interval. The earlier version, being the more interesting, is given here.

LONG *Rutland*'s Fair had bless'd her Consort's Sight,
  With am'rous Pride, and undisturb'd Delight;
Till Death grown envious, with repugnant Flame,
Frown'd at their Joys, and urg'd a Tyrant's Claim.
He summons each *Disease*!—the noxious Crew,   5
Writhing, in dire Distortions, strike his View!
From various Plagues, which various Natures know,
Forth rushes Beauty's fear'd, and fervent Foe.
Fierce to the Fair, the missile Mischief flies,
The sanguine Streams in raging Ferments rise!   10
It drives, Ignipotent, through ev'ry Vein,
Hangs on the Heart, and burns around the Brain!
Now a chill Damp the Charmer's Lustre dims!
Sad o'er her Eyes, the livid Languor swims!

---

1 *Rutland*'s Fair] a *lov'd fair GM*, 36; *LM*, 36.
3 Flame] aim *GM*, 36; *LM*, 36.

Her Eyes, that with a Glance could Joy inspire, 15
Like setting Stars, scarce shoot a glimm'ring Fire.
Now their pale Lights th'encroaching Fiend forbids,
Quench'd are their Beams, and clos'd th'unwilling Lids.
    Here *Rutland* stands, with gen'rous Anguish prest,
Grief in his Eye, and Terror in his Breast. 20
Th'enfeebled Graces, smit with anxious Care,
In silent Sorrow, weep the waining Fair.
Eight Suns, successive, roll their Fires away,
And eight slow Nights see their deep Shades decay.
While these revolve, though mute each Muse appears, 25
Their speaking Eyes drop Eloquence in Tears.
On the ninth Noon, his Ear their *Phœbus* bends!
Now from their Chief the Voice of Prayer ascends!
'Great God of Light, of Wit, and Physick's Art,
'To the lov'd, languid Fair Relief impart! 30
'New Charms awake! new-warm her chearless Breast!
'His Grief alleviate, who the Muse redrest!
'There Beauty, Wit, and Virtue, claim thy Care,
'And thy own Bounty's almost rivall'd there.'
    She said—the God assents—Death aims t'advance! 35
Phœbus unseen arrests the threat'ning Lance!
Down from his Orb a vivid Radiance streams,
While Herbs impregnate with salubrious Beams;
Each wholsome Plant Encrease of Virtue knows,
And Art, inspir'd, with its God's Wisdom, glows; 40

17–18] *Omitted in* GM, *36 and* LM, *36*.
19] Here stands her *consort*, sore, with anguish, prest, GM, 36; LM, 36.
21 Th'enfeebled Graces] The *Paphian graces* GM, 36; LM, 36.
23 Fires] fire GM, 36.   *24* see] let GM, 36; LM, 36.
26] Each speaking eye drops eloquence in tears; GM, 36; LM, 36.
27–8] On the ninth noon, great *Phœbus*, list'ning bends; / On the ninth noon, each voice in prayer ascends. GM, 36; LM, 36.
29 of Wit, and] of song, of GM, 36; LM, 36.
30–2 'Restore the languid pair! new soul impart! GM, 36; LM, 36.
33 There] Here GM, 36; LM, 36.
35] *Each* paused. The *god* assents. Wou'd *death* advance? GM, 36; LM, 36.
37 Radiance] influence GM, 36; LM, 36.
38] And quick'ning earth imbibes salubrious beams. GM, 36; LM, 36.
39 wholsome] balmy GM, 36; LM, 36.
40] And *art* inspir'd, with *all* her *Patron*, glows. GM, 36; LM, 36.

At each griev'd Pore instill'd, It Hope reveals;
Each Nerve's new-strung, each Vein new Vigour feels!
Wish'd Health absorbs the moist Disease away,
The Fair-One's Eyes, unseal'd, new Beams display.
From *Rutland*, swift recedes corroding Care: 45
Now Joy returns to chace away Despair!
Each Grace revives, each Muse resumes the Lyre,
Each Beauty brightens with re-kindled Fire.
As Health's assembled Charms a Bloom display,
Death, sullen at the Sight, stalks slow away.   50

41–6] The *charmer*'s opening eye, kind hope, reveals, / Kind hope, her *consort*'s
breast enlivening, feels. *GM*, 36; *LM*, 36.
48 re-kindled] re-lumin'd *GM*, 36; *LM*, 36.
49 As *health*'s auspicious *pow'rs*, gay *life*, display, *GM*, 36; *LM*, 36.

THE Authors of the Town; A SATIRE:
Inscribed to the AUTHOR *of* The UNIVERSAL PASSION.

TEXT: *THE Authors of the Town; A SATIRE.... 1725 [Anon.].

This poem was recognized as the work of RS by G. F. Whicher, who in
his *Life and Romances of Mrs Eliza Haywood* (New York, 1915), pp. 106 ff.,
noted the similarity between one passage in it (ll. 45–64) and a part of
On False Historians (ll. 63–70). He might have found another part
(ll. 125–6) embedded in *The Progress of a Divine* (ll. 397–8). There are
many other echoes of RS's poems and interests, such as the passage
on Eliza Haywood and Clio (ll. 157–72).

This is RS's first venture into satire, inspired particularly by the
example of his friend Edward Young, the first four of whose satires
appeared in the same year under the title of *The Universal Passion* (in later
editions, *Love of Fame, the Universal Passion*). RS's anonymity, unusual
with him, must have been the result of a rare fit of discretion, owing to
the number of persons he attacked, particularly old friends like John
Gay. His motive for attacking Gay must have been envy, for Gay
was being received in fashionable circles into which RS had not
penetrated. He must have known Gay intimately, for he was acquainted
with his poetical plans (ll. 211 ff. and n.) Moreover, in 1736 he was
asked by Thomas Birch to revise the life of Gay for the *General
Dictionary* (see *AB*, pp. 122–3, and E. L. Ruhe, in *Review of English*

Studies, n.s. v (1954), 171). His sketch of Gay in this poem, however envious, is not unfair.

The originals of some of the other satirical sketches contained in this poem are hard to identify. Matthew Concanen, for example, in an 'Essay on Satyrists' in *The Speculatist* (1730), p. 29, wrote that he was attacked in *The Authors of the Town*, but 'as his [the Author's] hand at drawing Characters keeps the Originals from a Danger of being discovered, I have no Wrath against him'. He was almost right; but see ll. 151–2 and n.

RS's lines on historians (ll. 45–64) were suggested to him by his reading for *Sir Thomas Overbury* (1724), in such writers as Echard (whom he mentions by name), Oldmixon, Howel, Coke, and others. These lines became the nucleus of *On False Historians* (1741) which, along with *A Character*, evidently formed part of some 'epistles upon authors', that he was never able to publish, and had possibly never completed (Johnson, *Account*, pp. 355 n., 392). Much of *The Authors of the Town* probably went into these epistles.

Concanen's essay, which was taken from a newspaper dated 4 September 1725, establishes the date of publication of *The Authors of the Town*. It has never been reprinted.

> —*Stulta est clementia cum tot ubique*
> *Vatibus occurras periturœ parcere chartœ.*   Juvenal.

> —*Tenet insanabile multos*
> *Scribendi cacoethes—*   *Ibid.*

> *Quod si dolosi spes refulserit nummi,*
> *Corvos poetas, & poetridas picas*
> *Cantare credas Pegaseium melos.*   Persius.

B RIGHT Arts, abus'd, like Gems, receive their Flaws;
  Physick has Quacks, and Quirks obscure the Laws.
Fables to shade Historic Truths combine,
And the dark Sophist dims the Text Divine.
The Art of Reasoning in Religion's Cause,   5
By Superstition's Taint a Blindness draws.
The *Art* of *Thinking Free* (Man's noblest Aim!)
Turns, in *Half-thinking* Souls, his equal Shame.
Colours, ill-mingled, coarse, and lifeless grow!

Mottos: Juvenal, *Satires*, I, 17–18; VII, 51–2; and Persius, *Choliambi*, ll. 13–15.

Violins squeak, when Scrapers work the Bow!　　10
Distortion deadens Action's temper'd Fire!
Belab'ring Poetasters *thrum* the Lyre!
Gesture shuns Strut, and Elocution, Cant!
Passion lies murder'd by unmeaning Rant!
Wit we debase, if Ribaldry we praise,　　15
And Satire fades, when Slander wears the Bays.

　　YOU, to whose Scrolls a just Neglect is shewn,
Whose Names, though printed oft, remain unknown;
I war not with the Weak, if wanting Fame,
The Proud, and Prosp'rous Trifler is my Game.　　20
With usual Wit, unfelt while you assail,
Remark unanswer'd, and unheeded Rail!
Or heeded, know I can your Censure prize,
For a Fool's Praise is Censure from the Wise;
If then my Labour your kind Malice draws,　　25
Censure from you is from the Wise Applause.

　　YOU, who delineate strong our Lust of Fame,
These mimic Lays your kind Protection claim!
My Frown, like yours, would to Improvement tend,
You but assume the Foe, to act the Friend.　　30
Pleasing, yet wounding, you our Faults rehearse,
Strong are your Thoughts! Inchanting rolls your Verse!
Deep, clear, and sounding! decent, yet sincere;
In Praise impartial, without Spleen severe.

　　'HOLD, Criticks cry—Erroneous are your Lays,　　35
'Your Field was Satire, your Pursuit is Praise.'
True, you Profound!—I praise, but yet I sneer;
You're dark to Beauties, if to Errors clear!
Know my Lampoon's in Panegyric seen,
For just Applause turns Satire on your Spleen.　　40

　　SHALL Ignorance and Insult claim my Rage?
Then with the World a gen'ral War I wage!
No—to some Follies Satire scorns to bend,
And Worth (or press'd, or prosp'rous) I commend.

---

27 Edward Young. Cf. *The Wanderer* (1729), I, 325–6.

FIRST, let me view what noxious Nonsense reigns,   *45*
While yet I loiter on Prosaic Plains;
If Pens impartial active Annals trace,
Others, with secret Hist'ry, Truth deface:
Views and Reviews, and wild Memoirs appear,
And Slander darkens each recorded Year.   *50*
Each Prince's Death to Poison they apply,
No Royal Mortals sure by Nature die.
Fav'rites or Kindred artful Deaths create,
A Father, Brother, Son, or Wife is Fate.
In a past Reign was form'd a secret League,   *55*
Some Ring, or Letter, now reveals th'Intrigue:
A certain Earl a certain Queen enjoys,
A certain Subject Fair her Peace destroys;
The jealous Queen a vengeful Art assumes,
And scents her Rival's Gloves with dire Perfumes: *60*
Queens, with their Ladies, work unseemly things,
And Boys grow Dukes, when Catamites to Kings.
A lying Monk on Miracles refines,
And Vengeance glares from violated Shrines.
   THUS Slander o'er the Dead-One's Fame prevails, *65*
And easy Minds imbibe Romantic Tales:
Thus from feign'd Facts a false Reflection flows,
And by Tradition Superstition grows.
   NEXT, Pamphleteers a Trade licentious drive,
Like wrangling Lawyers, they by Discord thrive.   *70*
If *Hancock* proves *Cold Water's* Virtue clear,
His Rival prints a Treatise on *Warm Beer*.

49–50 Cf. *On False Historians*, ll. 63–4.
51–2 Cf. *On False Historians*, ll. 69–70, and *Religion and Liberty*, ll. 79–80.
55–6 Cf. *On False Historians*, ll. 65–6.
60 Cf. [William] Howel, *The Ancient and Present State* (7th ed. 1719), p. 185:
'A.D. 1612....On *November* the Sixth following, Prince *Henry* died of a malignant
Fever, which Reigned that Year in most Parts of the Land. Some said that he died by
poisoned Grapes which he eat; others, by Gloves of a poisoned Perfume given him
for a Present.'
61–2 Cf. *On False Historians*, ll. 67–8.   64 Cf. *On False Historians*, l. 8.
71–2 John Hancocke, *Febrifugum Magnum: Or, Common Water the best Cure for
Fevers, and probably for the Plague*...(1722). I have not seen a copy of the pamphlet
on warm beer, but in the *Weekly Journal* for 22 February 1724 (no. 278) there is the

If next Inoculation's Art spreads wide,
(An Art, that mitigates Infection's Tide)
Loud *Pamphleteers* 'gainst *Innovation* cry,   75
Let Nature work—'Tis natural to die.

    IF Heav'n-born Wisdom, gazing Nature through,
Through Nature's Optics forms Religion's View,
Priestcraft opposes Demonstration's Aid,
And with dark Myst'ry dignifies her Trade.   80

    IF Ruin rushes o'er a Statesman's Sway,
Scribblers, like Worms, on tainted Grandeur pre[y].
While a poor Felon waits th' impending Stroke,
Voracious Scribes, like hov'ring Ravens, croak.
In their dark Quills a dreary Insult lies,   85
Th' Offence lives recent, though th' Offender dies;
In his last Words they suck his parting Breath,
And gorge on his loath'd Memory after Death.

    WRETCHES, like these, no Satire wou'd chastise,
But Follies here to ruthless Insult rise;   90
Distinguished Insult taints a Nation's Fame,
And various Vice deserves a various Shame.

    PAMPHLETS I leave—sublime my Fancy grows!
No more she sweeps the humble *Vale* of *Prose*.
Now I trace swift the *Muse*'s airy Clime,   95
The Dance of Numbers, and the Change of Rhime!
In measur'd Rounds Imagination swims,

---

following advertisement (p. 1654): 'Newly publish'd WARM BEER; or a Treatise
wherein is shewn by many Reasons, that Beer, so qualified, is far more wholesome
than that which is drank cold. Interspersed with divers Observations touching the
drinking of cold Water, and published for the Preservation of Health.'

73-6 There had been a pamphlet controversy on the subject of inoculation ever
since Lady Mary Wortley Montagu introduced the art into England in 1719, the
opposition maintaining that diseases are punishments inflicted by God, and that
man should not interfere with the divine order. Cf. headnote to *The Animalcule*.

77 By 'Nature's Optics' RS means primarily 'eyes' and secondarily 'common
sense', i.e. natural reason. These lines are the first indication of his drifting away from
the High-Church party, toward the latitudinarian school represented by Dr Samuel
Clarke.

83 Edmund Curll did a good business in biographies of condemned felons. When
RS was in prison in 1727 awaiting execution, he was approached by a bookseller
wishing to bring out his biography.

And the Brain whirls with new, surprizing Whims!
Poets are mad! 'tis granted:—So are you,
Grave Critics, who those Lunatics pursue: *100*
You labour Comments dry on *Classic* Lays,
Partial alike in Censure, and in Praise;
Where moſt abſtruse, you moſt assert they shine,
Where *Homer* raves, his *Allegory*'s fine!
But if a *Modern* with an *Ancient* vies,   *105*
Spirit grows Phrensy, to a Wit so wise.

      PHLEGM without Fire, your flat Encomiums bear,
When you declaim, a Mark revers'd you wear;
If not inspir'd, at leaſt possess'd you seem,
You boil with Choler, and *dismiss* your Phlegm.   *110*
None unprefer'd, in Parliament more loud!
No worn-out Fair more peevish, or more proud!
No City-Dame, when to the Birth-Night drawn,
More vain of Gems!—(some Female Courtier's Pawn!)
Proud as a Judge, when Equity's a Trade,   *115*
Or Lord, whose Guilt was with a Title paid.

      MARK cautious *Cinna* mimic Poesy's Flame,
Coarse are his Colours, and obscure his Aim!
Cinna, thy Genius weds not with the Muse;
No longer then thy well-known Parts misuse!   *120*
Cinna, thus *doctor'd*, stifles all he writ,
But sneers malignant at another's Wit.
Some beauteous Piece applauded, He replies,
The Sun has Spots, and a wish'd Error spies.

---

101 Comments] Comments, *1725*.

117 'Cautious *Cinna*' may have been intended to represent Addison, who, according to Pope, 'without sneering' could teach others how to sneer. Addison was cautious to a fault, and, like the historical Cinna, held public office. That he stifled all he wrote is not true; but RS may be referring to an episode in which he was suspected by some people of having either destroyed or refrained from writing a very large quantity of verse. He was thought to have been the real author of Tickell's translation of the first book of the *Iliad* (1715), a legend mentioned by Thomas Cooke in his *Battle of the Poets* (1725). Tickell's rivalry with Pope, who had published his own translation a few days before, caused much bitterness. Pope's work swept all before it, and no more of Tickell's translation was published. Thus RS, accepting the theory that Addison was the real author, could write of Cinna that he 'stifles all he writ'. Cf. George Sherburn, *Early Career of Alexander Pope* (1934), chap. v.

SO some warm Lass grows pregnant ere she marries, *125*
Takes *Physic*, and for *Honour's* sake *miscarries*;
Jealous of Praise, pale Envy taints her Lip,
And her Tongue tattles of each Virgin's Trip.
   THEOCRITUS's Ape, dry, proud, and vain,
Shews the ſtiff Quaker for the simple Swain. *130*
In Tragic Scenes, how *soft* he moves Diſtress?
His *Lamb-like Princess* in the *Pure-one's Dress*:
Plain in Expression, and in Passion tame,
Propriety of Words is all his Aim.
   SCRIBLERS grow faſt—One, who gains leaſt
      Applause, *135*
(His Works reprinting) a Subscription draws.
Ape of an Ape! How is the Species grown!
Inferior Apes this Ape a *Viceroy* own!
O'er a learn'd Tribe, He *Grand Dictator* plays,
And points young Wits new Models in his Lays. *140*
Flat Odes, Epiſtles, and Translations rise,
And a new Preface words it with the Wise!
Art is School Trash—*Horace* and *Pope* are Fools.
Sonnets and Madrigals require no Rules.
Milton runs *rough*—Here *plainer* Lays allure! *145*
Nor Low, nor Grand, nor Simple, nor Impure.

125-6 Cf. *The Progress of a Divine*, ll. 397-8.
129 Theocritus's Ape. Ambrose Philips. Cf. *An Apology to Brillante*. His tragic
'scenes' are his blank verse adaptation of Racine's *Andromaque*, entitled *The Distrest
Mother* (1712). Andromache, the most reserved and lamb-like character in his play,
appears in bridal costume in acts IV and V.
135-46 Leonard Welsted published his *Epistles, Odes, &c. Written on Several Subjects*
in 1724. Though not published on subscription, otherwise it fits RS's description.
Perhaps RS was confused with the proposals Welsted published for his abortive
translation of Horace, which appeared in the same number of the *Weekly Journal*
(no. 334, 20 March 1725, p. 2071) as the advertisement for his *Epistles, Odes, &c.*
(2nd ed. 1725). The following extracts from the introductory dissertation show the
point of RS's various remarks: He refers to the 'phrase and stile of MILTON' as
'an uncouth and unnatural jargon', and then goes on to depreciate the various arts
of poetry, including Horace's, and remarks: 'as to the numerous treatises, essays, arts,
&c. both in verse and prose, that have been written by the moderns on this ground-
work, they do but hackney the same thoughts over again, making them still more
trite' (p. xv). Although he does not refer to Pope's *Essay on Criticism*, the application to it is obvious. 'As the common rules of logic serve only for disputing,' he
concludes, 'so the common rules of poetry serve only for pedantry' (p. xxviii).

A Love-sick Youth, who sighs about Eighteen,
Whines in Blank Verse, and tries a Tragic Scene.
One Poet, damn'd, turns Critick, ſtorms in Prose;
His railing Pamphlet his wrong'd Merit shows.   *150*
A trading Bard salutes the Lord in Place,
Whom he insults with Satire, in Disgrace.
One, jocund, sings Birth-Days, and Nuptial Rites:
One, of the Dead, a doleful Dirge recites,
Dull as deep Bells, that toll the Fun'ral's Time,   *155*
Or drowzy Echoes from the Bell-Man's Rhime.
    A caſt-off Dame, who of Intrigues can judge,
Writes Scandal in Romance—A Printer's Drudge!
Flush'd with Success, for Stage-Renown she pants,
And melts, and swells, and pens luxurious Rants.   *160*
    BUT while her Muse a sulph'rous Flame displays,
Glows ſtrong with Luſt, or burns with Envy's Blaze!
While some black Fiend, that hugs the haggar'd Shrew,
Hangs his colleſted Horrors on her Brow!
Clio, descending Angels sweep thy Lyre,   *165*
Prompt thy soft Lays, and breathe *Seraphic* Fire.
Tears fall, Sighs rise, obedient to thy Strains,
And the Blood dances in the mazy Veins!
Crown'd with the Palm, Bays, Myrtle, and the Vine;
Love, Pity, Friendship, Music, Wit, and Wine,   *170*
In social Spirits, lead thy Hours along,
Thou Life of Loveliness, thou Soul of Song!

147–8 Perhaps Moses Browne, who published his *Polidus: or, Distress'd Love, a Tragedy*, in 1723, at the age of 19.

149–50 John Dennis had written many railing pamphlets. When he read a couplet in the *Essay on Criticism* (ll. 36–7), he is said to have 'flung down the book in a terrible fury, and cried, By G—d he means me' (*The Works of Pope*, ed. Elwin and Courthope (1886), x, 459).

151–2 This is the only place in the poem into which I can fit Matthew Concanen. RS, in *An Author to be Let* (ll. 154–5), wrote: 'Concanen is a precious Fellow! I once loved him for his Ingratitude to *Dean Swift*: I now adore him for his dull Humour, and malevolent blundering *Billingsgate* against Lord *Bolingbroke*.' The charge reappears in a note to the *Dunciad* (*c.* 1733), at II, 287.

153 Probably the poet-laureate, Laurence Eusden.

154–6 Joseph Mitchell published *Lugubres Cantus* in 1719 on the death of his brother, John, which certainly merits this description.

157–64 Mrs Eliza Haywood.   *165–72* Clio is Mrs Martha Fowke Sansom.

73

A Blade whose Life a Turn of Humour takes,
Cocks smart, trims fine, treats Harlots, scours with Rakes!
When his drain'd Purse no new Expence supplies,   175
Fond Madam frowns, each dear Companion flies!
Duns clamour, Bailiffs lurk, and Clothes decay,
Coin ebbs, he muſt recruit—He writes a Play.
'Bold task! a Play?—Mark our young Bard proceed!
'A Play?—Your Wits in Want are Wits indeed.'   180
Here the Punk's Jokes are for Politeness wrote,
Some inconsiſtent Novel forms a Plot.
In the Gallant, his own wise Conduct glares!
Smut is sheer Wit!—Each Prank a Merit wears!
Bright Youth! He ſteals, to make the Piece entire,   185
A Cuckold, Beau, pert Footman, and a Squire.
        WHEN Bards thus patch up Plays from various
              Scraps,
They dream of crouded Houses! thundring Claps!
False Hope! Poets are poor, and Fortune's blind,
Actors are saucy—or the Town's unkind.   190
        BUT why should Satire war with ill Success?
Why should I add Affliction to Diſtress?
'Tis bold t'assail proud Vice with ſtinging Lays!
'Tis bolder yet, to give wrong'd Merit Praise!
Few dare accuse what ſtately Wits defend!   195
Few dare againſt the gen'ral Vogue commend!
        JOHNNY's fine Works at Court obtain Renown!

173–86 This may be a fling at Christopher Bullock, who was accused of stealing
Woman is a Riddle from RS. Cf. *AB*, pp. 38–40.

197–236 'Aaron' is Aaron Hill, whose poetry was never popular. The 'Lampoons,
that lash *My Lady*'s Airs' and 'the Satire on the *Duke's white Staff*' are not titles to
be found among Hill's poems, but his point of view is correctly indicated in them.
Cf. RS's *The Friend* and Hill's *The Happy Man*.

        'Johnny' is John Gay. Hill and Gay had been school fellows. In *Britannia's
Miseries* RS quoted a line or two from *Trivia*, and here he seems to be aware that Gay
is working on the fables that he published the following year. Gay, of course, did
'obtain Renown' at court, wrote panegyrics on the Duke of Marlborough and other
celebrities, and was caressed by duchesses. His early poetry, like *The Flea*, is definitely
imitative of Pope ('that bright Genius, that has charm'd the Age') and subsequently
he did become more original. But the statement that he became less popular as
a result is probably not true. Gay's delicate craftsmanship, gentle irony, and apparent
ease of writing stand out in sharp contrast to Hill's laborious efforts to reach the

Aaron writes Trash—He ne'er collogues the Town.
How Grand the Verse which *My Lord*'s Feats declares!
Rude are Lampoons, that lash *My Lady*'s Airs.   200
How arch the Wit, when *Her Grace* deigns a Laugh[!]
Dull is the Satire on the *Duke's white Staff.*
Oh, You *Polite!* Your Smiles are Fame's sweet Road;
We praise, subscribe, or damn—because the *Mode.*

     JOHNNY no more reflects a shining Page,   205
From that bright Genius, that has charm'd the Age!
More conscious now, his single Worth he rates!
Verses are made, like Med'cines, by Receipts.
Soft Phrases he collects—to scan, to chime,
Reads deep, and weighs vast *Lexicons* of Rhyme.   210
Hints from *Fontaine*, some smart Design compleat;
The Whim is pretty, and the Language neat.
Though smart, neat, pretty; yet ev'n Courtiers own,
It glitters not with *Pope*—aside 'tis thrown.

     JOHNNY, who fosters next his Patron's Wit,   215
Strikes out a Play, with Thought, and Spirit writ!
To first-rank Beaus our artful Bard applies,
One writes to charm the Fair, and One the Wise.
Beaus fly the Fame, yet secret Talents know,
And read, revise, and ev'n Co-Authors grow;   220
And now anew th'inverted Work they frame,
New Thoughts they hatch!—But *Johnny* holds the *Name.*
So fruitful Madams, their Amours unknown,
Bear private Babes, which, born, their Midwives own.
At Grand Assemblies, Play and Bard appear,   225
Cabals are form'd, our *Johnny*'s Debts to clear;
'Tis read, prais'd, acted!—Now the Poet's Trap!
Beaus heed your *Scenes!* You know your *Cues* to *clap.*

---

sublime. Gay's play, *Three Hours after Marriage*, produced in Drury Lane on 16 January 1717, was the result of collaboration with Pope and Arbuthnot, the first of
whom might be said to have written 'to charm the fair' and the other 'the wise'.
But that Gay was in the habit of fathering other people's literary bastards is not
true, and he was himself mainly responsible for the writing of this play. George
Sherburn, 'The Fortunes and Misfortunes of *Three Hours after Marriage*', *Modern
Philology*, XXVI (1926), 91–109.

THUS through nine Nights loud Party-Praises roar,
Then die away at once, to noise no more.   230
In vain such Authors hope substantial Fame,
Such Praise must usher in a sequent Shame.
To the next Age, the present proves disgrac'd,
With the mean Wits we priz'd, it ranks our Taste;
But through a third, not ev'n their Shame they boast,   235
Their Names, their Works, and Shame alike are lost.
    CALL you these Witlings a Poetic Brood?
Are Pies and Daws the Songsters of the Wood?
For Wit, not Nonsense, first was form'd the Stage,
Not to infect, but to refine the Age!   240
Here soften'd Virtue Rigour's Frown declines!
Precept, enforc'd by just Example, shines!
In each rais'd Tear a gen'rous Meaning flows!
In each pleas'd Smile a fair Instruction grows!
When we strike Nature, and improve the Mind,   245
Those deathless Works a sweet Remembrance find;
No chearless Merit unrewarded toils,
Still *Compton* lives and still a *Dorset* smiles:
Some Noble Spirits still adorn the *Great*,
Still shines *Argyle* with ev'ry Grace of State;   250
Wisdom and Bounty sweet on *Rutland* sit,
And *Howard*'s the lovely Patroness of Wit.
    BUT say, whence liberal Arts thus feel Decay?
Why melt their Charms, like Fairy Towers, away?
Not Ignorance, oppos'd, their Strength impairs,   255
They break, they perish by intestine Jars.
Artists on Artists scoul with jealous Eyes,
And *Envy Emulation*'s place supplies.
With *Envy*'s Influence the dark Bosom's fraught,
But *Emulation* brightens ev'ry Thought!   260
Pale *Envy* pines, if Excellence aspires,
And most she slanders what she most admires;
Charm'd *Emulation* can, with Transport, gaze,
Yet wou'd outsoar the Worth, she loves to praise.

* Colonel HOWARD's Lady. [RS]

THUS thou, our *Universal Passion*'s Foe,   265
Canst thy own Height, by praising Others, show.
Young well may *Pope*'s and *Congreve*'s Charms admire,
Young glows distinguish'd with an equal Fire:
So strong thy Learning, Wit, and Friendship shine,
What Praise true Merit claims, is justly thine.   270

---

267 Cf. Young, *Universal Passion*, Satire 1:

> Why slumbers *Pope*, who leads the tuneful Train,
> Nor hears that Virtue, which He loves, complain?...
> *Congreve*, who crown'd with Laurels fairly won,
> Sits smiling at the Goal while Others run,
> He will not Write; and (more provoking still!)
> Ye Gods, He will not write, and *Mævius* will.

The ANIMALCULE.

A TALE.

Occasion'd by his Grace the Duke of Rutland*'s receiving the Small Pox by Inoculation.*

TEXT: **MP* (1726), pp. 129–34.

The Duke of Rutland submitted to inoculation in April 1725 (*Weekly Journal*, no. 337, 10 April 1725). But in his poem RS is less concerned with inoculation than with the spermatic animalcule, recently found in the semen by Leeuwenhoek and other microscopists, which figured in early theories of heredity. RS shows little scientific knowledge, his poem being an elaborate conceit, in which he traces the descent of the gene of literary patronage from the Greeks to the Duke of Rutland, who had become his patron in 1724.

I

IN *Animalcules*, Muse display
  Spirits, of Name unknown in Song!
Reader a kind Attention pay,
  Nor think an useful Comment long.

II

Far less than Mites, on Mites they prey;   5
  Minutest Things may Swarms contain:

When o'er your Iv'ry Teeth they stray,
    Then throb your little Nerves with Pain.

III

Fluids, in Drops, minutely swell;
    These subtil Beings Each contains;   *10*
In the small sanguine Globes they dwell,
    Roll from the Heart, and trace the Veins.

IV

Through ev'ry tender Tube they rove,
    In finer Spirits, strike the Brain;
Wind quick through ev'ry fibrous Grove,   *15*
    And seek, through Pores, the Heart again.

V

If they with purer Drops dilate,
    And lodge where Entity began,
They actuate with a genial Heat,
    And kindle into future *Man*.   *20*

VI

But, when our Lives are Nature's Due,
    Air, Seas, nor Fire, their Frames dissolve;
They Matter, through all Forms, pursue,
    And oft to genial Heats revolve.

VII

Thus once an *Animalcule* prov'd,   *25*
    When *Man*, a Patron to the Bays;
This Patron was in *Greece* belov'd;
    Yet Fame was faithless to his Praise.

VIII

In *Rome*, this *Animalcule* grew,
    Mæcenas, whom the Classics rate!   *30*

---

16 Pores. Passages or ducts. *OED* (sb. sense 2) considers the word obsolete in this
sense in RS's time, but Thomson so used it in *Spring*, l. 43 (ed. 1728 only).

Among the *Gauls*, it prov'd *Richlieu*,
 In Learning, Pow'r, and Bounty Great.

IX

In *Britain*, *Hallifax* it rose;
 (By *Hallifax*, bloom'd *Congreve*'s Strains)
And now it re-diminish'd glows,   *35*
 To glide through godlike *Rutland*'s Veins.

X

A Plague there is, too Many know;
 Too seldom perfect Cures befall it.
The *Muse* may term it *Beauty's Foe*;
 In *Physick*, the *Small Pox* we call it.   *40*

XI

From *Turks* we learn this Plague t'asswage,
 They, by admitting, turn its Course:
Their Kiss will tame the Tumor's Rage;
 By yielding, they o'ercome the Force.

XII

Thus *Rutland* did its Touch invite,   *45*
 While, watchful in the ambient Air,
This little, guardian, subtil Spright
 Did with the Poison *in* repair.

XIII

Th' Infection from the Heart it clears;
 Th' Infection, now dilated thin,   *50*
In pearly Pimples but appears,
 Expell'd upon the Surface Skin.

XIV

And now it, mould'ring, wasts away:
 'Tis gone!—doom'd to return no more!
Our *Animalcule* keeps its Stay,   *55*
 And must new Labyrinths explore.

XV

And now the *Noble's* Thoughts are seen,
　Unmark'd, it views his Heart's Desires!
It now reflects what It has been,
　And, rapt'rous, at its Change admires!   *60*

XVI

Its pristine Virtues, kept, combine,
　To be again in *Rutland* known;
But they, immers'd, no longer shine,
　Nor equal, nor encrease his own.

Unconstant.

TEXTS: (1) *Grub-street Journal*, 23 August 1733: '*To a YOUNG LADY*.'
　(2) *GM*, 33, 433–4.
　(3) *LM*, 33, 418–19.
　(4) **GM*, 34, 157: 'VERSES *to a* YOUNG LADY.'

Although all texts have as title either 'To a Young Lady', or 'Verses to a Young Lady', the Index to the Poetical Essays in *GM*, 34 calls it *Unconstant*. This is important, because it must be an author's correction, and because it gives a clue to the identity of the young lady. She was Clio (Martha Fowke Sansom) and in the manuscript 'Clio' may have stood where 'Polly' stands now. RS must have sent her his poem in manuscript, for she replied with one of hers entitled *The Innocent Inconstant*, which he printed in *MP* (1726), pp. 100–1. In 1722, in a letter to Aaron Hill, he mentions that Clio had written a poem about him, which may be this one (*European Magazine*, VI (1784), 189–90).

Part of the tangled bibliographical history of this poem is given in the *Autobiography of Sylvanus Urban*, *GM*, n.s. 1 (1856), 268, where it is stated, among other things, that it led to the acquaintance between RS and Edward Cave.

POLLY from me, though now a lovesick youth;
　Nay though a poet, hear the voice of truth!
POLLY you're not a beauty, yet you're pretty;
So grave, yet gay, so silly, yet so witty;

A heart of softness, yet a tongue of satire;   5
You've cruelty, yet, ev'n in *that*, good nature:
Now you are free, and now reserv'd a while;
Now a forc'd frown betrays a willing smile.
Reproach'd for absence, yet your sight denied;
My tongue you silence, yet my silence chide.   10
How wou'd you praise me, shou'd your sex defame!
Yet, shou'd they praise, grow jealous, and exclaim.
If I despair, with some kind look you bless;
But if I hope, at once all hope suppress.
You scorn; yet shou'd my passion change, or fail,   15
Too late you'd whimper out a softer tale.
You love; yet from your lover's wish retire,
Doubt, yet discern; deny, and yet desire.
Such POLLY, are your sex—part truth, part fiction,
Some thought, much whim, and all a contradiction.   20

17–18] You love; and yet your lover's plea reject; / Shun, yet desire; discern, and
yet suspect. *1733*; *GM*, 33; *LM*, 33.

The GENTLEMAN.
Address'd to JOHN JOLIFFE, *Esq;* commissioner of the Wine-licence.

TEXTS: (1) *London Journal*, 18 September 1725: '*The* GENTLEMAN;
Address'd to J— J—e *Esq;*'
  (2) *MP* (1726), pp. 38–9: '*The* GENTLEMAN. *Address'd to* John
Joliffe, *Esq;*'
  (3) **Grub-street Journal*, 12 December 1734.
  (4) *GM*, 34, 694.
  (5) *LM*, 34, 661.

A decent mien, and elegance of dress;
Words, which, at ease, each winning grace, express;
A life, where love, by wisdom polish'd, shines;
Where wisdom's self again, by love, refines;

1 and] an *1725*; *MP*.

Where we to chance for friendship never trust;   5
Nor ever dread from sudden whim disgust;
Where social manners, ever fix'd, remain;
A nature ever great, and never vain;
A wit, that no licentious pertness knows;
The sense, that unassuming candour shows;   10
Reason, by narrow principles uncheck'd,
Slave to no party, bigot to no sect;
Knowledge of various life, of learning too;
Thence taste; thence truth, which will from taste ensue;
Unwilling censure, though a judgment clear;   15
A smile indulgent, and that smile sincere;
An humble, though an elevated mind;
A pride; its pleasure but to serve mankind;
If these, esteem, and admiration, raise,
Give true delight, and gain unflatt'ring praise,   20
In one, wish'd view, th' accomplish'd man we see;
These graces all are thine, and Thou art he.

5–6 *Added in 1734.*
7] A Mind, where Pity, Mirth, and Friendship reign: *1725; MP*; The social manners,
and the heart humane; *GM, 34; LM, 34.*
11–14] A Love of Learning; Knowledge of Mankind; / Meekness unservile, and
a Taste refin'd; *1725; MP.*
15 though] yet *1725; MP.*   16 that smile sincere;] a Soul Sincere: *1725; MP.*
17–18] *Added in 1734.*
20] If where These live, they form a living Praise; *1725; MP.*
21 wish'd] bright *1725; MP.*   22 graces] Virtues *1725; MP.*

A POEM,
Sacred to the Glorious MEMORY
Of our Late *Most Gracious*
SOVEREIGN LORD King GEORGE.
Inscribed to the Right Honourable
GEORGE DODINGTON, Esq;

TEXT: *A POEM, etc. . . . MDCCXXVII.

This poem is an appeal for patronage, aimed at George II and Bubb
Dodington, who had recently become Lord Lieutenant of Somerset,

member of parliament for Bridgwater, and lord of the Treasury under
Walpole. He was also setting himself up as a literary patron. Pope's
'Bufo' was generally taken to be a portrait of him. Edward Young
dedicated his *Third Satire* to him in 1725, and James Thomson his
Summer in 1727. Dodington did not respond to RS in any way, so far
as is known, and neither did the new king.

L ET gaudy *Mirth*, to the blithe Carrol-song,
   In loose light-measur'd Numbers dance along;
Thou, *Muse*[,] no flow'ry fancies here display,
Nor warble with the chearful *Lark* thy Lay.
In the dark Cypress Grove, or moss-grown Cell,   5
Where dreary *Ravens* haunt, would *Sorrow* dwell!
Where *Ghosts*, that shun the Day, come sweeping by,
Or fix in melancholy *Frenzy*'s Eye;
Yet now she turns her flight to Scenes of State,
Where *Wealth* and *Grandeur* weep the frowns of Fate!   10
Wealth, Want, Rank, Power, here each alike partakes,
As the Shrub bends, the lofty Cedar shakes;
To her wide view is no contraction known,
'Tis Youth, 'tis Age, the Cottage and the Throne.
     O *Exclamation*! lend thy sad Relief!   15
O *Dodington*! indulge the righteous Grief!
Distant, I've long beheld, in *Thee*, transcend
The Poet, Patron, Patriot, and the Friend.
Thou, who must live in *Truth*'s remotest Page,
Form'd to delight, and dignify an Age;   20
Whose words, whose manners, and whose mind declare,
Each grace, each moral, and each muse are there;
Accept this Po'esy, void of venal aim,
Made sacred by thy *Royal Master*'s Name.
     But why, O *Muse*! are songful Hours thy choice?   25
Lost is the Life, whose glory lifts thy voice!
GEORGE is no more! As at the doomful sound
Of the last Trump, all *Nature* feels the wound!
Each private, each distinguish'd *Virtue* bleeds!
And what but *Lamentation* long succeeds?   30
Where wilt thou then for apt Allusions fly?

What Eloquence can throbbing Grief supply?
    Late, golden *Pleasures* urg'd their shining way,
With GEORGE they flourish'd, and with GEORGE decay!
Now dusky *Woes*, o'er varied scenes extend,   35
Groans rise! Rocks echo! and chill Damps descend!
Grief strikes my View with ever-weeping Eyes,
At her wan Look, each lively *Fancy* dies.
In fear, in hope, dull rest, or ruf[f]ling storms,
Thus *Woe* besets us, though in various forms!   40
That dire event of Youth's ungovern'd rage!
That dear-bought knowledge to declining Age!
In *want*, in *scorn*, it haunts an humble State,
'Tis *care*, 'tis *envy*, to perplex the Great!
A Kingdom's curse, it in *Dissention* brings;   45
Or heavier falls, when falls the best of Kings!
Worth it exalts, when aiming to debase;
'Tis Virtue's triumph, or 'tis Guilt's disgrace!
It humbles Life, yet dignifies our End;
Reflection's torment, yet Reflection's Friend!   50
Then let the *Muse* her meaning notes resume,
And pay due sorrows to the hallow'd Tomb.
    Was there a Glory, yet to Greatness known,
That not in *Brunswick*'s Soul superior shone?
Ill fare the *Man*, who, robed in purple pride,   55
To wounded *Worth* has no relief apply'd!
Benevolence makes *Pow'r* to *Prudence* dear,
When *Pity* weeps, what Pearl excells the Tear?
When not one *Virtue* glows to bless Mankind,
When *Pride*'s cold influence *petrifies* the Mind;   60
Let the *Prince* blaze with Jems!—in *Wisdom*'s view,
An Emblem of the Rock, where once they grew!
Yet springs gush out, to prove ev'n Rocks can flow
In Rills refreshful to the Vales below.
Why has he pow'r, and why no heart to chear,   65
Unseeing Eyes, and Ears that will not hear?
Swift, as his Bliss, shall his light name decay,
Who, self-indulgent, *sports* his hours away!

But, Oh!—what Love, what Honour shall he claim,
Whose Joy is Bounty, and whose Gift is Fame?   70
He (truly great!) his useful pow'r refines,
By him discover'd *Worth* exalted shines;
Exalted *Worth*, th' enlivening act, repeats,
And draws *new Virtues* from obscure retreats;
He, as the first, creative Influence, prais'd,   75
Smiles o'er the *Beings*, which his Bounty rais'd.
Such *Dodington*, thy Royal Master shin'd,
Such Thou, the Image of thy *Monarch*'s mind.
    Nations were ballanc'd by his guardian skill,
Like the pois'd *Planets* by the all-pow'rful Will.   80
Mark the *Swede* succour'd[!] mark the aspiring CZAR!
Check'd are his hopes, and shun'd the naval War.
By GEORGE the *Austrian Eagle* learns to tower,
While the proud *Turk* shakes conscious of her power;
But when her Menace braves our envied shore,   85
She trembles at the *British Lyon*'s Roar;
Trembles, though aided by the force of *Spain*,
And *India*'s wealth!—'gainst *Brunswick*, All how vain!
He bad *thy* Honour, *Albion*, foremost shine!
His was the Care, unmeasur'd Bliss was Thine!   90
Yet oft against his Virtue *Faction* rose!

_____

79–80 English foreign policy under the Whigs during the reign of George I was
mostly concerned with matching any possible combination of hostile powers with
an equally powerful group of allies.

81–2 Charles XII had been in exile and a virtual prisoner in Turkish territory from
1709 to 1714. On his return he began to try to win back his lost outlying possessions,
and declared war on George I as Elector of Hanover. He even threatened to ally
himself with his former arch-enemy, the Tsar, for the purpose of landing the Pretender in Scotland. This plan was frustrated by an immediate display of naval
strength by England, and eventually by the Triple Alliance between England, France,
and Holland, 1716–17.

83 Austrian Eagle. In 1716 the Emperor, Charles VI, threatened by a Turkish
war, made the treaty of Westminster with England, guaranteeing the Hanoverian
succession in exchange for a guarantee of his own gains in the treaties of Utrecht
and Baden. Hence the Quadruple Alliance in 1718. After the close of the Turkish
war in that year, the Emperor tried to back out of the Alliance, formed the Ostend
Company to rival the East India Company, and came to an agreement with Spain.
Hostilities broke out on a small scale in 1726, but England, in alliance with Prussia,
was victorious, and peace was signed in 1727.

An *Angel*, if *thy* Monarch, would have Foes.
    Come *Charity*, First-born of Virtue's Line!
Come meek-ey'd *Mercy* from the Seat Divine!
Pure *Temp'rance*, Mistress of a tranquil Mind,   *95*
By whom each sensual *Passion* stands confin'd!
Fix'd *Fortitude*, from whom fierce *Peril* flies!
By whom (O Soul of Action!) Empires rise!
Fair *Justice*, Author of a Godlike Reign!
Peace, *Plenty*, *Liberty* adorn *thy* Train!   *100*
Lov'd *Prudence*! Queen of Virtues! blissful Dame!
Parent, and Guide of each illustrious Aim!
From whose firm Step *Confusion* turns in Flight,
That shapeless Spawn of *Anarchy* and *Night*!
From whom kind *Harmony* deduc'd her Race,   *105*
Then *Order*, all in one united Grace!
And thou, *Religion*! truest, Heav'nly Friend!
Whom *These* alone establish, *These* defend!
Assemble to the wailing Muse's Call!
Weep o'er the clay-cold Breast, that held you *All*!   *110*
    O *Death*, rouze all those *Terrors* to thy Aid,
Weak *Fear*, or wisest *Valour* wou'd evade!
Whether foul *Pestilence*, in dire Array,
Red *War*, or pale-ey'd *Famine*, point your Way,
What can you more than Kingdoms overthrow?   *115*
What aim'd you less, when *Brunswick* felt the Blow?
But mark!—AUGUSTUS, still above thy Rage,
Steps forth to give a second, GOLDEN AGE.
    Ye great *Plantagenets*! distinguish'd Race!
One greater meets you on cœlestial Space.   *120*
And thou, *Nassau*! the fairest, noblest Name!
Ev'n mid the Blest, superior still thy Flame!
Behold an *Equal* now!—How dear th'Embrace!
Oh, flye!—present him at the Throne of Grace!
'Tis done!—He's crown'd with a resplendant Joy, *125*

---

121 *Nassau*! William III, whose family name was Orange-Nassau. Cf. *Genius of Liberty*, l. 31.

Which Care shall never dim, nor Time destroy.
   See!—from yon Golden Cloud, amidst a Band
Of Angel-Pow'rs, once *Patriots* of the Land,
Soft-leaning o'er *Britannia*'s weeping Isle,
And shedding, sweet, a fond, paternal Smile;   *130*
Pointing, the visionary *Seraph* cries,
Suspend thy Tears!—Behold a *Sov'reign* rise,
Thy *Second* GEORGE! whose Reign shall soon disclose
All that Mine gave, and Heav'n, in Grace, bestows.
   He said.—Again, with Majesty refin'd,   *135*
Up-wing'd to Realms of Bliss, th'*Ætherial Mind*.

The BASTARD.

A POEM inscrib'd with all due reverence to Mrs BRET, *once Countess of* Macclesfield.

TEXTS: (1) THE BASTARD, etc. 1728. (Advertised in *Monthly Chronicle*, 18 April 1728)   [1728*a*]
   (2) THE BASTARD, etc. The SECOND EDITION. 1728. (Advertised in *Mist's Weekly Journal*, 11 May 1728.)   [1728*b*]
   (3) THE BASTARD, etc. The THIRD EDITION, 1728. (Advertised in *Mist's Weekly Journal*, 8 June 1728.)   [1728*c*]
   (4) THE BASTARD, etc. The FOURTH EDITION. 1728. (Advertised in *Mist's Weekly Journal*, 3 August 1728.)   [1728*d*]
   (5) THE BASTARD, etc. The FIFTH EDITION. 1728.
   (I have not noticed any advertisements.)   [1728*e*]
   (6) *GM*, 37, 113–14. (Lacks preface, but has introductory note.)

The text given below is the revised one in *GM*, 37, supplemented by the preface in 1728*a*. RS's revisions consist merely of three small changes in words or word-order, the only interesting one being the substitution of 'other' for 'nobler' in line 43.

From both the poem and the preface it is clear that composition began 'in gayer hours' before the murder of Sinclair, and that it was completed after RS's pardon in January 1728. It was probably begun at Richmond, where RS was living before his arrest, and completed in London, at Lord Tyrconnel's house. RS's authorship of it was disputed by I.K., in his 'Life of Aaron Hill' prefixed to *The Dramatick Works of Aaron Hill* (1760), who said that Hill wrote *The Bastard* 'to serve Mr Savage'. This statement cannot be taken seriously. Hill himself never laid claim to the poem, and it does not appear in his posthumously published *Poetical Works.* Cf. *Volunteer Laureat*, no. 1.

Decet hæc dare Dona Novercam. *Ov. Met.*

THE PREFACE.

*T*HE *Reader will easily perceive these Verses were begun, when my Heart was Gayer, than it has been of late; and finish'd in Hours of the deepest Melancholy.*

I hope the World will do me the Justice to believe, that no part of this flows from any real Anger *against the* Lady, *to whom it is* 5 *inscrib'd. Whatever undeserv'd Severities I may have receiv'd at her Hands, wou'd she deal so Candidly as to acknowledge Truth, she very well knows, by an* Experience *of many Years, that I have ever behaved my self towards her, like one, who thought it his Duty to support with Patience all Afflictions from that* Quarter. *Indeed* 10 *if I had not been capable of* forgiving *a* Mother, *I must have blush'd to receive Pardon my self at the Hands of my* Sovereign.

Neither to say Truth, were the manner of my Birth All, shou'd I have any Reason for complaint—when I am a little disposed to a gay turn of Thinking, I consider, as I was a De-relict *from my* 15 *Cradle, I have the Honour of a* lawful Claim *to the best Protection in* Europe. *For being a* Spot of Earth, *to which no Body* pretends *a* Title, *I devolve naturally upon the* KING, *as one of the* Rights of His *Royalty.*

While I presume to Name his MAJESTY, *I look back, with* 20 *Confusion, upon the* Mercy *I have lately experienc'd, because it is impossible to* remember *it, but* with *something I would fain* forget; *for the sake of my future Peace, and Alleviation of my past Misfortune.*

I owe my Life to the Royal Pity; *if a Wretch can, with Pro-* 25 *priety, be said to live, whose Days are fewer than his Sorrows; and to whom* Death *had been but a* Redemption *from* Misery.

But I will Suffer *my* Pardon, *as my* Punishment, *till that Life, which has so graciously been given me, shall become considerable enough* not to be useless *in His Service, to Whom it was forfeited.* 30

Motto: Ovid, *Metamorphoses*, IX, 181.

Under Influence of these Sentiments, with which his MAJESTY'S *great Goodness has inspired me, I consider my Loss of Fortune, and Dignity, as my Happiness; to which, as I was born without Ambition, I am thrown from them without Repining.—Possessing those Advantages, my Care had been, perhaps, but how to enjoy 35 Life; by the want of them I am taught this nobler Lesson, to study how to deserve it.*   R. Savage.

IN gayer hours, when high my fancy ran,
The muse, exulting, thus her lay began.
   Blest be the *Bastard's* birth! through wondr'ous ways,
He shines eccentric like a Comet's blaze.
No sickly fruit of faint compliance he;   5
He! stampt in nature's mint of extasy!
He lives to build, not boast, a gen'rous race:
No tenth transmitter of a foolish face.
His daring hope, no sire's example bounds;
His first-born lights, no prejudice confounds.   10
He, kindling from within, requires no flame;
He glories in a *Bastard's* glowing name.
   Born to himself, by no possession led,
In freedom foster'd, and by fortune fed;
Nor Guides, nor Rules, his sov'reign choice controul,   15
His body independant, as his soul.
Loos'd to the world's wide range—enjoyn'd no aim;
Prescrib'd no duty, and assign'd no Name:
Nature's unbounded son, he stands alone,
His heart unbiass'd, and his mind his own.   20
   O *Mother*, yet *no* Mother!—'tis to you,
My thanks for such distinguish'd claims are due.
You, unenslav'd to nature's narrow laws,
Warm championess for *freedom's* sacred cause,
From all the dry devoirs of blood and line,   25
From ties maternal, moral and divine,
Discharg'd my grasping soul; push'd me from shore,
And launch'd me into life without an oar.

---

1 ran] run *1728a*.   2 began] begun *1728a*.

What had I lost, if conjugally kind,
By nature hating, yet by vows confin'd,   30
Untaught the matrimonial bounds to slight,
And coldly conscious of a husband's right,
You had *faint-drawn* me with a *form* alone,
A lawful lump of life by force your own!
Then, while your backward will retrench'd desire,   35
And unconcurring spirits lent no fire,
I had been born your dull, domestic heir;
Load of your life, and motive of your care;
Perhaps been poorly rich, and meanly great;
The slave of pomp, a cypher in the state;   40
Lordly neglectful of a worth unknown,
And slumb'ring in a *seat*, by *chance* my own.

  Far other blessings wait the *Bastard*'s lot;
Conceiv'd in rapture, and with fire begot!
Strong, as necessity, he starts away,   45
Climbs against wrongs, and brightens into day.

  Thus unprophetic, lately misinspir'd,
I sung; gay, flatt'ring hope my fancy fir'd;
Inly secure, through conscious scorn of ill;
Nor taught by wisdom how to ballance will,   50
Rashly deceiv'd, I saw no *pits* to shun;
But thought to *purpose*, and to *act* were *one*;
Heedless what pointed cares pervert his way,
Whom caution arms not, and whom woes betray;
But now expos'd and shrinking from distress,   55
I fly to shelter, while the tempests press;
My muse to grief resigns the varying tone,
The raptures languish, and the numbers groan.

  O memory!—thou soul of joy and pain!
Thou actor of our passions o'er again!   60
Why dost thou aggravate the wretch's woe?
Why add continuous smart to ev'ry blow?
Few are my joys; alas! how soon forgot!

---

43 other] nobler *1728a, b, c, d, e.*

On that *kind* quarter thou invad'st me not,
While sharp and numberless my sorrows fall[;]   65
Yet thou repeat'st and multiply'st 'em all.

    Is chance a guilt? that my disastrous heart,
For mischief never meant must ever smart?
Can self-defence be sin?—Ah, plead no more!
What though no purpos'd malice stain'd thee o'er?   70
Had heav'n befriended thy unhappy side,
Thou had'st not been provok'd—Or *thou* had'st died.

    Far be the guilt of home-shed blood from all,
On whom unsought, embroiling dangers fall!
Still the pale *dead* revives and lives to me,   75
To me! through *Pity*'s eye condemn'd to see.
Remembrance veils his rage, but swells his fate;
Griev'd I forgive, and am grown cool too late.
Young and unthoughtful then; who knows, one day,
What rip'ning virtues might have made their way!   80
He might have liv'd till folly died in shame,
Till kindling wisdom felt a thirst for fame.
He might perhaps his country's friend have prov'd,
Been gen'rous, happy, candid and belov'd.
He might have sav'd some worth, now doom'd to fall,   85
And I, perchance, in him have *murder'd* all.

    O fate of late Repentance! always vain:
Thy remedies but lull undying pain.
Where shall my hope find rest?—No mother's care
Shielded my infant innocence with prayer: 90
No father's guardian hand my youth maintain'd,
Call'd forth my virtues, and from vice restrain'd.
Is it not time to snatch some pow'rful arm,
First to advance, then screen from future harm?
Am I return'd from death, to live in pain?   95
Or would *imperial pity* save in vain?
Distrust it not!—What blame can *mercy* find,
Which gives at once a life, and rears a mind?

---

84 gen'rous, happy] happy, gen'rous *1728a, b, c, d, e.*
92 and] or *1728a, b, c, d, e.*

Mother, miscall'd, farewell—Of soul severe,
This sad reflection yet may force one tear: 100
All I was wretched by to You I ow'd,
Alone from strangers ev'ry comfort flow'd.

    Lost to the life *you* gave, *your* son no more,
And now *adopted*, who was *doom'd* before,
New-born I may a nobler mother claim;   105
But dare not whisper her immortal *name*;
Supreamly lovely, and serenely great!
Majestic *mother* of a kneeling *state*!
Queen of a people's hearts, who ne'er before
Agreed—yet now with one consent *adore*!   110
One contest yet remains in this desire,
Who most shall give applause, where all admire.

FULVIA.
A Poem.

TEXT: *GM*, 37, 312.

Though not published until long afterwards, this poem must have been
written when RS was at the height of his popularity, immediately
after the publication of *The Bastard*.

LET *Fulvia*'s wisdom be a slave to will,
   Her darling passions, scandal and Quadrille;
On friends and foes her tongue a satire known,
Her deeds a satire on herself alone.
On her poor kindred deigns she word or look?   5
'Tis cold respect, or 'tis unjust rebuke;
Worse when good-natur'd than when most severe;
The jest impure then pains the modest ear.
How just the sceptic? the divine how odd?
What turns of wit play smartly on her God?   10

    The fates, my nearest kindred, foes decree:
Fulvia, when piqu'd at them, strait pities me.
She, like benevolence, a smile bestows,

Favours to me indulge her spleen to those.
The banquet serv'd, with peeresses I sit: *15*
She tells my ſtory, and repeats my wit.
With mouth diſtorted, through a sounding nose
It comes, now homeliness more homely grows.
With see-saw sounds and nonsense not my own,
She screws her features, and she cracks her tone.   *20*
'How fine your BASTARD! why so soft a ſtrain?
'What *such* a *Mother*? satirize again!'
Oft I objeɕt, but fix'd is *Fulvia*'s will:
Ah! though unkind, she is my *mother* ſtill!
　　The verse now flows, the manuscript she claims. *25*
'Tis fam'd—The fame, each curious fair enflames:
The wildfire runs; from copy, copy grows:
The *Brets* alarm'd, a sep'rate peace propose.
'Tis ratified—How alter'd Fulvia's look?
My wit's degraded, and my cause forsook.   *30*
Thus she: 'What's poetry but to amuse?
'Might I advise—there are more solid views.'
With a cool air she adds: 'This tale is old:
'Were it *my* case, it should no more be told.
'Complaints—had I been worthy to advise—   *35*
'You know—But when are wits, like women, wise?
'True it may take, but think whate'er you liſt,
'All love the satire, none the satiriſt.'
　　I ſtart, I ſtare, ſtand fix'd, then pause awhile;
Then hesitate, then ponder well, then smile.   *40*
'Madam—a pension loſt—and where's amends?'
'Sir (she replies) indeed you'll lose your friends.'
Why did I ſtart? 'twas but a change of wind—
Or the same thing—the Lady chang'd her mind.
I bow, depart, despise, discern her all: *45*
Nanny revisits, and disgrac'd I fall.
　　Let *Fulvia*'s friendship whirl with ev'ry whim!
A reed, a weathercock, a shade, a dream:

---

28 The *Brets*. Perhaps Mrs Brett (the former Lady Macclesfield) and her daughter.

No more the friendship shall be now display'd
By weathercock or reed or dream or shade;   *50*
To *Nanny* fix'd unvarying shall it tend,
For souls, so form'd alike, were form'd to blend.

A Grace after Dinner,
spoken *Extempore* at a *Miser's Feaſt.*

TEXT: *MS 5832 (British Museum), f. 169.

This MS is volume XXXI of the MSS of Rev. Wm. Cole, which contains
a miscellaneous collection of prose and verse. How Cole got a copy of
RS's epigram is not known, nor on what occasion it was composed.
Cole, however, did note that RS was the author. I date it conjecturally
at the same time as *Fulvia*.

T Hanks for this Miracle! for 'tis no less
  Thus sumptuously at a miser's Board to feaſt.
In Land of Famine we have found Relief,
  And seen the wonders of a Chine of Beef.
Chimneys have smoak'd, which never smoak'd before;   *5*
  And we have din'd—where we shall dine no more.

THE WANDERER: A VISION.

TEXT: *THE WANDERER: A POEM. In FIVE CANTO's.... 1729.
    (Advertised in *Fog's Weekly Journal*, 18 January 1729).

On the title-page this poem is called THE WANDERER: A POEM,
but the title given at the head of each canto is THE WANDERER:
A VISION. This has been adopted here as the title most likely to have
been intended by RS.
    Composition was begun at Richmond in 1726–7. See note to I, 179 ff.
The greatest part, however, must have been written at Lord Tyrconnel's
house in Arlington Street in 1728. Professor W. M. Sale believes that
the poem was actually printed off early in 1728 or even late in 1727
(*Samuel Richardson, Master Printer* (Ithaca, 1950), pp. 258–60). But late
1727 is out of the question, since at that time RS was being tried for murder and condemned to death. After his pardon in January 1728, he had
ample leisure for composition, once he had completed *The Bastard*.

The editor of the *European Magazine* (VI (1784), 191) suggested that
The Wanderer may have been the same poem as a now lost one entitled
The Enthusiast, of which RS sent a copy to Aaron Hill in 1721. But
that poem was in stanzas and its subject was the history of enthusiasm
from the Garden of Eden down. Consequently it cannot have been
even an early version of *The Wanderer*.

In writing this poem, RS was evidently influenced strongly by his
friend James Thomson, who had recently published the greater part
of *The Seasons*. Cf. A. D. McKillop, *The Background of Thomson's*
SEASONS (Minneapolis, 1942).

Nulla mali *nova mî facies inopinave* surgit. Virg.

To the Right Honourable *JOHN*, *Lord Viscount* Tyrconnel, *Baron* Charleville, *and Lord* Brownlowe: *Knight of the* Bath.

My LORD,

PART of this POEM had the Honour of your Lordship's 5
Perusal when in Manuscript, and it was no small Pride
to me, when it met with Approbation from so diſtinguishing
a Judge: Should the reſt find the like Indulgence, I shall
have no Occasion (whatever its Success may be in the World)
to repent the Labour it has coſt me.—But my Intention is 10
not to pursue a Discourse on my own Performance; No,
my Lord, it is to embrace this Opportunity of throwing out
Sentiments that relate to your Lordship's Goodness, the
Generosity of which, give me Leave to say, I have greatly
experienc'd. 15

I offer it not as a new Remark, that Dependance on the
Great, in former Times, generally terminated in Disappointment; nay, even their Bounty (if it could be called such) was
in its very Nature ungenerous. It was, perhaps, with-held
through an indolent, or wilful Negleƈt, 'till those, who 20
lingered in the Want of it, grew almoſt paſt the Sense of
Comfort. At length it came, too often, in a Manner, that
half cancell'd the Obligation, and, perchance, muſt have been

---

Motto: Vergil, *Aeneid*, VI, 103–4: 'non ulla laborum / O virgo, nova mi facies
inopinave surgit.'

acquired too by some previous Act of Guilt in the Receiver, the Consequence of which was Remorse and Infamy.   25

But *that I live*, my Lord, is a Proof that Dependance on your Lordship, and the present Ministry, is an Assurance of Success. I am persuaded Distress, in many other Instances, affects your Soul with a Compassion, that always shews itself in a manner most humane and active; that to forgive 30 Injuries, and confer Benefits, is your Delight; and that to deserve your Friendship is to deserve the Countenance of the best of Men: To be admitted into the Honour of your Lordship's Conversation (permit me to speak but Justice) is to be elegantly introduced into the most instructive, as well 35 as entertaining, Parts of Literature; it is to be furnish'd with the finest Observations upon human Nature, and to receive from the most unassuming, sweet, and winning Candour, the worthiest and most polite Maxims—Such as are always enforc'd by the Actions of your own Life. I could also take 40 Notice of your many publick-spirited Services to your Country in Parliament, and your constant Attachment to Liberty, and the Royal, Illustrious House of our Most *Gracious Sovereign*; But, my Lord, believe me, your own Deeds are the noblest and fittest Orators to speak your Praise, and will elevate 45 it far beyond the Power of a much abler Writer than I am.

I will therefore turn my View from your Lordship's Virtues to the kind Influence of them, which has been so lately shed upon me; and then, if my future Morals and Writings shall gain any Approbation from Men of Parts and 50 Probity, I must acknowledge all to be the Product of your Lordship's Goodness to me. I must, in fine, say with *Horace*,

Quod spiro, & placeo (si placeo) tuum est.

I am, with the highest Gratitude and Veneration,
My LORD,   55
Your Lordship's most Dutiful
And Devoted Servant,
R. SAVAGE.

_____

53 Horace, *Odes*, IV, iii, 24.

96

FAIN wou'd my Verse, TYRCONNEL, boaſt thy Name,
BROWNLOW, at once my Subjeƈt, and my Fame!
Oh! cou'd that Spirit, which thy Bosom warms,
Whose Strength surprizes, and whose Goodness charms!
That various Worth!—cou'd that inspire my Lays,   5
Envy shou'd smile, and Censure learn to praise:
Yet, though unequal to a Soul, like thine,
A generous Soul, approaching to Divine,
When bless'd beneath such Patronage I write,
Great my Attempt, though hazardous my Flight.   10
    O'er ample Nature I extend my Views;
Nature to rural Scenes invites the Muse:
She flies all public Care, all venal Strife,
To try the *Still*, compar'd with *Aƈtive* Life;
To prove, by these the Sons of Men may owe   15
The Fruits of Bliss to burſting Clouds of Woe,
That ev'n Calamity, by Thought refin'd,
Inspirits, and adorns the thinking Mind.
    Come, CONTEMPLATION, whose unbounded Gaze,
Swift in a Glance, the Course of Things, surveys;   20
Who in *Thy-self* the various View can'ſt find
Of Sea, Land, Air, and Heav'n, and human Kind;
What Tides of Passion in the Bosom roll;
What Thoughts debase, and what exalt the Soul;
Whose Pencil paints, obsequious to thy Will,   25
All thou survey'ſt, with a creative Skill!
Oh, leave a-while thy lov'd, sequeſter'd Shade!
A-while in wintry Wilds vouchsafe thy Aid!
Then waft me to some olive, bow'ry Green;
Where, cloath'd in white, thou shew'ſt a Mind serene;   30
Where kind *Content* from Noise, and Court retires,
And smiling sits, while Muses tune their Lyres:
Where *Zephyrs* gently breathe, while *Sleep* profound
To their soft Fanning nods, with Poppies crown'd,
Sleep on a Treasure of bright Dreams reclines,   35

By *thee* bestow'd; whence *Fancy* colour'd shines,
And flutters round his Brow a hov'ring Flight,
Varying her Plumes in visionary Light.

The solar Fires now faint, and watry burn,
Just where with Ice *Aquarius* frets his Urn!   40
If thaw'd, full-issue from its Mouth severe,
Raw Clouds, that sadden all th'inverted Year.

When FROST and FIRE with martial Pow'rs engag'd,
FROST, northward, fled the War, unequal wag'd!
Beneath the Pole his Legions urg'd their Flight,   45
And gain'd a Cave profound, and wide as Night.
O'er chearless Scenes by Desolation own'd,
High on an Alp of Ice he sits enthron'd!
One clay-cold Hand, his crystal Beard, sustains,
And scepter'd One, o'er Wind, and Tempest, reigns;   50
O'er stony Magazines of Hail, that storm
The blossom'd Fruit, and flow'ry Spring deform.
His languid Eyes, like frozen Lakes, appear,
Dim-gleaming all the Light, that wanders here.
His Robe snow-wrought, and hoar'd with Age; his Breath   55
A nitrous Damp, that strikes petrific Death.

Far hence lies, ever-freez'd, the Northern Main,
That checks, and renders Navigation vain;
That, shut against the Sun's dissolving Ray,
Scatters the trembling Tides of vanquish'd Day,   60
And stretching *Eastward* half the World secures,
Defies Discov'ry, and like Time endures!

Now FROST sent boreal Blasts to scourge the Air,
To bind the Streams, and leave the Landscape bare;
Yet when *far-west*, his Violence declines;   65
Though here the Brook, or Lake, his Pow'r confines;
To rocky Pools, to Cat'racts are unknown
His Chains!—to Rivers, rapid like the *Rhone!*

The falling Moon cast cold, a quiv'ring Light,
Just silver'd o'er the Snow, and sunk!—Pale Night   70
Retir'd. The Dawn in light-grey Mists arose!
Shrill chants the Cock!—the hungry Heifer lows!

Slow blush yon breaking Clouds!—the Sun's up-roll'd!
Th' expansive *Grey* turns azure, chac'd with Gold;
White-glitt'ring Ice, chang'd like the *Topaz*, gleams,   *75*
Reflecting Saffron Lustre from his Beams.
 O *Contemplation*, teach me to explore,
From *Britain* far remote, some distant Shore!
From *Sleep* a Dream distinct, and lively Claim;
Clear let the Vision strike the Moral's Aim!   *80*
It comes! I feel it o'er my Soul serene!
Still *Morn* begins, and *Frost* retains the Scene!
 Hark!—the loud Horn's enlivening Note's begun!
From Rock to Vale sweet-wand'ring Echoes run!
Still floats the Sound shrill-winding from afar!   *85*
Wild Beasts astonish'd dread the Sylvan War!
Spears to the Sun in Files embattled play,
March on, charge briskly, and enjoy the Fray!
Swans, Ducks, and Geese, and the wing'd, Winter Brood,
Chatter discordant on yon echoing Flood!   *90*
At *Babel* thus, when Heav'n the Tongue confounds,
Sudden a thousand different, jargon Sounds,
Like jangling Bells, harsh-mingling, grate the Ear!
All stare! all talk! all mean; but none cohere!
Mark! wiley Fowlers meditate their Doom,   *95*
And smoky *Fate* speeds thundr'ing though the Gloom!
Stop'd short, they cease in airy Rings to fly,
Whirl o'er, and o'er, and, flutt'ring, fall and die.
 Still Fancy wafts me on! deceiv'd I stand,
Estrang'd, adventrous on a foreign Land!   *100*
Wide and more wide extends the Scene unknown!
Where shall I turn, a *Wanderer*, and alone?
 From hilly Wilds, and Depths where Snows remain,
My winding Steps up a steep Mountain strain!
Emers'd a-top I mark the Hills subside,   *105*
And Tow'rs aspire but with inferior Pride!
On this bleak Height tall Firs, with Ice-work crown'd,
Bend, while their flaky Winter shades the Ground!
Hoarse, and direct, a blust'ring North-wind blows!

On Boughs, thick-rustling, crack the crispid Snows!   110
Tangles of Frost half fright the wilder'd Eye,
By Heat oft blacken'd like a low'ring Sky!
Hence down the Side two turbid Riv'lets pour,
And devious Two, in one huge Cat'ract, roar!
While pleas'd the watry Progress I pursue,   115
Yon Rocks in rough Assemblage rush in View!
In form an Amphitheatre they rise;
And a dark Gulph in their broad Center lies.
There the dim'd Sight with dizzy Weakness fails,
And Horror o'er the firmest Brain prevails!   120
Thither these Mountain-streams their Passage take,
Headlong foam down, and form a dreadful Lake!
The Lake, high-swelling, so redundant grows,
From the heap'd Store deriv'd a River flows;
Which deep'ning travels through a distant Wood,   125
And, thence emerging, meets a Sister-flood;
Mingled they flash on a wide-opening Plain,
And pass yon City to the far-seen Main.
　　So blend two Souls by Heav'n for Union made,
And strength'ning forward, lend a mutual Aid,   130
And prove in ev'ry transient Turn their Aim,
Through finite Life to infinite the same.
　　Nor ends the Landscape—Ocean, to my Sight,
Points a blue Arm, where sailing Ships delight,
In Prospect lessen'd!—Now new Rocks, rear'd high,   135
Stretch a cross Ridge, and bar the curious Eye!
　　There lies obscur'd the ripening Diamond's Ray,
And thence red-branching Coral's rent away.
In conic Form there gelid Crystal grows;
Through such the Palace-Lamp, gay Lustre, throws!   140
Lustre, which, through dim Night, as various plays,
As play from yonder Snows the changeful Rays!

---

137 Compare the answer returned by Sir Philberto Vernatti, Resident in Batavia
in Java Major, to inquiries sent thither by order of the Royal Society: 'Q. I. *Whether
Diamonds and other precious Stones grow again, after three or four Years, in the same Places
where they have been digged out?* A. Never, or at least as the Memory of Man can attain
to' (Thomas Sprat, *The History of the Royal Society of London* (3rd ed. 1722), p. 158).

For nobler Use the Cryſtal's Worth may rise,
If Tubes perſpeſtive hem the spotless Prize;
Through these the Beams of the far-lengthen'd Eye   *145*
Measure known Stars, and new remoter spy.
Hence *Commerce* many a shorten'd Voyage ſteers,
Shorten'd to Months, the Hazard once of Years;
Hence HALLEY's Soul etherial Flight essays;
Inſtruſtive there from Orb to Orb she ſtrays;   *150*
Sees, round new countless Suns, new Syſtems roll!
Sees God in *All*! and magnifies the Whole!
Yon rocky Side enrich'd the Summer Scene,
And Peasant's Search with Herbs of healthful Green;
Now naked, pale, and comfortless it lies,   *155*
Like Youth extended cold in Death's Disguise.
There, while without the sounding Tempeſt swells,
Incav'd secure th'exulting Eagle dwells;
And there, when Nature owns prolific Spring,
Spreads o'er her Young a fondling Mother's Wing.   *160*
Swains on the Coaſt the far-fam'd Fish descry,
That gives the fleecy Robe the *Tyrian* Dye;
While Shells, a scatter'd Ornament, beſtow;
The tinſtur'd Rivals of the show'ry Bow.
Yon limeless Sands, loose-driving with the Wind,   *165*
In future Cauldrons useful Texture find,
Till, on the Furnace thrown, the glowing Mass
Brightens, and bright'ning hardens into Glass.
When winter Halcyons, flick'ring on the Wave,
Tune their Complaints, yon Sea forgets to rave;   *170*
Though lash'd by Storms, which naval Pride o'erturn,
The foaming Deep in Sparkles seems to burn,

---

144 'Tubes perspective' are telescopes. Note the influence in this passage of
Newton's *Opticks*. Marjorie Nicolson, *Newton Demands the Muse* (Princeton, 1946),
p. 29.
   161 Far-fam'd Fish. The murex, from which the famous purple dye was made in
ancient times.
   165 Limeless. RS may mean either *without limit*, a rare use of the word according
to *OED*, or *without cohesiveness* (cf. 'bird-lime').

Loud Winds turn Zephyrs to enlarge their Notes,
And each safe Nest on a calm Surface floats.
　　Now veers the Wind full East; and keen, and sore, *175*
Its cutting Influence akes in ev'ry Pore!
How weak thy Fabrick, Man!—A Puff, thus blown,
Staggers thy Strength, and echoes to thy Groan.
A Tooth's minutest Nerve let Anguish seize,
Swift kindred Fibres catch! (so frail our Ease!)　　　　*180*
Pinch'd, pierc'd, and torn, enflam'd, and unassuag'd,
They smart, and swell, and throb, and shoot enrag'd!
From Nerve to Nerve fierce flies th'exulting Pain!
—And are we of this mighty Fabrick vain?
Now my Blood chills! scarce through my Veins it glides! *185*
Sure on each Blast a shiv'ring Ague rides!
Warn'd let me this bleak Eminence forsake,
And to the Vale a diff'rent Winding take!
　　Half I descend: My Spirits fast decay;
A Terrass now relieves my weary Way.　　　　　　　*190*
Close with this Stage a Precipice combines;
Whence still the spacious Country far declines!
The Herds seem Insects in the distant Glades,
And Men diminish'd, as at Noon their Shades!
Thick on this Top o'ergrown for Walks are seen　　　*195*
Grey, leafless Wood, and winter Greens between!
The red'ning Berry, deep-ting'd Holly shows,
And matted Misleto, the white, bestows!
Though, lost the Banquet of autumnal Fruits,
Though on broad Oaks, no vernal Umbrage shoots; *200*
These Boughs, the silenc'd, shiv'ring Songsters seek!
These foodful Berries fill the hungry Beak.
　　Beneath appears a Place, all outward bare,
Inward the dreary Mansion of Despair!

---

179 ff. These lines were evidently written before August 1726. James Thomson,
writing to Mallet at that time, said: 'I have racked my Brain about the common
Blessing of the Sun You say is forgot, as much as ever S. did his in that elaborate
Description of the Tooth-Ach Dr Young disconcerted, without being able to hit
on it' (*James Thomson* (1700–1748); *Letters & Documents*, ed. A. D. McKillop (Lawrence,
Kansas, 1958), p. 40).

The Water of the Mountain-Road, half stray'd,   *205*
Break's o'er it wild, and falls a brown Cascade.
    Has Nature this rough, naked Piece design'd,
To hold Inhabitant of mortal Kind?
She has. Approach'd, appears a deep Descent,
Which opens in a Rock a large Extent!   *210*
And hark!—its hollow Entrance reach'd, I hear
A trampling Sound of Footsteps hast'ning near!
A death-like Chillness thwarts my panting Breast:
Soft! the wish'd Object stands at length confest!
Of Youth his Form!—But why with Anguish bent? *215*
Why pin'd with sallow Marks of Discontent?
Yet Patience, lab'ring to beguile his Care,
Seems to raise Hope, and smiles away Despair.
Compassion in his Eye surveys my Grief,
And in his Voice invites me to Relief.   *220*
Preventive of thy Call, behold my haste,
(He says.) Nor let warm Thanks thy Spirits waste!
All Fear forget—Each Portal I possess,
Duty wide-opens to receive Distress.
Oblig'd, I follow, by his Guidance led: *225*
The vaulted Roof re-echoing to our Tread!
And now, in squar'd Divisions, I survey
Chambers sequester'd from the Glare of Day;
Yet needful Lights, are taught to intervene,
Through Rifts; each forming a perspective Scene. *230*
    In front a Parlour meets my ent'ring View;
Oppos'd, a Room to sweet Refection due.
Here my chill'd Veins are warm'd by chippy Fires,
Through the bor'd Rock above, the Smoke expires;
Neat, o'er a homely Board, a Napkin's spread, *235*
Crown'd with a heapy Canister of Bread.
A Maple Cup is next dispatch'd, to bring
The Comfort of the salutary Spring:
Nor mourn we absent Blessings of the Vine,
Here laughs a frugal Bowl of rosy Wine;   *240*
And sav'ry Cates, upon clear Embers cast,

Lie hissing, till snatch'd off; a rich Repast!
Soon leap my Spirits with enliven'd Pow'r,
And in gay Converse glides the feastful Hour.
    The *Hermit*, thus: Thou wonder'st at thy Fare: *245*
On me, yon City, kind, bestows her Care;
Meat for keen Famine, and the gen'rous Juice,
That warms chill'd Life, her Charities produce:
Accept without Reward; unask'd 'twas mine;
Here what thy Health requires, as free be thine.   *250*
Hence learn that GOD, (who, in the Time of Need,
In frozen Desarts can the Raven feed)
Well-sought, will delegate some pitying Breast,
His second Means, to succour Man distrest.
He paus'd. Deep Thought upon his Aspect gloom'd;   *255*
Then He, with Smile humane, his Voice resum'd.
I'm just inform'd, (and laugh me not to scorn)
By One unseen by thee, thou'rt *English-born.*
Of *England* I—To me the *British* State,
Rises, in dear Memorial, ever great!   *260*
Here stand we conscious!—Diffidence suspend!
Free flow our Words!—Did ne'er thy Muse extend
To Grots, where *Contemplation* smiles serene,
Where Angels visit, and where Joys convene?
To Groves, where more than mortal Voices rise,   *265*
Catch the rapt Soul, and waft it to the Skies?
This Cave!—Yon Walks!—But ere I more unfold,
What artful Scenes, thy Eyes shall here behold,
Think Subjects of my Toil: nor wond'ring gaze!
What cannot *Industry* completely raise?   *270*
Be the whole Earth in one great Landscape found,
By *Industry* is all with Beauty crown'd!
He, He alone explores the Mine for Gain,
Hues the hard Rock, or harrows up the Plain;
He forms the Sword to smite; He sheaths the Steel,   *275*

---

270 ff. Compare with these lines on Industry the whole of RS's later poem *Of Public Spirit in Regard to Public Works.*

Draws Health from Herbs, and shews the Balm to heal;
Or with loom'd Wool the native Robe supplies;
Or bids young Plants in future Forests rise;
Or fells the monarch Oak; which, borne away,
Shall with new Grace the distant Ocean sway; *280*
Hence golden *Commerce* views her Wealth encrease,
The blissful Child of Liberty and Peace.
He scoops the stubborn *Alps*, and, still employ'd,
Fills with soft, fertile Mold the steril Void;
Slop'd up white Rocks, small, yellow Harvests grow, *285*
And, green on terrass'd Stages, Vineyards blow!
By him fall Mountains to a level Space,
An *Isthmus* sinks, and sunder'd Seas embrace!
He founds a City on the naked Shore,
And Desolation starves the Tract no more. *290*
From the wild Waves he won the *Belgic* Land;
Where wide they foam'd, her Towns, and Trafficks stand;
He clear'd, manur'd, enlarg'd the furtive Ground,
And firms the Conquest with his fenceful Mound.
Ev'n *Mid* the watry World his *Venice* rose, *295*
Each Fabric there, as *Pleasure*'s Seat he shows!
There Marts, Sports, Councils are for Action sought,
Landscapes for Health, and Solitude for Thought.
What wonder then I, by his potent Aid,
A Mansion in a barren Mountain made? *300*
Part thou hast view'd!—If further we explore,
Let *Industry* deserve Applause the more.
   No frowning Care yon blest Apartment sees,
There *Sleep* retires, and finds a Couch of Ease.
Kind Dreams, that fly Remorse, and pamper'd Wealth, *305*
There shed the Smiles of Innocence, and Health.
   Mark!—Here descends a Grot, delightful Seat!

---

288 Most of the great canals of England were built after this time, but the Canal du Midi, connecting the Mediterranean with the Atlantic through the Garonne, had been completed in 1681. Peter the Great was also planning a series of canals to connect the Baltic with the Black Sea (A. D. McKillop, *The Background of Thomson's 'Seasons'*, p. 108). Cf. *Of Public Spirit in Regard to Public Works* (second version), l. 28.

Which warms ev'n Winter, tempers Summer's Heat!
See!—Gurgling from a Top, a Spring distils!
In mournful Measures wind the dripping Rills;   310
Soft Cooes of distant Doves, receiv'd around,
In soothing Mixture, swell the wat'ry Sound;
And hence the Streamlets seek the terrass Shade,
Within, without, alike to all convey'd.
Pass on—New Scenes, by my creative Pow'r,   315
Invite Reflection's sweet, and solemn Hour.
      We enter'd, where in well-rang'd Order, stood
Th'instructive Volumes of the Wise and Good.
These Friends (said he) though I desert Mankind,
Good Angels never wou'd permit behind.   320
Each Genius, Youth conceals, or Time displays,
I know; each Work, some Seraph here conveys,
Retirement thus presents my searchful Thought,
What Heav'n inspir'd, and what the Muse has taught;
What YOUNG Satiric, and Sublime has writ,   325
Whose Life is Virtue, and whose Muse is Wit.
Rapt I foresee thy *MALLET's early Aim
Shine in full Worth, and shoot at length to Fame.
Sweet Fancy's Bloom in FENTON's Lay appears,
And the ripe Judgment of instructive Years.   330
In HILL is all, that gen'rous Souls revere,
To Virtue, and the Muse for ever dear:
And THOMSON, in this Praise, thy Merit see,
The Tongue, that praises Merit, praises thee.
      These scorn (said I) the *Verse-Wright* of their Age, 335
Vain of a labour'd, languid, useless Page;
To whose dim Faculty the meaning Song
Is glaring, or obscure, when clear, and strong;
Who in cant Phrases gives a Work Disgrace;
His Wit, an Odness of his Tone, and Face;   340
Let the weak Malice, nurs'd to an Essay,

* Author of a Poem, call'd, The *Excursion*. [RS]

---

335 I do not know whom RS means here.

106

In some low Libel a mean Heart display;
Those, who once prais'd, now, undeceiv'd despise,
It lives contemn'd a Day, then harmless dies.
Or shou'd some nobler Bard, their Worth, unpraise,   *345*
Deserting Morals, that adorn his Lays,
Alas! too oft each Science shews the same,
The Great grow jealous of a greater Name:
Ye Bards, the Frailty mourn; yet brave the Shock:
Has not a STILLINGFLEET oppos'd a LOCKE?   *350*
Oh, still proceed, with sacred Rapture fir'd!
Unenvied had ye liv'd, if unadmir'd.

 Let *Envy*, he replied, all-ireful rise,
Envy pursues alone the Brave, and Wise;
MARO, and SOCRATES inspire her Pain,   *355*
And POPE, the *Monarch* of the tuneful Train;
To whom be *Nature*'s, and *Britannia*'s Praise!
All their bright Honours rush into his Lays!
And all that glorious Warmth his Lays reveal,
Which only Poets, Kings, and Patriots feel!   *360*
Though gay as Mirth, as curious Thought sedate,
As Elegance polite, as Pow'r elate;
Profound as Reason, and as Justice clear;
Soft as Compassion; yet as Truth severe;
As Bounty copious, as Persuasion sweet,   *365*
Like Nature various, and like Art complete;
So fine her Morals, so sublime her Views,
His Life is almost equal'd by his Muse.

 O POPE!—Since Envy is decreed by Fate,
Since she pursues alone the Wise, and Great;   *370*
In one small, emblematic Landscape see,
How vast a Distance 'twixt thy Foe, and Thee!
Truth from an Eminence surveys our Scene,
(A Hill, where all is clear, and all serene.)

---

350 Edward Stillingfleet, Bishop of Worcester, engaged in a controversy with John
Locke in 1696–7 over the doctrine of the trinity.

 374 Cf. Bacon, 'Of Truth': 'A hill not to be commanded, and where the air is always clear and serene.'

Rude, earth-bred Storms o'er meaner Valleys blow,   375
And wand'ring Mists roll, black'ning, far below;
Dark, and debas'd, like them, is *Envy*'s Aim,
And clear, and eminent, like Truth, thy Fame.
      Thus, I. From what dire Cause can Envy spring?
Or why embosom we a Viper's Sting?   380
'Tis Envy stings our darling Passion, Pride.
Alas! (the Man of mighty Soul replied)
Why chuse we Mis'ries? Most derive their Birth
From one bad Source; we dread superior Worth;
Prefer'd, it seems a Satire on our own;   385
Then heedless to excel, we meanly moan:
Then we abstract our Views, and Envy show,
Whence springs the Mis'ry, Pride is doom'd to know.
Thus Folly pain creates: By Wisdom's Pow'r,
We shun the Weight of many a restless Hour—   390
Lo! I meet Wrong, perhaps the Wrong, I feel,
Tends by the Scheme of Things to publick Weal.
I of the Whole am Part—the Joy, Men see,
Must circulate, and so revolve to me.
Why shou'd I then of private Loss complain?   395
Of Loss, that proves, perchance, a Brother's Gain?
The Wind, that binds one Bark within the Bay,
May waft a richer Freight its wish'd-for Way.
If Rains, redundant, flood the abject Ground,
Mountains are but supplied, when Vales are drown'd;   400
If, with soft Moisture swell'd, the Vale looks gay,
The Verdure of the Mountain fades away.
Shall Clouds, but at *my* Welfare's Call descend?
Shall *Gravity* for me her Laws suspend?
For me shall Suns their Noon-tide Course forbear?   405
Or *Motion* not subsist to influence Air?
Let the Means vary, be they Frost, or Flame,
Thy End, O Nature! still remains the same!
Be This the Motive of a wise Man's Care,
To shun deserving Ills, and learn to bear.   410

WHILE thus a Mind Humane, and wise, he shows,
All-eloquent of Truth his Language flows.
Youth, though depress'd, through all his Form, appears;
Through all his Sentiments the Depth of Years.
Thus He—Yet farther *Industry* behold,   5
Which conscious waits new Wonders to unfold.
Enter my Chapel next—Lo! here begin
The hallow'd Rites, that check the Growth of Sin.
When first we met, how soon you seem'd to know
My Bosom, lab'ring with the Throbs of Woe!   10
Such racking Throbs!—soft! when I rouze those Cares,
On my chill'd Mind pale *Recollection* glares!
When moping *Frenzy* strove my Thoughts to sway,
Here prudent Labours chac'd her Pow'r away.
Full, and rough-rising from yon sculptur'd Wall,   15
Bold Prophets, Nations to Repentance, call!
Meek Martyrs smile in Flames! gor'd Champions groan!
And Muse-like Cherubs tune their Harps in Stone!
Next shadow'd Light, a rounding Force, bestows,
Swells into Life, and speaking Action grows!   20
Here pleasing, melancholy Subjects find,
To calm, amuse, exalt the pensive Mind!
This Figure, tender Grief, like mine, implies,
And semblant Thoughts, that earthly Pomp despise.
Such penitential *Magdalene* reveals: 25
Loose-veil'd, in Negligence of Charms she kneels.
Though Dress, near-stor'd, its Vanity supplies,
The Vanity of Dress unheeded lies.
The sinful World in sorrowing Eye she keeps,
As o'er *Jerusalem*, *Messiah* weeps.   30
One Hand, her Bosom smites; in One appears
The lifted Lawn, that drinks her falling Tears.
        Since Evil outweighs Good, and sways Mankind,
True Fortitude assumes the patient Mind:
Such prov'd *Messiah*'s, though to suff'ring born,   35

To Penury, Repulse, Reproach, and Scorn.
Here by the Pencil mark his Flight design'd;
The wearied Virgin by a Stream reclin'd,
Who feeds the Child. Her Looks a Charm express,
A modeſt Charm, that dignifies Diſtress.   40
Boughs o'er their Heads with blushing Fruits depend,
Which Angels to her busied Consort bend.
Hence by the smiling Infant seems discern'd,
Trifles, concerning him, all Heav'n, concern'd.

    Here the transfigur'd Son, from Earth, retires: 45
See! the white Form in a bright Cloud aspires!
Full on his Foll'wers burſts a Flood of Rays,
Proſtrate they fall beneath th'o'erwhelming Blaze!
Like Noon-tide Summer-Suns the Rays appear,
Unsuff'rable, magnificent, and near!   50

    What Scene of Agony the Garden brings;
The Cup of Gall; the suppliant King of Kings;
The Crown of Thorns; the Cross, that felt him die;
These, languid in the Sketch, unfinish'd, lye.

    There from the Dead Centurions see him rise,   55
See! but ſtruck down with horrible Surprize!
As the firſt Glory seem'd a Sun at Noon,
This caſts the Silver Splendor of the Moon.

    Here peopled Day, th'ascending God surveys!
The Glory varies, as the Myriads gaze!   60
Now soften'd, like a Sun at Diſtance seen,
When through a Cloud bright-glancing, yet serene!
Now faſt-encreasing to the Croud amaz'd,
Like some vaſt Meteor high in Ether rais'd!

    My Labour, yon high-vaulted Altar, ſtains   65
With Dies, that emulate etherial Plains.
The convex Glass, which in that Opening glows,
Mid circling Rays a piĉtur'd *Saviour* shows!
Bright It colleĉts the Beams, which, trembling All,

65–72 According to Marjorie Nicolson, this is an adaptation of the camera obscura
(*Newton Demands the Muse*, p. 80).

Back from the God, a show'ry Radiance, fall,   70
Ligh'tning the Scene beneath! a Scene divine!
Where Saints, Clouds, Seraphs intermingled shine!
     Here Water-falls, that play melodious round,
Like a sweet Organ, swell a lofty Sound!
The solemn Notes bid earthly Passions fly,   75
Lull all my Cares, and lift my Soul on High!
     This monumental Marble—this I rear
To One—Oh! ever mourn'd!—Oh! ever dear!
He ſtopt—pathetic Sighs the Pause supply,
And the prompt Tear ſtarts, quiv'ring, on his Eye!   80
     I look'd—two Columns near the Wall were seen,
An imag'd *Beauty* ſtretch'd at length between.
Near the wept Fair, her harp *Cecilia* ſtrung,
Leaning, from high, a liſt'ning Angel hung!
Friendship, whose Figure at the Feet remains,   85
A Phœnix, with irradiate Creſt, suſtains:
This grac'd one Palm, while One extends t'impart
Two foreign Hands, that clasp a burning Heart.
A pendent Veil two hov'ring Seraphs raise,
Which, opening Heav'n, upon the Roof displays!   90
And two, benevolent, less-distant, hold
A Vase, colleǎive of Perfumes up-roll'd!
These from the Heart, by *Friendship* held, arise;
Od'rous as Incense gath'ring in the Skies.
In the fond Pelican is Love expreſt,   95
Who opens to her Young her tender Breaſt.
Two mated Turtles hov'ring hang in Air,
One by a Faulcon ſtruck!—in wild Despair,
The Hermit cries,—So Death, alas! deſtroys
The tender Consort of my Cares, and Joys!   100
Again soft Tears upon his Eye-lid hung,
Again check'd Sounds dy'd, flutt'ring, on his Tongue.
Too well his pining, inmoſt Thought I know!
Too well ev'n Silence tells the ſtory'd Woe!
To his my Sighs, to his my Tears reply!   105
I ſtray o'er all the Tomb a watry Eye!

Next, on the Wall, her Scenes of Life I gaz'd,
The Form back-leaning, by a Globe half-rais'd!
Cherubs a proffer'd Crown of Glory show,
Ey'd wistful by th'admiring Fair below.   *110*
In Action eloquent dispos'd her Hands,
One shows her Breast, in Rapture One expands!
This the fond Hermit seiz'd!—o'er all his Soul,
The soft, wild, wailing, am'rous Passion stole!
In stedfast Gaze his Eyes her Aspect keep,   *115*
Then turn away, a-while dejected weep;
Then he reverts 'em; but reverts in vain,
Dim'd with the swelling Grief, that streams again.
Where now is my Philosophy? (he cries)
My Joy, Hope, Reason, my *Olympia* dies!   *120*
Why did I e'er that Prime of Blessings know?
Was it, ye cruel Fates! t'imbitter Woe?
Why wou'd your Bolts not level first *my* Head?
Why must I live to weep *Olympia* dead?
—Sir, I had once a Wife! fair bloom'd her Youth,   *125*
Her Form was Beauty, and her Soul was Truth!
Oh, she was dear!—How dear, what Words can say?
She dies!—My Heav'n at once is snatch'd away!
Ah! what avails, that, by a Father's Care,
I rose a wealthy, and illustrious Heir?   *130*
That early in my Youth I learn'd to prove
Th'instructive, pleasing, academic Grove?
That in the Senate Eloquence was mine?
That Valour gave me in the Field to shine?
That Love showr'd Blessings too—far more than All, *135*
High-rapt Ambition e'er cou'd happy call?
Ah!—What are These, which ev'n the Wise adore?
Lost is my Pride!—*Olympia* is no more!
Had I, ye persecuting Pow'rs! been born
The World's cold Pity, or, at best, its Scorn;   *140*
Of Wealth, of Rank, of kindred Warmth bereft;
To Want, to Shame, to ruthless Censure left;
Patience, or Pride, to this, Relief, supplies!

But a loſt Wife!—there! there Diſtraction lies!
    Now three sad Years I yield me all to Grief,   *145*
And fly the hated Comfort of Relief.
Though rich, great, young, I leave a pompous Seat,
(My Brother's now) to seek some dark Retreat:
Mid cloiſter'd, solitary Tombs I ſtray,
Despair, and Horror lead the chearless Way!   *150*
My Sorrow grows to such a wild Excess,
Life, injur'd Life muſt wish the Passion less!
Olympia!—My *Olympia*'s loſt (I cry)
Olympia's loſt, the hollow Vaults reply!
Louder I make my lamentable Moan;   *155*
The swelling Echoes learn like me to groan;
The Ghoſts to scream, as through lone Isles they sweep;
The Shrines to shudder, and the Saints to weep!
    Now Grief, and Rage, by gath'ring Sighs, suppreſt,
Swell my full Heart, and heave my lab'ring Breaſt!   *160*
With ſtruggling Starts, each vital String they ſtrain,
And ſtrike the tott'ring Fabric of my Brain!
O'er my sunk Spirits frowns a vap'ry Scene,
Woe's dark Retreat! the madding Maze of *Spleen*!
A deep, damp Gloom o'erspreads the murky Cell;   *165*
Here pining Thoughts, and secret Terrors dwell!
Here learn the Great unreal Wants to feign!
Unpleasing Truths here mortify the Vain!
Here *Learning*, blinded firſt, and then beguil'd,
Looks dark as *Ignorance*, as *Frenzy* wild!   *170*
Here firſt *Credulity* on *Reason* won!
And here *false Zeal* myſterious Rants begun!
Here *Love* impearls each Moment with a Tear,
And *Superſtition* owes to *Spleen* her Fear!
    Fantaſtic Lightnings, through the dreary Way,   *175*
In swift, short Signals, flash the burſting Day!
Above, beneath, across, around, they fly!
A dire Deception ſtrikes the mental Eye!
By the Blue Fires, pale Phantoms grin severe!
Shrill-fancied Echoes wound th'affrighted Ear!   *180*

Air-banish'd Spirits flag in Fogs profound,
And all-obscene, shed baneful Damps around!
Now Whispers, trembling in some feeble Wind,
Sigh out prophetic Fears, and freeze the Mind!
    Loud laughs the Hag!—She mocks Complaint away,   *185*
Unroofs the Den, and lets in more than Day.
Swarms of Wild *Fancies*, wing'd in various Flight,
Seek emblematic Shades, and myſtic Light!
Some drive with rapid Steeds the shining Car!
These nod from Thrones! Those thunder in the War!   *190*
Till, tir'd, they turn from the delusive Show,
Start from wild Joy, and fix in ſtupid Woe.
    Here the lone Hour, a Blank of Life, displays,
Till now bad Thoughts a Fiend more aſtive raise;
A Fiend in evil Moments ever nigh!   *195*
Death in her Hand, and Frenzy in her Eye!
Her Eye all red, and sunk!—A Robe she wore,
With Life's Calamities embroider'd o'er.
A Mirror in one Hand colleſtive shows,
Varied, and multiplied that Group of Woes.   *200*
This endless Foe to gen'rous Toil and Pain
Lolls on a Couch for Ease; but lolls in vain;
She muses o'er her woe-embroider'd Veſt,
And Self-Abhorrence heightens in her Breaſt.
To shun her Care, the Force of Sleep she tries,   *205*
Still wakes her Mind, though Slumbers doze her Eyes:
She dreams, ſtarts, rises, ſtalks from Place to Place,
With reſtless, thoughtful, interrupted Pace;
Now eyes the Sun, and curses ev'ry Ray,
Now the green Ground, where Colour fades away.   *210*
Dim Speſtres dance! Again her Eye she rears;

---

193 ff. Mrs Thrale believed that these lines on suicide, which Johnson considered
'terriffick' (*Account*, p. 366), were suggested by a passage in Robert Burton's *Anatomy
of Melancholy*—'towards the 216th page'. *Letters of Mrs Thrale*, ed. R. B. Johnson
(1926), p. 75. See *Anatomy* (7th ed. 1660), pp. 213–16. Though there is some similarity in thought and treatment, no actual indebtedness is apparent. Miss K. C.
Balderston suggests instead as a source the description of Despair in the *Faerie
Queene*, I, 9 (*Thraliana*, 2nd ed. 1951, p. 537). Cf. *Wanderer*, v, 475–96.

Then from the blood-shot Ball wipes purpled Tears;
Then presses hard her Brow, with Mischief fraught,
Her Brow half bursts with Agony of Thought!
From me (she cries) pale Wretch thy Comfort claim,   215
Born of *Despair*, and *Suicide* my Name!
Why shou'd thy Life a Moment's Pain endure?
Here ev'ry Object proffers Grief a Cure.
She points where Leaves of Hemlock black'ning shoot!
Fear not! pluck! eat (said she) the sov'reign Root!   220
Then *Death*, revers'd, shall bear his ebon Lance!
Soft o'er thy Sight shall swim the shadowy Trance!
Or leap yon Rock, possess a watry Grave,
And leave wild Sorrow to the Wind and Wave!
Or mark—this Ponyard thus from Mis'ry frees!   225
She wounds her Breast!—the guilty Steel I seize!
Straight, where she struck, a smoking Spring of Gore
Wells from the Wound, and floats the crimson'd Floor.
She faints! She fades!—Calm Thoughts the Deed revolve,
And now, unstartling, fix the dire Resolve!   230
Death drops his Terrors, and, with charming Wiles,
Winning, and kind, like my *Olympia* smiles!
He points the Passage to the Seats divine,
Where Poets, Heroes, sainted Lovers shine!
I come, *Olympia*!—My rear'd Arm extends;   235
Half to my Breast the threat'ning Point descends!
Straight Thunder rocks the Land! new Lightnings play!
When, lo! a Voice resounds, Arise! away!
Away! nor murmur at th'afflictive Rod!
Nor tempt the Vengeance of an angry God!   240
Fly'st thou from *Providence* for vain Relief?
Such ill-sought Ease shall draw avenging Grief.
Honour, the more obstructed, stronger shines,
And Zeal by Persecution's Rage refines.
By Woe, the Soul to daring Action swells;   245
By Woe, in plaintless Patience It excels;
From Patience, prudent, clear Experience springs,
And traces Knowledge through the Course of Things;

Thence Hope is form'd, thence Fortitude, Success,
Renown:—What'er Men covet and caress.   250
      The vanish'd Fiend thus sent a hollow Voice,
Woud'st thou be happy? Straight be Death thy Choice;
How mean are those, who passively complain,
While active Souls, more free, their Fetters strain?
Though Knowledge thine, Hope, Fortitude, Success,   255
Renown—Whate'er Men covet, and caress;
On Earth Success must in its Turn give way,
And ev'n Perfection introduce Decay.
Never the World of Spirits thus—their Rest
Untouch'd! entire!—once happy, ever blest!   260
      Earnest the heav'nly Voice responsive cries,
Oh, listen not to Subtilty unwise!
Thy guardian Saint, who mourns thy hapless Fate,
Heav'n grants to prop thy Virtue, ere too late.
Know, if thou wilt thy dear-lov'd Wife deplore,   265
Olympia waits thee on a foreign Shore;
There in a Cell thy last Remains be spent;
Away! deceive Despair, and find Content!
      I heard, obey'd; nor more of Fate complain'd;
Long Seas I measur'd, and this Mountain gain'd.   270
Soon to a yawning Rift, Chance turn'd my Way;
A Den it prov'd, where a huge Serpent lay!
Flame-ey'd he lay!—He rages now for Food,
Meets my first Glance, and meditates my Blood!
His Bulk, in many a gather'd Orb up-roll'd,   275
Rears Spire on Spire! His Scales, be-dropt with Gold,
Shine burnish'd in the Sun! Such Height they gain,
They dart green Lustre on the distant Main!
Now writh'd in dreadful Slope, he stoops his Crest,
Furious to fix on my unshielded Breast!   280
Just as he springs, my Sabre smites the Foe!
Headless he falls beneath th'unerring Blow!
Wrath yet remains, though Strength his Fabric leaves,
And the meant Hiss, the gasping Mouth, deceives;
The length'ning Trunk slow-loosens ev'ry Fold,   285

Lingers in Life; then stretches stiff, and cold.
Just as th'invet'rate Son of Mischief ends,
Comes a white Dove, and near the Spot descends.
I hail this Omen! all bad Passions cease,
Like the slain *Snake*, and all within is *Peace*.   290
      Next, to *Religion*, this plain Roof I raise!
In duteous Rites, my hallow'd Tapers blaze!
I bid due Incense on my Altar smoke;
Then, at this Tomb, my promis'd *Love* invoke!
She hears!—She comes!—My Heart what Raptures
      warm?   295
All my *Olympia* sparkles in the Form!
No pale, wan, livid Mark of Death she bears!
Each roseate Look, a quick'ning Transport, wears!
A Robe of Light, high-wrought, her Shape, invests;
Unzon'd the swelling Beauty of her Breasts!   300
Her auburn Hair, each flowing Ring, resumes,
In her fair Hand, Love's Branch of Myrtle blooms!
Silent, a-while, each well-known Charm, I trace;
Then thus, (while nearer she avoids th'Embrace)
Thou dear Deceit!—must I a Shade pursue?   305
Dazzled I gaze!—thou swim'st before my View!
Dipt in etherial Dews, her Bough divine
Sprinkles my Eyes, which, strengthen'd, bear the Shine:
Still thus I urge, (for still the shadowy Bliss
Shuns the warm Grasp, nor yields the tender Kiss.)   310
Oh, fly not!—fade not! listen to Love's Call!
She lives!—no more I'm Man!—I'm Spirit all!
Then let me snatch thee!—press thee!—take me whole!
Oh, close!—yet closer!—closer to my Soul!
Twice, round her Waist, my eager Arms entwin'd,   315
And, twice deceiv'd, my Frenzy clasp'd the Wind!
Then thus I rav'd—Behold thy Husband kneel,

315–16 This incident may have been suggested by the familiar story of Orpheus
and Eurydice. Cf. Virgil, *Georgics*, iv (trans. Dryden, 1697):
  'In vain, with folding arms, the youth essayed
  To stop her flight, and strain the flying shade.'

And judge! O judge what Agonies I feel!
Oh be no longer, if unkind, thus fair;
Take Horror's Shape, and fright me to Despair!   *320*
Rather, than thus, unpitying, see my Moan,
Far rather frown, and fix me here in Stone!
But mock not thus—Alas! (the Charmer said,
Smiling; and, in her Smile, soft Radiance play'd)
Alas! no more eluded Strength employ,   *325*
To clasp a Shade!—What more is mortal Joy?
Man's Bliss is, like his Knowledge, but surmis'd;
One Ignorance, the other Pain disguis'd;
Thou wert (had all thy Wish been ſtill posseſt)
Supreamly curſt from being greatly bleſt;   *330*
For oh! so fair, so dear was I to Thee,
Thou hadſt forgot thy God, to worship me;
This he foresaw, and snatch'd me to the Tomb;
Above I flourish in unfading Bloom.
Think me not loſt; for thee I Heav'n implore!   *335*
Thy guardian Angel, though a Wife no more!
I, when abſtracted from this World you seem,
Hint the pure Thought, and frame the heav'nly Dream!
Close at thy Side, when Morning ſtreaks the Air,
In Musick's Voice I wake thy Mind to Prayer!   *340*
By me, thy Hymns, like pureſt Incense, rise,
Fragrant with Grace, and pleasing to the Skies!
And when that Form shall from its Clay refine,
(That only Bar betwixt my Soul, and Thine!)
When thy lov'd Spirit mounts to Realms of Light,   *345*
Then shall *Olympia* aid thy earlieſt Flight;
Mingled we'll flame in Raptures, that aspire
Beyond all Youth, all Sense, and all Desire.
　　　She ended. Still such Sweetness dwells behind,
Th'inchanting Voice ſtill warbles in my Mind,   *350*
But lo! th'unbodied Vision fleets away!—
—Stay my *Olympia*!—I conjure thee, ſtay!
Yet ſtay—for thee my Mem'ry learns to smart!
Sure ev'ry Vein contains a bleeding Heart!

Sooner shall Splendor leave the Blaze of Day,   355
Than Love, so pure, so vast as mine, decay!
From the same heav'nly Source its Lustre came,
And glows, immortal, with congenial Flame!
Ah!—let me not with Fires neglected, burn!
Sweet Mistress of my Soul, return, return!   360
      Alas!—she's fled!—I traverse now the Place,
Where my enamour'd Thoughts, her Footsteps trace.
Now, o'er the Tomb, I bend my drooping Head,
There Tears, the Eloquence of Sorrow, shed.
Sighs choak my Words, unable to express   365
The Pangs, the Throbs of speechless Tenderness!
Not with more ardent, more transparent Flame,
Call dying Saints on their Creator's Name,
Than I on hers!—But, through yon yielding Door,
Glides a new Phantom o'er th'illumin'd Floor!   370
The Roof swift-kindles from the beaming Ground,
And Floods of living Lustre flame around!
In all the Majesty of Light array'd,
Awful it shines!—'tis *Cato*'s honour'd Shade!
As I, the Heav'nly Visitant, pursue,   375
Sublimer Glory opens to my View!
He speaks!—But, oh! what Words shall dare repeat
His Thoughts?—They leave me fir'd with Patriot Heat!
More than poetic Raptures now I feel,
And own that godlike Passion, Publick Zeal!   380
But from my Frailty it receives a Stain,
I grow, unlike my great Inspirer, vain;
And burn, once more, the busy World to know,
And wou'd, in Scenes of Action, foremost glow!
Where proud Ambition points her dazzling Rays!   385
Where Coronets, and Crowns, attractive, blaze!
When my *Olympia* leaves the Realms above,
And lures me back to solitary Love.

---

374 ff. *Cato*'s honour'd Shade! Addison's *Cato* was revived on the London stage
in 1728. RS uses the vision of Cato as a symbol of self-control and forgetfulness of
self in public service.

She tells me Truth, prefers an humble State,
That genuine Greatness shuns the being Great! 390
That mean are those, who false-term'd Honour prize;
Whose Fabricks, from their Country's Ruins, rise;
Who look the Traytor, like the Patriot, fair;
Who to enjoy the Vineyard, wrong the Heir.
    I hear!—through all my Veins new Transports roll! 395
I gaze!—Warm Love comes rushing on my Soul!
Ravish'd I gaze!—Again her Charms decay!
Again my Manhood to my Grief gives way!
Cato returns!—Zeal takes her Course to reign;
But Zeal is in Ambition loſt again! 400
I'm now the Slave of Fondness!—now of Pride!
—By Turns they conquer, and by Turns subside!
These ballanc'd Each by Each, the golden Mean,
Betwixt 'em found, gives Happiness serene;
This I'll enjoy!—He ended!—I replied, 405
O Hermit! thou art Worth severely tried!
But had not innate Grief produc'd thy Woes,
Men, barb'rous Men had prey'd on thy Repose.
When seeking Joy, we seldom Sorrow miss,
And often Mis'ry points the Path to Bliss. 410
The Soil, moſt worthy of the thrifty Swain,
Is wounded thus, ere truſted with the Grain;
The ſtrugling Grain muſt work obscure, its way,
Ere the firſt Green springs upward to the Day;
Up-sprung, such weed-like Coarseness it betrays, 415
Flocks on th'abandon'd Blade permissive graze;
Then shoots the Wealth, from Imperfeċtion clear,
And thus a grateful Harveſt crowns the Year.

CANTO III

THUS free our social Time from Morning flows,
'Till rising Shades attempt the Day to close.
Thus my new Friend: Behold the Light's Decay:
Back to yon City let me point thy Way.

South-West, behind yon Hill, the sloping Sun,   5
To Ocean's Verge, his fluent Course, has run:
His parting Eyes a watry Radiance shed,
Glance through the Vale, and tip the Mountain's Head:
To which oppos'd, the shad'wy Gulphs, below,
Beauteous, reflect the party-colour'd Snow.   10
    Now dance the Stars, where *Vesper* leads the Way;
Yet all, faint-glimm'ring with Remains of Day.
Orient, the Queen of Night emits her Dawn,
And throws, unseen, her Mantle o'er the Lawn.
Up the blue Steep, her crimson Orb now shines;   15
Now on the Mountain-top her *Arm* reclines,
In a *red Crescent* seen: Her *Zone* now gleams,
Like *Venus*, quiv'ring in reflecting Streams.
Yet red'ning, yet round-burning up the Air,
From the white Cliff, her *Feet* slow-rising glare!   20
See! Flames, condens'd, now vary her Attire;
Her *Face*, a broad Circumference of Fire.
Dark Firs seem kindled in nocturnal Blaze;
Through Ranks of Pines, her broken Lustre plays,
Here glares, there brown-projecting Shade bestows,   25
And glitt'ring sports upon the spangled Snows.
    Now Silver turn her Beams!—Yon Den they gain;
The big, rouz'd *Lion* shakes his brinded Main.
Fierce, fleet, gaunt Monsters, All, prepar'd for Gore,
Rend Woods, Vales, Rocks, with wide-resounding Roar.   30
O dire Presage!—But fear not thou, my Friend,
Our Steps the Guardians of the Just attend.
Home-ward I'll wait thee on—and now survey,
How Men, and Spirits chace the Night away!
    Yon Nymphs, and Swains in am'rous Mirth advance;   35
To breathing Musick moves the circling Dance.
Here the bold Youth in Deeds adventrous glow,
Skimming in rapid Sleds the crackling Snow.

---

11 ff. Notice the accuracy of RS's description of the rising of the moon, especially his observation of its gradually changing colour as the angle of refraction alters: first crimson (l. 15), then silver (l. 27), and finally white (l. 77).

Not when *Tidides* won the fun'ral Race,
Shot his light Car along in swifter Pace.   40
Here the glaz'd Way with Iron Feet they dare,
And glide, well-pois'd, like *Mercuries* in Air.
There Crouds, with stable Tread, and levell'd Eye,
Lift, and dismiss the Quoits, that whirling fly.
With Force superior, not with Skill so true,   45
The pond'rous Disk from *Roman* Sinews flew.
Where neighb'ring Hills some cloudy Sheet sustain,
Freez'd o'er the nether Vale a pensile Plain,
Cross the roof'd Hollow rolls the massy Round,
The crack'd Ice rattles, and the Rocks resound;   50
Censures, Disputes, and Laughs, alternate, rise;
And deaf'ning Clangor thunders up the Skies.

    Thus, amid crouded Images, serene,
From Hour to Hour we pass'd, from Scene to Scene:
Fast wore the Night. Full long we pac'd our way;   55
Vain Steps! the City yet far-distant lay.
While thus the Hermit, ere my Wonder spoke,
Methought, with new Amusement, Silence broke,
Yon amber-hued Cascade, which fleecy flies
Through Rocks, and strays along the trackless Skies,   60
To frolick Fairies marks the mazy Ring,
Forth to the Dance from little Cells they spring,
Measur'd to pipe, or harp!—and next they stand,
Marshall'd beneath the Moon, a radiant Band!
In Frost-work now delight the sportive kind: 65
Now court wild *Fancy* in the whistling Wind.

    Hark!—the funereal Bell's deep-sounding Toll,
To Bliss from Mis'ry, calls some righteous Soul!
Just freed from Life, like swift-ascending Fire,
Glorious it mounts, and gleams from yonder Spire!   70
Light clapt its Wings!—It views, with pitying Sight,
The friendly Mourner pay the pious Rite;
The Plume high-wrought, that black'ning nods in Air;

---

39 *Tidides*. Diomedes. *Iliad*, XXIII, 373 ff.

The slow-pac'd, weeping Pomp; the solemn Prayer,
The decent Tomb; the Verse, that *Sorrow* gives;   75
Where, to Remembrance sweet, fair Virtue lives.
    Now to mid Heav'n the whiten'd Moon inclines,
And Shades contraƈt, mark'd out in clearer Lines;
With noiseless Gloom the Plains are delug'd o'er:
See!—from the North, what ſtreaming Meteors pour!   80
Beneath *Bootes* spring the radiant Train,
And quiver through the Axle of his Wain.
O'er Altars thus, impainted, we behold
Half-circling Glories shoot in Rays of Gold.
Cross *Ether* swift elance the vivid Fires!   85
As swift again each pointed Flame retires!
In *Fancy*'s Eye encount'ring Armies glare,
And sanguine Ensigns wave unfurl'd in Air!
Hence the weak Vulgar deem impending Fate,
A Monarch ruin'd, or unpeopled State.   90
Thus Comets, dreadful Visitants! arise
To them wild Omens, Science to the Wise!
These mark the Comet to the Sun incline,
While deep-red Flames around its Center shine!
While its fierce Rear, a winding Trail, displays,   95
And lights all *Ether* with the sweepy Blaze!
Or when compell'd, it flies the torrid *Zone*,
And shoots by Worlds un-number'd, and unknown;
By Worlds, whose People, all-aghaſt with Fear,
May view that Miniſter of Vengeance near!   100
Till now the transient Glow, remote, and loſt,
Decays, and darkens mid-involving Froſt!
Or when it, Sun-ward, drinks rich Beams again,
And burns imperious on th'etherial Plain!
The Learn'd-One curious eyes it from afar,   105
Sparkling through Night, a new, illuſtrious Star!
    The Moon, descending, saw us now pursue
The various Talk:—the City near in view!

---

80 ff. Cf. *Britannia's Miseries*, l. 13 n.
85 Elance. Shoot, dart, glance. *OED* quotes this line.

Here from *Still Life* (he cries) avert thy Sight,
And mark what *Deeds* adorn, or shame the Night!   110
But heedful each immodest Prospect fly;
Where Decency forbids Enquiry's Eye.
Man were not Man, without Love's wanton Fire,
But Reason's Glory is to quell Desire.
What are thy Fruits, O *Lust*? Short Blessings, bought   115
With long Remorse, the Seed of bitter Thought;
Perhaps some *Babe* to dire Diseases born,
Doom'd for *Another*'s Crimes, through Life, to mourn;
Or *murder'd*, to preserve a *Mother's Fame*;
Or cast obscure; the *Child* of *Want*, and *Shame*!   120
False Pride! What Vices on our Conduct steal,
From the World's Eye one Frailty to conceal?
Ye *cruel Mothers*!—Soft! those Words command!
So near, shall *Cruelty*, and *Mother* stand?
Can the Dove's Bosom snaky Venom draw?   125
Can its Foot sharpen, like the Vultur's Claw?
Can the fond Goat, or tender, fleecy Dam
Howl, like the Wolf, to tear the Kid, or Lamb?
Yes, there *are* Mothers—There I fear'd his Aim,
And, conscious, trembled at the coming Name;   130
Then with a Sigh his issuing Words oppos'd!
Straight with a falling Tear the Speech he clos'd.
That Tenderness, which Ties of Blood deny,
Nature repaid me from a Stranger's Eye.
Pale grew my Cheeks!—But now to gen'ral Views   135
Our Converse turns, which thus my Friend renews.

Yon Mansion, made by beaming Tapers gay,
Drowns the dim Night, and counterfeits the Day.
From lumin'd Windows glancing on the Eye,
Around, athwart, the frisking Shadows fly.   140
There Midnight *Riot* spreads illusive Joys,
And Fortune, Health, and dearer Time destroys.

---

123 Ye *cruel Mothers*! RS is drawing attention to himself here. It must be remembered that these lines were probably written in Lord Tyrconnel's house, or at least
published while he was living there.

Soon Death's dark Agent, to luxuriant Ease,
Shall wake sharp Warnings in some fierce Disease.
    O Man! thy Fabrick's like a well-form'd State;   *145*
Thy *Thoughts*, first-rank'd, were sure design'd the *Great!*
Passions Plebeians are, which *Faction* raise;
Wine, like pour'd Oil, excites the raging Blaze:
Then giddy *Anarchy's* rude Triumphs rise:
Then sov'reign *Reason* from her Empire flies: *150*
That *Ruler* once depos'd, *Wisdom*, and *Wit*
To *Noise*, and *Folly*, Place, and Pow'r, submit;
Like a frail Bark thy weaken'd Mind is tost,
Unsteer'd, unballanc'd, 'till its Wealth is lost.
    The *Miser-spirit* eyes the spend-thrift *Heir*,   *155*
And mourns, too late, Effects of sordid Care.
His Treasures fly to cloy each fawning Slave;
Yet grudge a Stone, to dignify his Grave.
For this, low-thoughted Craft his Life employ'd;
For this, though wealthy, he no Wealth enjoy'd;   *160*
For this, he grip'd the Poor, and Alms denied,
Unfriended liv'd, and unlamented died.
Yet smile, griev'd Shade! when that unprosp'rous Store
Fast-lessens, when gay Hours return no more;
Smile at thy Heir, beholding, in his Fall,   *165*
Men once oblig'd, like him, ungrateful All!
Then Thought-inspiring *Woe* his Heart shall mend,
And prove his only wise, unflatt'ring Friend.
    Folly exhibits thus unmanly Sport,
While plotting *Mischief* keeps reserv'd her Court.   *170*
Lo! from that Mount, in blasting Sulphur broke,
Stream Flames voluminous, enwrap'd with Smoke!
In Chariot-shape they whirl up yonder Tow'r,
Lean on its Brow, and like Destruction lour!
From the black Depth a fiery Legion springs;   *175*
Each bold, bad Spectre claps her sounding Wings;
And straight beneath a summon'd, trait'rous Band,
On Horror bent, in dark Convention stand:
From each Fiend's Mouth a ruddy Vapour flows,

Glides through the Roof, and o'er the Council glows: *180*
The Villains, close beneath th'Infection pent,
Feel, all-possess'd, their rising Galls ferment;
And burn with Faction, Hate, and vengeful Ire,
For Rapine, Blood, and Devastation dire;
But *Justice* marks their Ways: She waves, in Air,   *185*
The Sword, high-threat'ning like a Comet's Glare.
　　While here dark *Villany* her self deceives,
There studious *Honesty* our View relieves.
A feeble Taper, from yon lonesome Room,
Scatt'ring thin Rays, just glimmers through the Gloom. *190*
There sits the sapient *BARD* in museful Mood,
And glows impassion'd for his Country's Good!
All the bright *Spirits* of the *Just*, combin'd,
Inform, refine, and prompt his tow'ring Mind!
He takes his *gifted Quill* from *Hands divine*,   *195*
Around his Temples Rays refulgent shine!
Now rapt! now more than Man!—I see him climb,
To view this Speck of Earth from Worlds sublime!
I see him now o'er Nature's Works preside!
How clear the Vision! and the Scene how wide!   *200*
Let some a Name by Adulation raise,
Or Scandal, meaner than a venal Praise!
My *Muse* (he cries) a nobler Prospect view!
Through Fancy's Wilds some Moral's Point pursue!
From dark Deception clear-drawn Truth display,   *205*
As from black Chaos rose resplendent Day!
Awake Compassion, and bid Terror rise!
Bid humble Sorrows strike superior Eyes!
So pamper'd *Pow'r*, unconscious of *Distress*,
May see, be mov'd, and being mov'd, redress.   *210*
　　Ye Traytors, Tyrants, fear his stinging Lay!
Ye Pow'rs unlov'd, unpitied in Decay!
But know, to *you* sweet-blossom'd Fame he brings,
Ye Heroes, Patriots, and paternal Kings!
　　O *Thou*, who form'd, who rais'd the Poet's Art,   *215*
(*Voice* of *thy Will!*) unerring Force impart!

If wailing Worth can gen'rous Warmth excite,
If Verse can gild Instruction with Delight,
Inspire his honest Muse with *orient* Flame,
To rise, to dare, to reach the noblest Aim!   220
  But, O my Friend! mysterious is our Fate!
How mean his Fortune, though his Mind elate!
Æneas-like he passes through the Croud,
Unsought, unseen beneath Misfortune's Cloud;
Or seen with slight Regard: Unprais'd his Name: 225
His after-Honour, and our after-Shame.
The *doom'd Desert* to *Av'rice* stands confess'd;
Her Eyes averted are, and steel'd her Breast.
Envy asquint the *future Wonder* eyes:
Bold *Insult*, pointing, hoots him as he flies;   230
While coward *Censure*, skill'd in darker Ways,
Hints sure Detraction in dissembled Praise!
Hunger, Thirst, Nakedness there grievous fall!
Unjust Derision too!—That Tongue of Gall!
Slow comes *Relief*, with no mild Charms endued,   235
Usher'd by *Pride*, and by *Reproach* pursued.
Forc'd Pity meets him with a cold Respect,
Unkind as *Scorn*, ungen'rous as *Neglect*.
  Yet, *suff'ring Worth*! thy Fortitude will shine!
Thy Foes are *Virtue*'s, and her Friends are thine!   240
Patience is thine, and Peace thy Days shall crown;
Thy Treasure Prudence, and thy Claim Renown:
Myriads unborn, shall mourn thy hapless Fate,
And Myriads grow by thy Example Great!
  Hark! from the Watch-Tow'r rolls the Trumpet's
   Sound,   245
Sweet through still Night, proclaiming Safety round!
Yon Shade illustrious quits the Realms of Rest,
To aid some Orphan of its Race distrest,
Safe winds him through the subterraneous Way,
That mines yon Mansion, grown with Ruin grey,   250
And marks the wealthy, unsuspected Ground,
Where green with Rust, long-buried Coins abound.

127

This plaintive Ghost, from Earth when newly fled,
Saw those, the Living trusted, wrong the Dead;
He saw, by Fraud abus'd, the lifeless Hand   255
Sign the false Deed, that alienates his Land;
Heard on his Fame injurious Censure thrown,
And mourn'd the beggar'd Orphan's bitter Groan:
Commission'd now the Falsehood He reveals,
To Justice soon th'enabled Heir appeals;   260
Soon by this Wealth are costly Pleas maintain'd,
And by discover'd Truth lost Right regain'd.

    But why (may some enquire) why kind Success,
Since mystic Heav'n gives Mis'ry oft to bless?
Though Mis'ry leads to Happiness, and Truth,   265
Unequal to the Load this languid Youth.
Unstrengthen'd Virtue scarce his Bosom fir'd,
And fearful from his growing Wants retir'd.
(Oh, let none censure if, untried by Grief,
If amidst Woe untempted by Relief!   270
He stoop'd reluctant to low Arts of Shame,
Which then, ev'n then he scorn'd, and blush'd to name.)
Heav'n sees, and makes th'imperfect Worth its Care,
And chears the trembling Heart, unform'd to bear.
Now rising Fortune elevates his Mind,   275
He shines unclouded, and adorns Mankind.

    So in some Engine, that denies a Vent,
If unrespiring is some Creature pent,
It sickens, droops, and pants, and gasps for Breath,
Sad o'er the Sight swim shad'wy Mists of Death;   280
If then kind Air pours pow'rful in again,
New Heats, new Pulses quicken ev'ry Vein,
From the clear'd, lifted, life-rekindled Eye,
Dispers'd, the dark and dampy Vapours fly.

    From trembling Tombs the Ghosts of Greatness rise, 285
And o'er their Bodies hang with wistful Eyes;
Or discontented stalk, and mix their Howls

---

270 Relief!] Relief!) *1729.*   272 name.)] name. *1729.*

With howling Wolves, their Screams with screaming Owls.
The Interval 'twixt Night and Morn is nigh,
Winter more nitrous chills the shadow'd Sky.   290
Springs with soft Heats no more give Borders green,
Nor smoaking breathe along the whiten'd Scene;
While steamy Currents sweet in Prospect charm,
Like Veins blue-winding on a Fair-one's Arm.
Now *Sleep* to *Fancy* parts with half his Pow'r,   295
And broken Slumbers drag the restless Hour.
The Murder'd seems alive, and ghastly glares,
And in dire Dreams the conscious Murd'rer scares,
Shews the yet-spouting Wound, th' ensanguin'd Floor,
The Walls yet-smoaking with the spatter'd Gore;   300
Or shrieks to dozing Justice, and reveals
The Deed, which fraudful Art from Day conceals;
The Delve obscene, where no Suspicion pries;
Where the disfigur'd Coarse unshrouded lies;
The sure, the striking Proof, so strong maintain'd,   305
Pale Guilt starts self-convicted, when arraign'd.
These Spirits Treason of its Pow'r divest,
And turn the Peril from the Patriot's Breast.
Those solemn Thought inspire, or bright descend,
To snatch in Vision sweet the dying Friend.   310
But we deceive the Gloom, the Matin Bell
Summons to Prayer!—Now breaks th'Inchanter's Spell!
And now—But yon fair Spirit's Form survey!
'Tis she! *Olympia* beckons me away!
I haste! I fly!—adieu!—and when you see   315
The Youth, who bleeds with Fondness, think on me!
Tell him my Tale, and be his Pain carest;
By Love I tortur'd was, by Love I'm blest.
When worship'd Woman we entranc'd behold,
We praise the Maker in his fairest Mold;   320
The Pride of Nature, Harmony combin'd,
And Light immortal to the Soul refin'd!
Depriv'd of charming Woman, soon we miss
The Prize of Friendship, and the Life of Bliss!

Still through the Shades *Olympia* dawning breaks! *325*
What Bloom, what Brightness lusters o'er her Cheeks!
Again she calls!—I dare no longer stay!
A kind Farewell—*Olympia*, I obey.
He turn'd, no longer in my Sight remain'd,
The Mountain he, I safe the City gain'd. *330*

CANTO IV

STILL o'er my Mind wild *Fancy* holds her Sway,
Still on strange, visionary Land I stray.
Now Scenes crowd thick! Now indistinct appear!
Swift glide the *Months*, and turn the varying Year!
Near the *Bull*'s Horn Light's rising Monarch draws; *5*
Now on its Back the *Pleiades* he thaws!
From vernal Heat pale *Winter* forc'd to flie,
Northward retires, yet turns a watry Eye;
Then with an aguish Breath nips infant Blooms,
Deprives unfolding Spring of rich Perfumes, *10*
Shakes the slow-circling Blood of human Race,
And in sharp, livid Looks contracts the Face.
Now o'er *Norwegian* Hills he strides away:
Such slipp'ry Paths *Ambition*'s Steps betray.
Turning with Sighs, far, spiral Firs he sees, *15*
Which bow obedient to the Southern Breeze.
Now from yon *Zemblan* Rock his Crest he shrouds,
Like *Fame*'s, obscur'd amid the whitening Clouds;
Thence his lost Empire is with Tears deplor'd:
Such Tyrants shed o'er Liberty restor'd. *20*
Beneath his Eye (that throws malignant Light
Ten Times the measur'd Round of mortal Sight)
A waste, pale-glimm'ring, like a Moon, that wanes,
A wild Expanse of frozen Sea contains.
It cracks! vast, floating Mountains beat the Shore! *25*
Far off he hears those icy Ruins roar,
And from the hideous Crash distracted flies,
Like One, who feels his dying Infant's Cries.

Near, and more near the rushing Torrents sound,
And one great Rift runs through the vast Profound, 30
Swift as a shooting Meteor; groaning loud,
Like deep-roll'd Thunder through a rending Cloud.
The late-dark *Pole* now feels unsetting Day:
In Hurricanes of Wrath he whirls his Way;
O'er many a polar *Alp* to *Frost* he goes, 35
O'er crackling Vales, embrown'd with melting Snows;
Here Bears stalk Tenants of the barren Space,
Few Men, unsocial Those!—a barb'rous Race!
At length the Cave appears! the Race is run:
Now he recounts vast Conquests lost, and won, 40
And taleful in th'Embrace of *Frost* remains,
Barr'd from our Climes, and bound in icy Chains.

Mean while the Sun his Beams on *Cancer* throws,
Which now beneath his warmest Influence glows.
From glowing *Cancer* fall'n the King of Day, 45
Red through the kindling *Lyon*, shoots his Ray.
The tawny Harvest pays the earlier Plough,
And mellowing Fruitage loads the bending Bough.
'Tis Day-spring. Now green Lab'rinths I frequent,
Where *Wisdom* oft retires to meet *Content*. 50

The mounting Lark her warbling Anthem lends,
From Note to Note the ravish'd Soul ascends;
As thus it wou'd the Patriarch's Ladder climb,
By some good Angel led to Worlds sublime:
Oft (Legends say) the Snake, with waken'd Ire, 55
Like *Envy* rears in many a scaly Spire;
Then Songsters drop, then yield their vital Gore,
And Innocence, and Musick are no more.

Mild rides the Morn in orient Beauty drest,
An azure Mantle, and a purple Vest, 60
Which blown by Gales her gemmy Feet display,
Her amber Tresses negligently gay.
Collected now her rosy Hand they fill,
And, gently wrung, the pearly Dews distill.
The songful Zephyrs, and the laughing Hours 65

Breathe sweet; and ſtrew her opening Way with Flowers.
    The chatt'ring Swallows leave their neſted Care,
Each promising Return with plenteous Fare.
So the fond Swain, who to the Market hies,
Stills with big Hopes his Infant's tender Cries.   *70*
    Yonder two Turtles, o'er their callow Brood,
Hang hov'ring, ere they seek their guiltless Food.
Fondly they bill. Now to their morning Care,
Like our firſt Parents part the am'rous Pair:
But ah!—a Pair no more!—with spreading Wings,   *75*
From the high, sounding Cliff a Vultur springs;
Steady he sails along th' aërial Grey,
Swoops down, and bears yon tim'rous Dove away.
Start we, who, worse than Vulturs, *Nymrods* find,
Men meditating Prey on human Kind?   *80*
    Wild Beaſts to gloomy Dens re-pace their Way,
Where their couch'd Young demand the slaughter'd Prey.
Rooks from their nodding Neſts black-swarming fly,
And in hoarse Uproar tell the Fowler nigh.
    Now in his Tabernacle rouz'd, the Sun   *85*
Is warn'd the blue, ætherial Steep to run:
While on his Couch of floating Jasper laid,
From his bright Eye *Sleep* calls the dewy Shade.
The cryſtal Dome transparent Pillars raise,
Whence beam'd from Saphirs living Azure plays: *90*
The liquid Floor, in-wrought with Pearls divine,
Where all his Labours in Mosaic shine.
His Coronet, a Cloud of Silver-white;
His Robe with unconsuming Crimson bright,
Varied with Gems, all Heaven's collected Store;   *95*
While his loose Locks descend, a golden Shower.
If to his Steps compar'd, we tardy find
The *Grecian* Racers, who outſtript the Wind.
Fleet to the glowing Race behold him ſtart!
His quick'ning Eyes a quiv'ring Radiance dart,   *100*
And, while the laſt, noƈturnal Flag is furl'd,
Swift into Life and Motion look the World.

The Sun-flow'r now averts her blooming Cheek
From West, to view his Eastern Lustre break.
What gay, creative Pow'r his Presence brings!   *105*
Hills, Lawns, Lakes, Villages!—the Face of Things,
All Night beneath successive Shadows miss'd,
Instant begins in Colours to exist:
But absent these from Sons of Riot keep,
Lost in impure, unmeditating Sleep.   *110*

  T'unlock his Fence, the new-ris'n Swain prepares,
And ere forth-driv'n recounts his fleecy Cares;
When, lo! an ambush'd Wolf, with Hunger bold,
Springs at the Prey, and fierce invades the Fold!
But by the Pastor not in vain defied,   *115*
Like our arch Foe by some cœlestial Guide.

  Spread on yon Rock the Sea-Calf I survey,
Bask'd in the Sun his Skin reflects the Day:
He sees yon tow'r-like Ship the Waves divide,
And slips again beneath the glassy Tide.   *120*

  The watry Herbs, and Shrubs, and Vines, and Flowers
Rear their bent Heads, o'ercharg'd with nightly Showers.

  Hail glorious Sun! to whose attractive Fires,
The waken'd, vegetative Life aspires!
The Juices, wrought by thy directive Force,   *125*
Through Plants, and Trees, perform their Genial Course,
Extend, in Root, with Bark unyielding bind
The hearted Trunk; or weave the branching Rind;
Expand in Leaves, in flow'ry Blossoms shoot,
Bleed in rich Gums, and swell in ripen'd Fruit.   *130*
From thee, bright, universal Pow'r! began
Instinct in Brute, and gen'rous Love in Man.

  Talk'd I of Love?—Yon Swain, with am'rous Air,
Soft swells his Pipe, to charm the rural Fair.
She milks the Flocks; then, list'ning as he plays,   *135*
Steals in the running Brook a conscious Gaze.

  The Trout, that deep, in Winter, ooz'd remains,
Up-springs, and Sunward turns its crimson Stains.

  The Tenants of the Warren, vainly chac'd,

Now lur'd to ambient Fields for green Repast,   *140*
Seek their small, vaulted Labyrinths in vain;
Entangling Nets betray the skipping Train;
Red Massacres through their Republic fly,
And Heaps on Heaps by ruthless Spaniels dye.

    The Fisher, who the lonely Beech has stray'd,   *145*
And all the live-long Night his Net-work spread,
Drags *in*, and bears the loaded Snare away;
Where flounce deceiv'd th'expiring, finny Prey.

    Near *Neptune*'s Temple, (*Neptune*'s now no more)
Whose Statue plants a Trident on the Shore,   *150*
In sportive Rings the gen'rous Dolphins wind,
And eye, and think the Image human-Kind:
Dear, pleasing Friendship!—See! the Pile commands
The Vale, and grim as *Superstition* stands!
Time's Hand there leaves its Print of mossy green,   *155*
With Hollows, carv'd for Snakes, and Birds obscene.

    O *Gibbs*, whose Art the solemn Fane can raise,
Where *God* delights to dwell, and *Man* to praise;
When moulder'd thus the Column falls away,
Like some great Prince, majestic in Decay;   *160*
When *Ignorance*, and *Scorn* the Ground shall tread,
Where *Wisdom* tutor'd, and *Devotion* pray'd;
Where shall thy pompous Work our Wonder claim?
What, but the Muse alone, preserve thy Name?

    The Sun shines, broken, though yon Arch, that rears *165*
This once-round Fabric, half-depriv'd by Years,
Which rose a stately Colonade, and crown'd
Encircling Pillars, now unfaithful found;
In Fragments, these the Fall of those forebode,
Which, nodding, just up-heave their crumbling Load.   *170*
High, on yon Column, which has batter'd stood,

171–6 'The Dutch are very solicitous for the preservation of the stork in every part of their republic.... They have even got an opinion that it will only live in a republic...' (Oliver Goldsmith, *A History of the Earth and Animated Nature* (1866), II, 177). Cf. A. C. McKillop, *Background of Thomson's Seasons* (Minneapolis, 1942), p. 132.

Like some stripp'd Oak, the Grandeur of the Wood,
The Stork inhabits her aërial Nest;
By her are Liberty and Peace carest;
She flies the Realms, that own despotick Kings,   *175*
And only spreads o'er free-born States her Wings.
The Roof is now the Daw's, or Raven's Haunt,
And loathsome Toads in the dark Entrance pant;
Or Snakes, that lurk to snap the heedless Fly,
And fated Bird, that oft comes flutt'ring by.   *180*
    An Aqueduct across yon Vale is laid,
Its Channel through a ruin'd Arch betray'd;
Whirl'd down a Steep, it flies with torrent-Force,
Flashes, and roars, and plows a devious Course.
    Attracted Mists a golden Cloud commence,   *185*
While through high-colour'd Air strike Rays intense.
Betwixt two Points, which yon steep Mountains show,
Lies a mild Bay, to which kind Breezes flow.
Beneath a Grotto, arch'd for calm Retreat,
Leads length'ning in the Rock—Be this my Seat.   *190*
Heat never enters here; but *Coolness* reigns
O'er Zephyrs, and distilling, watry Veins.
Secluded now I trace th'instructive Page,
And live o'er Scenes of many a backward Age;
Through Days, Months, Years, through Time's whole
        Course I run,   *195*
And present stand where Time it self begun.
    Ye mighty *Dead* of just, distinguish'd Fame,
Your thoughts, (ye bright Instructers!) here I claim.
Here ancient Knowledge opens Nature's Springs;
Here Truths historic give the Hearts of Kings.   *200*
Hence Contemplation learns white Hours to find,
And labours Virtue on th'attentive Mind.
O lov'd Retreat! thy Joys Content bestow,
Nor Guilt, nor Shame, nor sharp Repentance know.
What the fifth *Charles* long aim'd in Power to see,   *205*

205-6 The Emperor Charles V abdicated in 1555 and retired to a little house
attached to a monastery at Yuste in Estremadura.

135

That Happiness he found reserv'd in Thee.
  Now let me change the Page—Here *Tully* weeps,
While in Death's icy Arms his *Tullia* sleeps,
His Daughter dear!—Retir'd I see him mourn,
By all the Frenzy now of Anguish torn.   210
Wild his Complaints! Nor sweeter *Sorrow*'s Strains,
When *Singer* for *Alexis* loſt complains.
Each Friend condoles, expoſtulates, reproves:
More than a Father raving *Tully* loves;
Or *Salluſt* censures thus!—Unheeding Blame,   215
He schemes a Temple to his *Tullia*'s Name.
Thus o'er my *Hermit* once did Grief prevail,
Thus rose *Olympia*'s Tomb, his moving Tale,
The Sighs, Tears, frantic Starts, that banish Reſt,
And all the burſting Sorrows of his Breaſt.   220
  But hark! a sudden Pow'r attunes the Air!
Th'inchanting Sound enamour'd Breezes bear;
Now low, now high, they sink, or lift the Song,
Which the Cave echoes sweet, and sweet the Creeks
              prolong.
  I liſten'd, gaz'd, when, wondrous to behold!   225
From Ocean ſteam'd a Vapour gath'ring roll'd:
A blue, round Spot on the Mid-roof it came,
Spread broad, and redden'd into dazzling Flame.
Full-orb'd it shone, and dimm'd the swimming Sight,
While doubling Objeéts danc'd with darkling Light. 230
Amaz'd I ſtood!—amaz'd I ſtill remain!
What earthly Pow'r this Wonder can explain?
Gradual at length the Luſtre dies away:
My Eyes reſtor'd a mortal Form survey.
My Hermit-Friend? 'Tis He.—All hail! (he cries.)   235

---

207 Tullia died 46 B.C. Cicero (Tully) wrote a treatise *De Consolatione* in her
memory.

212 Elizabeth Singer Rowe wrote a poem *On the anniversary return of the day on
wh ch Mr* ROWE *died,* in which she called him Alexis. See her *Works* (1796), III, 152–6.
Cf. *Plain Dealer,* 21 December 1724.

215 In the pseudo-Sallustian *In M. Tullium Ciceronem Oratio*: 'filia matris praelex,
tibi iucundior atque obsequentior quam parenti par est' (II, 1).

I see, and wou'd alleviate thy Surprize.
The vanish'd Meteor was Heaven's Message meant,
To warn thee hence; I knew the high Intent.
Hear then! In this sequester'd Cave retir'd,
Departed Saints converse with Men inspir'd.   240
'Tis sacred Ground; nor can thy Mind endure,
Yet unprepar'd, an Intercourse so pure.
Quick let us hence—And now extend thy Views
O'er yonder Lawn; there find the heav'n-born *Muse*!
Or seek her, where she trusts her tuneful Tale   245
To the mid, silent Wood, or vocal Vale;
Where Trees half check the Light with trembling Shades,
Close in deep Glooms, or open clear in Glades:
Or where surrounding Vistas far descend,
The Landscape varied at each less'ning End!   250
She, only *She* can mortal Thought refine,
And raise thy Voice to Visitants divine.

CANTO V

WE left the Cave. Be Fear (said I) defied!
Virtue (for thou art Virtue) is my Guide.
    By time-worn Steps a steep Ascent we gain,
Whose Summit yields a Prospect o'er the Plain.
There bench'd with Turf, an Oak our Seat extends,   5
Whose top a verdant, branch'd Pavilion bends.
Vistas with Leaves diversify the Scene,
Some pale, some brown, and some of lively green.
    Now from the full-grown Day a beamy Shower
Gleams on the Lake, and gilds each glossy Flower.   10
Gay Insects sparkle in the genial Blaze,
Various as Light, and countless as its Rays.
They dance on ev'ry Stream, and pictur'd play,
Till by the watry Racer snatch'd away.
    Now, from yon Range of Rocks, strong Rays
            rebound,   15
Doubling the Day on flow'ry Plains around:

Kingcups beneath far-striking Colours glance,
Bright as th'etherial glows the green Expanse.
Gems of the Field!—The *Topaz* charms the Sight,
Like these, effulging yellow Streams of Light.   20
From the same Rocks fall Rills with soften'd Force,
Meet in yon Mead, and well a River's Source.
Through her clear Chanel shine her finny Shoals,
O'er Sands, like Gold, the liquid Crystal rolls.
Dim'd in yon coarser Moor her Charms decay,   25
And shape through rustling Reeds a ruffled Way.
Near Willows short and bushy Shadows throw:
Now lost, she seems through nether Tracts to flow;
Yet, at yon Point, winds out in Silver State,
Like Virtue from a Labyrinth of Fate.   30
In length'ning Rows prone from the Mountains run
The Flocks:—their Fleeces glist'ning in the Sun;
Her Streams they seek, and, 'twixt her neighb'ring Trees,
Recline in various Attitudes of Ease.
Where the Herds sip, the little scaly Fry,   35
Swift from the Shore, in scatt'ring Myriads fly.
  Each liv'ried Cloud, that round th'Horizon glows,
Shifts in odd Scenes, like Earth, from whence it rose.
The Bee hums wanton in yon Jess'mine Bower,
And circling settles, and despoils the Flower.   40
Melodious there the plumy Songsters meet,
And call charm'd *Echo* from her arch'd Retreat.
Neat, polish'd Mansions rise in Prospect gay;
Time-batter'd Tow'rs frown awful in Decay;
The Sun plays glitt'ring on the Rocks, and Spires,   45
And the Lawn lightens with reflected Fires.
  Here *Mirth*, and *Fancy*'s wanton Train advance,
And to light Measures turn the swimming Dance.
Sweet, slow-pac'd *Melancholy* next appears,
Pompous in Grief, and Eloquent of Tears.   50
Here *Meditation* shines in Azure drest,
All-starr'd with Gems: A Sun adorns her Crest.
Religion, to whose lifted, raptur'd Eyes

Seraphic Hosts descend from opening Skies;
Beauty, who sways the Heart, and charms the Sight; 55
Whose tongue is Music, and whose Smile Delight;
Whose Brow is Majesty; whose Bosom Peace;
Who bad Creation be, and Chaos cease;
Whose Breath perfumes the Spring; whose Eye divine
Kindled the Sun, and gave its Light to shine. 60
Here in thy Likeness fair *Ophelia seen,
She throws kind Lustre o'er th'enliven'd Green.
Next her *Description*, robed in various Hues,
Invites Attention from the pensive *Muse*!
The *Muse*!—she comes! refin'd the *Passions* wait, 65
And *Precept*, ever winning, wise, and great.
The *Muse*! a thousand *Spirits* wing the Air:
(Once *Men*, who made like *her* Mankind their Care.)
Inamour'd round her press th'inspiring Throng,
And swell to Extacy her solemn Song. 70
　　　Thus in the Dame each nobler Grace we find,
Fair *Wortley*'s angel-Accent, Eyes, and Mind.
Whether her Sight the dew-bright Dawn surveys,
The Noon's dry Heat, or Evening's temper'd Rays,
The Hours of Storm, or Calm, the gleby Ground, 75
The corral'd Sea, gem'd Rock, or Sky profound,
A *Raphael*'s Fancy animates each Line,
Each Image strikes with Energy divine;
Bacon, and *Newton* in her Thought conspire;
Not sweeter than her Voice is *Hendel*'s Lyre. 80
　　　My Hermit thus. She beckons us away:
Oh, let us swift the high Behest obey!
　　　Now through a Lane, which mingling Tracks have
　　　　　crost,
The Way unequal, and the Landscape lost,
We rove. The Warblers lively Tunes essay, 85
The *Lark* on Wing, the *Linnet* on the Spray.

* Mrs. *Oldfield*. [RS]

---

72 Lady Mary Wortley Montagu.　　　　　83 Tracks] Tracts *1729*.

While Music trembles in their songful Throats,
The *Bullfinch* whistles soft his flute-like Notes.
The bolder *Blackbird* swells sonorous Lays;
The varying *Thrush* commands a tuneful Maze;   90
Each a wild Length of Melody pursues;
While the soft-murm'ring, am'rous *Wood-Dove* cooes.
And, when in Spring these melting Mixtures flow,
The *Cuckoo* sends her Unison of Woe.
    But as smooth Seas are furrow'd by a Storm;   95
As Troubles all our tranquil Joys deform;
So, loud through Air, unwelcome Noises sound,
And Harmony's, at once, in Discord, drown'd.
From yon dark Cypress croaks the Raven's Cry;
As dissonant the *Daw*, *Jay*, chatt'ring *Pye*:   100
The clam'rous *Crows* abandon'd Carnage seek,
And the harsh *Owl* shrills out a sharp'ning Shriek.
    At the Lane's End a high-lath'd Gate's prefer'd,
To bar the Trespass of a vagrant Herd.
Fast by, a meagre Mendicant we find,   105
Whose russet Rags hang flutt'ring in the Wind:
Years bow his Back, a Staff supports his Tread,
And soft white Hairs shade thin his palsied Head.
Poor Wretch!—Is this for Charity his Haunt?
He meets the frequent Slight, and ruthless Taunt.   110
On Slaves of Guilt oft smiles the squand'ring Peer;
But passing knows not common Bounty here.
Vain thing! in what dost thou superior shine?
His our first Sire: what Race more ancient thine?
Less backward trac'd, he may his Lineage draw   115
From Men, whose Influence kept the World in awe:
Whose worthless Sons, like thee, perchance consum'd
Their ample Store, their Line to Want was doom'd.
So thine may perish by the course of Things,
While his from Beggers re-ascend to Kings.   120
Now *Lazar*, as thy Hardships I peruse,

---

103 Prefer'd. Possibly an error for *proffer'd*.

On my own State instructed wou'd I muse.
When I view Greatness, I my Lot lament,
Compar'd to thee, I snatch supreme Content.
I might have felt, did Heav'n not gracious deal,   *125*
A Fate, which I must mourn to see thee feel.
But soft! the Cripple our Approach descries,
And to the Gate, though weak, officious hies.
I spring preventive, and unbar the Way,
Then, turning, with a Smile of Pity say,   *130*
Here, Friend!—this little, copper Alms receive;
Instance of Will, without the Pow'r to give.
Hermit, if here with Pity we reflect,
How must we grieve, when Learning meets Neglect?
When God-like Souls endure a mean Restraint;   *135*
When gen'rous Will is curb'd by tyrant Want;
He truly feels what to Distress belongs,
Who, to his private, adds a People's Wrongs;
Merit's a Mark, at which Disgrace is thrown,
And ev'ry injur'd Virtue is his own.   *140*
Such their own Pangs with Patience here endure,
Yet there weep Wounds, they are denied to cure.
Thus rich in Poverty, thus humbly Great,
And though depress'd superior to their Fate.
Minions in Pow'r, and Misers, mid their Store,   *145*
Are mean in Greatness, and in Plenty poor.
What's Pow'r, or Wealth? Were they not form'd for Aid,
A Spring for Virtue, and from Wrongs a Shade?
In Pow'r we salvage Tyranny behold,
And wily Av'rice owns polluted Gold.   *150*
From golden Sands her Pride cou'd *Lybia* raise,
Cou'd she, who spreads no Pasture, claim our Praise?
Loath'd were her Wealth, where rabid Monsters breed;
Where Serpents, pamper'd, on her Venom, feed.
No sheltry Trees invite the Wand'rer's Eye,   *155*
No Fruits, no Grain, no Gums, her Tracts supply;
On her vast Wilds no lovely Prospects run;
But all lies barren, though beneath the Sun.

My Hermit thus. I know thy Soul believes,
'Tis hard Vice triumphs, and that Virtue grieves;   160
Yet oft Affliction purifies the Mind,
Kind Benefits oft flow from Means unkind.
Were the whole known, what we uncouth suppose,
Doubtless, wou'd beauteous Symmetry disclose.
The naked Cliff, that singly rough remains,   165
In Prospect dignifies the fertile Plains;
Lead-colour'd Clouds, in scatt'ring Fragments seen,
Shew, though in broken Views, the blue serene.
Severe Distresses Industry inspire;
Thus Captives oft excelling Arts acquire,   170
And boldly struggle through a State of Shame,
To Life, Ease, Plenty, Liberty and Fame.
Sword-law has often *Europe*'s Ballance gain'd,
And one red Vict'ry Years of Peace maintain'd.
We pass through Want to Wealth, through dismal Strife 175
To calm Content, through Death to endless Life.
Lybia thou nam'st—Let *Africk*'s Wastes appear
Curst by those Heats, that fructify the Year;
Yet the same *Suns* her Orange-Groves befriend,
Where clust'ring Globes in shining Rows depend.   180
Here when fierce Beams o'er with'ring Plants are roll'd,
There the green Fruit seems ripen'd into Gold.
Ev'n Scenes, that strike with terrible Surprize,
Still prove a God, just, merciful, and wise.
Sad wintry Blasts, that strip the Autumn, bring   185
The milder Beauties of a flow'ry Spring.
Ye sulph'rous Fires in jaggy Lightnings break!
Ye Thunders rattle, and ye Nations shake!
Ye Storms of riving Flame the Forest tear!
Deep crack ye Rocks! rent Trees be whirl'd in Air!   190
Reft at a Stroke, some stately Fane we'll mourn;
Her Tombs wide-shatter'd, and her Dead up-torn;
Were noxious Spirits not from Caverns drawn,
Rack'd Earth wou'd soon in Gulphs enormous yawn:
Then all were lost!—Or shou'd we floating view   195

142

The baleful Cloud, there wou'd Destruction brew;
Plague, Fever, Frenzy close-engend'ring lie,
'Till these red Ruptures clear the sullied Sky.
Now a Field opens to enlarge my Thought,
In parcell'd Tracts to various Uses wrought.   200
Here hard'ning Ripeness the first Blooms behold,
There the last Blossoms Spring-like Pride unfold.
Here swelling Peas on leafy Stalks are seen,
Mix'd Flower's of Red and Azure shine between;
Whose waving Beauties, heighten'd by the Sun,   205
In colour'd Lanes along the Furrows run.
There the next Produce of a genial Shower,
The Bean fresh-blossoms in a speckled Flower;
Whose morning Dews, when to the Sun resign'd,
With undulating Sweets embalm the Wind.   210
Now daisy Plats of Clover square the Plain,
And part the bearded from the beardless Grain.
There fibrous Flax with Verdure binds the Field,
Which on the Loom shall art-spun Labours yield.
The Mulb'ry, in fair summer Green array'd,   215
Full in the midst starts up, a silky Shade.
For human Taste the rich-stain'd Fruitage bleeds;
The Leaf the silk-emitting Reptile feeds.
As Swans their Down, as Flocks their Fleeces leave,
Here Worms for Man their glossy Entrails weave.   220
Hence to adorn the Fair, in Texture gay,
Sprigs, Fruits, and Flow'rs on figur'd Vestments play:
But *Industry* prepares them oft to please
The guilty Pride of vain, luxuriant Ease.
Now frequent, dusty Gales offensive blow,   225
And o'er my Sight a transient Blindness throw.
Windward we shift. Near down th'etherial Steep,
The Lamp of Day hangs hov'ring o'er the Deep.
Dun Shades, in rocky Shapes up Ether roll'd,
Project long, shaggy Points, deep-ting'd with Gold.   230

---

217 rich-stain'd] rich'd-stain'd *1729*.

Others take faint th'unripen'd Cherry's Die,
And paint amusing Landscapes on the Eye.
There blue-veil'd Yellow, through a Sky serene,
In swelling Mixture forms a floating Green.
Streak'd through white Clouds a mild Vermilion shines, *235*
And the Breeze freshens, as the Heat declines.
      Yon crooked, sunny Roads change rising Views
From brown, to sandy-red, and chalky Hues.
One mingled Scene another quick succeeds,
Men, Chariots, Teams, yok'd Steers, and prancing Steeds, *240*
Which climb, descend, and, as loud Whips resound,
Stretch, sweat, and smoke along unequal Ground.
On winding *Thames*, reflecting radiant Beams,
When Boats, Ships, Barges mark the roughen'd Streams,
This Way, and that, they diff'rent Points pursue; *245*
So mix the Motions, and so shifts the View.
While thus we throw around our gladden'd Eyes,
The Gifts of Heav'n in gay Profusion rise;
Trees rich with Gums, and Fruits; with Jewels Rocks;
Plains with Flow'rs, Herbs, and Plants, and Beeves, and
         Flocks; *250*
Mountains with Mines; with Oak, and Cedar, Woods;
Quarries with Marble, and with Fish the Floods.
In dark'ning Spots, mid Fields of various Dies,
Tilth new-manur'd, or naked Fallow lies.
Near Uplands fertile Pride enclos'd display, *255*
The green Grass yellowing into scentful Hay,
And thick-set Hedges fence the full-ear'd Corn,
And Berries blacken on the virid Thorn.
Mark in yon Heath oppos'd the cultur'd Scene,
Wild Thyme, pale Box, and Firs of darker green. *260*
The native Strawberry red-ripening grows,
By Nettles guarded, as by Thorns the Rose.
There Nightingales in unprun'd Copses build,
In shaggy Furzes lies the Hare conceal'd.
'Twixt Ferns, and Thistles, unsown Flow'rs amuse, *265*
And form a lucid Chase of various Hues;

Many half-grey with Dust; Confus'd they lie,
Scent the rich Year, and lead the wand'ring Eye.
　　Contemplative, we tread the flow'ry Plain,
The *Muse* preceding with her heav'nly Train. 270
When, lo! the Mendicant, so late behind,
Strange View! now journeying in our Front we find!
And yet a View more strange our Heed demands;
Touch'd by the Muse's Wand transform'd he stands.
O'er Skin late-wrinkled, instant Beauty spreads; 275
The late-dimm'd Eye a vivid Lustre sheds;
Hairs, once so thin, now graceful Locks decline;
And Rags, now chang'd, in regal Vestments shine.
　　The Hermit thus. In him the *B A R D* behold,
Once seen by Midnight's Lamp in Winter's Cold; 280
The *Bard*, whose Want so multiplied his Woes,
He sunk a Mortal, and a Seraph rose.
See!—where those stately Yew-Trees darkling grow,
And, waving o'er yon Graves, brown Horrors throw,
Scornful he points—there, o'er his sacred Dust, 285
Arise the sculptur'd Tomb, and labour'd Bust.
Vain Pomp! bestow'd by ostentatious Pride,
Who to a Life of Want Relief deny'd.
　　But thus the *Bard*. Are these the Gifts of State?
Gifts unreceiv'd!—These? Ye ungen'rous Great! 290
How was I treated when in Life forlorn?
My Claim your Pity; but my Lot your Scorn.
Why were my studious Hours oppos'd by Need?
In me did Poverty from Guilt proceed?
Did I contemporary Authors wrong, 295
And deem their Worth, but as they priz'd my Song?
Did I sooth Vice, or venal Strokes betray
In the low-purpos'd, loud, polemic Fray?
Did e'er my Verse immodest Warmth contain,
Or, once licentious, heav'nly Truths prophane? 300
Never.—And yet when Envy sunk my Name,
Who call'd my shadow'd Merit into Fame?
When undeserv'd a Prison's Grate I saw,

What Hand redeem'd me from the wrested Law?
Who cloath'd me naked, or when hungry fed?   *305*
Why crush'd the Living? Why extoll'd the Dead?
But foreign Languages adopt my Lays,
And distant Nations shame you into Praise.
Why shou'd *unrelish'd* Wit these Honours cause?
Custom, not Knowledge, dictates your Applause: *310*
Or think you thus a self-Renown to raise,
And mingle your Vain-Glories with my Bays?
Be Yours the mould'ring Tomb! Be mine the Lay
Immortal!—Thus he scoffs the Pomp away.

  Though Words like these unletter'd Pride impeach,   *315*
To the meek Heart he turns with milder Speech.
Though now a Seraph, oft he deigns to wear
The Face of human Friendship, oft of Care;
To walk disguis'd an Object of Relief,
A learn'd, good Man, long exercis'd in Grief;   *320*
Forlorn, a friendless Orphan oft to roam,
Craving some kind, some hospitable Home;
Or, like *Ulysses*, a low Lazar stand,
Beseeching Pity's Eye, and Bounty's Hand;
Or, like *Ulysses*, Royal Aid request,   *325*
Wand'ring from Court to Court, a King distrest.
Thus varying Shapes, the seeming Son of Woe
Eyes the cold Heart, and Hearts that gen'rous glow;
Then to the *Muse* relates each lordly Name,
Who deals impartial Infamy, and Fame.   *330*
Oft, as when Man, in mortal State depress'd,
His Lays taught Virtue, which his Life confess'd,
He now forms visionary Scenes below,
Inspiring Patience in the Heart of Woe;
Patience that softens every sad Extreme,   *335*
That casts through Dungeon-Glooms a chearful Gleam,
Disarms Disease of Pain, mocks Slander's Sting,
And strips of Terrors the terrific King,
'Gainst *Want*, a sourer Foe, its Succour lends,
And smiling sees th'Ingratitude of Friends.   *340*

Nor are these Tasks to him alone consign'd,
Millions invisible befriend Mankind.
When watry Structures, seen cross Heav'n t'ascend,
Arch above Arch in radiant Order bend,
Fancy beholds, a-down each glitt'ring Side,   345
Myriads of missionary Seraphs glide;
She sees good Angels genial Show'rs bestow
From the red Convex of the dewy Bow.
They smile upon the Swain: He views the Prize;
Then grateful bends, to bless the bounteous Skies.   350
Some collect Winds, and send propitious Gales
Oft where *Britannia*'s Navy spreads her Sails;
There ever wafting, on the Breath of Fame,
Unequal'd Glory in her *Sovereign*'s Name.
Some teach young Zephyrs vernal Sweets to bear,   355
And float the balmy Health on ambient Air;
Zephyrs, that, oft where Lovers list'ning lie,
Along the Grove in melting Music die,
And in lone Caves to Minds poetic roll
Seraphic Whispers, that abstract the Soul.   360
Some range the Colours, as they parted fly,
Clear-pointed to the philosophic Eye,
The flaming *Red*, that pains the dwelling Gaze;
The stainless, lightsome *Yellow*'s gilding Rays;
The clouded *Orange*, that betwixt them grows,   365
And to kind Mixture tawny Lustre owes;
All-chearing *Green*, that gives the Spring its Dye;
The bright, transparent *Blue*, that robes the Sky;
And *Indico*, which shaded Light displays;
And *Violet*, which in the View decays.   370
Parental Hues, whence Others all proceed;
An ever-mingling, changeful, countless Breed;

343–74 The 'watry Structures' are rainbows, and the extended passage which
follows on the primary ('parental') colours of the spectrum must have been inspired
by Newton's *Opticks* (1704). The seraphs with which RS peoples the rainbow, however, were most likely modelled on Pope's sylphs and Jacob's angels.

369 *Indico*, the common spelling of 'indigo' in the sixteenth and seventeenth
centuries, survived into the eighteenth (*OED*).

Unravel'd, variegated Lines of Light,
When blended, dazzling in promiscuous *White*.
Oft through these Bows departed Spirits range,   *375*
New to the Skies, admiring at their Change;
Each Mind a Void, as when first-born to Earth,
Beheld a second Blank in second Birth;
Then, as yon *Seraph-Bard* fram'd Hearts below,
Each sees him here transcendant Knowledge show.   *380*
New Saints he tutors into Truth refin'd,
And tunes to rapt'rous Love the new-form'd Mind.
He swells the Lyre, whose loud, melodious Lays
Call high *Hosannahs* from the Voice of Praise;
Though one bad Age such Poësy cou'd wrong,   *385*
Now Worlds around retentive roll the Song:
Now God's high Throne the full-voic'd Raptures gain,
Cœlestial Hosts returning Strain for Strain.
　　　Thus he, who once knew Want without Relief,
Sees Joy resulting from well-suff'ring Grief.   *390*
Hark! while we talk, a distant, patt'ring Rain
Resounds!—See! up the broad etherial Plain
Shoots the bright Bow!—The Seraph flitts away;
The *Muse*, the Graces from our View decay.
　　　Behind yon western Hill the Globe of Light   *395*
Drops sudden; fast-pursued by Shades of Night.
　　　Yon Graves from winter-Scenes to Mind recall
Rebellion's Council, and Rebellion's Fall.
What Fiends in sulph'rous, Car-like Clouds upflew?
What midnight Treason glar'd beneath their View?   *400*
And now the Traytors rear their *Babel* Schemes,
Big, and more big, stupendous Mischief seems;
But *Justice*, rouz'd, superior Strength employs,
Their Scheme wide-shatters, and their Hope destroys.
Discord she wills; the missile Ruin flies;   *405*
Sudden, unnatural Debates arise,
Doubt, mutual Jealousy, and dumb Disgust,
Dark-hinted Mutt'rings, and avow'd Distrust;
To secret Ferment is each Heart resign'd;

Suspicion hovers in each clouded Mind;   410
They jar, accus'd accuse, revil'd revile,
And Wrath to Wrath oppose, and Guile to Guile;
Wrangling they part, themselves themselves betray;
Each dire Device ſtarts naked into Day;
They feel Confusion in the Van with Fear;   415
They feel the King of Terrors in the Rear.
    Of these were Three by diff'rent Motives fir'd,
Ambition One, and One Revenge inspir'd.
The Third, O *Mammon*, was thy meaner Slave;
Thou Idol seldom of the Great, and Brave.   420
    Florio, whose Life was one continu'd Feaſt,
His Wealth diminish'd, and his Debts increas'd,
Vain Pomp, and Equipage his low Desires,
Who ne'er to intelleƈtual Bliss aspires;
He, to repair by Vice what Vice has broke,   425
Durſt with bold Treasons Judgment's Rod provoke.
His Strength of Mind, by Lux'ry half-dissolv'd,
Ill brooks the Woe, where deep he ſtands involv'd.
He weeps, ſtamps wild, and to and fro now flies;
Now wrings his Hands, and sends unmanly Cries,   430
Arraigns his Judge, affirms unjuſt he bleeds,
And now recants, and now for Mercy pleads;
Now blames Associates, raves with inward Strife,
Upbraids himself; then thinks alone on Life.
He rolls red-swelling, tearful Eyes around,   435
Sore smites his Breaſt, and sinks upon the Ground.
He wails, he quite desponds, convulsive lies,
Shrinks from the fancied Ax, and thinks he dies:
Revives, with Hope enquires, ſtops short with Fear,
Entreats ev'n Flatt'ry, nor the worſt will hear;   440
The worſt, alas, his Doom!—What Friend replies?
Each speaks with shaking Head, and down-caſt Eyes.
One Silence breaks, then pauses, drops a Tear;

---

417 ff. So far as is known, the three rebels described here are imaginary, though
possibly Horatio (ll. 541 ff.) should be associated with the Horatius of *To a Young
Gentleman, a Painter*.

Nor Hope affords, nor quite confirms his Fear;
But what kind Friendship part reserves unknown   445
Comes thund'ring in his Keeper's surly Tone.
Enough—struck through and through, in ghastly Stare,
He stands transfixt, the Statue of Despair;
Nor ought of Life, nor ought of Death he knows,
Till Thought returns, and brings Return of Woes: 450
Now pours a Storm of Grief in gushing Streams:
That past—Collected in himself he seems,
And with forc'd Smile retires—His latent Thought
Dark, horrid, as the Prison's dismal Vault.

　　If with himself at Variance ever-wild,   455
With angry Heav'n how stands he reconcil'd?
No penitential Orisons arise;
Nay he obtests the Justice of the Skies.
Not for his Guilt, for sentenc'd Life he moans;
His Chains rough-clanking to discordant Groans,   460
To Bars harsh-grating, heavy-creaking Doors,
Hoarse-echoing Walls, and hollow-ringing Floors,
To Thoughts more dissonant, far, far less kind,
One *Anarchy*, one *Chaos* of the *Mind*.

　　At length, fatigu'd with Grief, on Earth he lies: 465
But soon as Sleep weighs down th'unwilling Eyes,
Glad Liberty appears, no Damps annoy;
Treason succeeds, and all transforms to Joy.
Proud Palaces their glitt'ring Stores display;
Gain he pursues, and Rapine leads the Way.   470
What Gold? What Gems?—He strains to seize the Prize;
Quick from his Touch dissolv'd, a Cloud it flies.
Conscious he cries.—And must I wake to weep?
Ah, yet return, return delusive Sleep!
Sleep comes; but Liberty no more:—Unkind,   475
The Dungeon-Glooms hang heavy on his Mind.
Shrill Winds are heard, and howling Dæmons call;
Wide-flying Portals seem unhing'd to fall;

475–96 Cf. II, 193 ff.

Then close with sudden Claps; a dreadful Din!
He starts, wakes, storms, and all is Hell within.   *480*
     His Genius flies—reflects he now on Prayer?
Alas! bad Spirits turn those Thoughts to Air.
What shall he next? What, straight relinquish Breath,
To bar a publick, just, though shameful Death?
Rash, horrid Thought! yet not afraid to live,   *485*
Murd'rous he strikes—may Heav'n the Deed forgive!
     Why had he thus false Spirit to rebel?
And why not Fortitude to suffer well?
Were his Success, how terrible the Blow?
And its Recoil on him eternal Woe.   *490*
Heav'n this Affliction then for Mercy meant,
That a good End might close a Life mispent.
     Where no kind Lips the hallow'd Dirge resound,
Far from the Compass of yon sacred Ground;
Full in the Center of three meeting Ways,   *495*
Stak'd through he lies.—Warn'd let the Wicked gaze!
     Near yonder Fane, where Mis'ry sleeps in Peace,
Whose Spire fast-lessens, as these Shades encrease,
Left to the North, whence oft brew'd Tempests roll,
Tempests, dire Emblems, *Cosmo*, of thy Soul!   *500*
There mark that *Cosmo*, much for Guile renown'd!
His Grave by unbid Plants of Poison crown'd.
When out of Pow'r, through him the Publick Good,
So strong his factious Tribe, suspended stood.
In Pow'r, vindictive Actions were his Aim,   *505*
And Patriots perish'd by th'ungenerous Flame.
If the best Cause he in the Senate chose,
Ev'n Right in him from some wrong Motive rose.
The Bad he loath'd, and wou'd the Weak despise;
Yet courted for dark Ends, and shun'd the Wise.   *510*
When ill his Purpose, eloquent his Strain;
His Malice had a Look, and Voice humane.
His Smile, the Signal of some vile Intent,
A private Ponyard, or empoison'd Scent;
Proud, yet to popular Applause a Slave;   *515*

No Friend he honour'd, and no Foe forgave.
His Boons unfrequent, or unjust to Need;
The Hire of Guilt, of Infamy the Meed,
But if they chanc'd on Learned Worth to fall,
Bounty in him was Ostentation all.   *520*
No true Benevolence his Thought sublimes,
His noblest Actions are illustrious Crimes.
Fine Parts, which Virtue might have rank'd with Fame,
Enhance his Guilt, and magnify his Shame.
When Parts, and Probity in Man combine,   *525*
In Wisdom's Eye, How charming must he shine?
Let him, less happy, Truth at least impart,
And what he wants in Genius bear in Heart.

    Cosmo, as Death draws nigh, no more conceals
That Storm of Passions, which his Nature feels;   *530*
He feels much Fear, more Anger, and most Pride;
But Pride and Anger make all Fear subside.
Dauntless He meets at length untimely Fate;
A desp'rate Spirit! rather Fierce, than Great.
Darkling he glides along the dreary Coast,   *535*
A sullen, wand'ring, self-tormenting Ghost.

    Where veiny Marble dignifies the Ground,
With Emblem fair in Sculpture rising round,
Just where a crossing, length'ning Isle we find,
Full East; whence God returns to judge Mankind,   *540*
Once-lov'd *Horatio* sleeps, a Mind elate!
Lamented Shade, *Ambition* was thy Fate!
Ev'n Angels, wond'ring, oft his Worth survey'd;
Behold a Man, like one of Us! they said.
Straight heard the Furies, and with Envy glar'd,   *545*
And to precipitate his Fall prepar'd:
First *Av'rice* came. In vain Self-Love she press'd;
The Poor he pitied still, and still redress'd:
Learning was his, and Knowledge to commend,
Of Arts a Patron, and of Want a Friend.   *550*
Next came *Revenge*: But her Essay, how vain?
Nor Hate, nor Envy, in his Heart remain.

No previous Malice cou'd his Mind engage,
Malice, the Mother of vindictive Rage.
No—from his Life his Foes might learn to live; 555
He held it still a Triumph to forgive.
At length *Ambition* urg'd his Country's Weal,
Assuming the fair Look of publick *Zeal*;
Still in his Breast so gen'rous glow'd the Flame,
The Vice, when there, a Virtue half became. 560
His pitying Eye saw Millions in Distress,
He deem'd it God-like to have Pow'r to bless,
Thus, when unguarded, Treason stain'd him o'er,
And Virtue, and Content were then no more.

But when to Death by rig'rous Justice doom'd, 565
His genuine Spirit Saint-like State resum'd.
Oft from soft Penitence distill'd a Tear;
Oft Hope in heav'nly Mercy lighten'd Fear;
Oft wou'd a Drop from strugling Nature fall,
And then a Smile of Patience brighten all. 570

He seeks in Heav'n a Friend, nor seeks in vain;
His guardian Angel swift descends again;
And Resolution thus bespeaks a Mind,
Not scorning Life, yet all to Death resign'd;
—Ye Chains, fit only to restrain the Will 575
Of common, desp'rate Veterans in Ill,
Though rankling on my Limbs ye lie, declare,
Did e'er my rising Soul your Pressure wear?
No!—free as Liberty, and quick as Light,
To Worlds remote she takes unbounded Flight. 580
Ye Dungeon-Glooms, that dim corporeal Eyes,
Cou'd ye once blot her Prospect of the Skies?
No!—from her clearer Sight, ye fled away,
Like Error, pierc'd by Truth's resistless Ray.
Ye Walls, that witness my repentant Moan! 585
Ye Echoes, that to midnight Sorrows groan!
Do I, in Wrath, to you of Fate complain?
Or once betray Fear's most inglorious Pain?
No!—Hail, twice hail then ignominious Death!

Behold how willing glides my parting Breath!   *590*
Far greater, better far,—Ay far indeed!
Like me, *have* suffer'd, and like me *will* bleed.
Apostles, Patriarchs, Prophets, Martyrs all,
Like me, once fell, nor murmur'd at their Fall.
Shall I, whose Days, at best, no Ill design'd,   *595*
Whose Virtue shone not, though I lov'd Mankind,
Shall I, now guilty Wretch, shall I repine?
Ah, no! to Justice let me Life resign!
Quick, as a Friend, wou'd I embrace my Foe!
He taught me Patience, who first taught me Woe;   *600*
But Friends are Foes, they render Woe severe,
For me they wail, from me extort the Tear.
Not those, yet-absent, missive Griefs controul;
These Periods weep, those rave, and these condole.
At Entrance shrieks a Friend, with pale Surprize;   *605*
Another panting, prostrate, speechless lies;
One gripes my Hand, one sobs upon my Breast!
Ah, who can bear?—It shocks, it murders Rest!
And is it yours, alas! my Friends to feel?
And is it mine to comfort, mine to heal?   *610*
Is mine the Patience, yours the Bosom-strife?
Ah! wou'd rash Love lure back my Thoughts to Life?
Adieu, dear, dang'rous Mourners! swift depart!
Ah, fly me! fly!—I tear ye from my Heart.
    Ye Saints, whom Fears of Death cou'd ne'er
        controul,   *615*
In my last Hour compose, support my Soul!
See my Blood wash repented Sin away!
Receive, receive me to eternal Day!
    With Words like these the destin'd Hero dies,
While Angels waft his Soul to happier Skies.   *620*
    Distinction now gives way; yet on we talk,
Full Darkness deep'ning o'er the formless Walk.
Night treads not with light Step the dewy Gale,
Nor bright-distends her Star-embroider'd Veil;
Her leaden Feet inclement Damps distill,   *625*

Clouds shut her Face, black Winds her Vesture fill;
An Earth-born Meteor lights the sable Skies,
Eastward it shoots, and, sunk, forgotten dies.
So Pride, that rose from Dust to guilty Pow'r,
Glares out in vain, so Dust shall Pride devour.   630
        Fishers, who yonder Brink by Torches gain,
With teethful Tridents strike the scaly Train.
Like Snakes in Eagles' Claws, in vain they strive,
When heav'd aloft, and quiv'ring yet-alive.
        While here, methought, our Time in Converse
                pass'd,   635
The Moon Clouds muffl'd, and the Night wore fast.
At prowling Wolves was heard the Mastiff's Bay,
And the warn'd Master's Arms forbad the Prey.
Thus Treason steals, the Patriot thus descries,
Forth-springs the Monarch, and the Mischief flies.   640
        Pale Glow-worms glimmer'd through the Depth of
                Night,
Scatt'ring, like Hope through Fear, a doubtful Light.
Lone *Philomela* tun'd the silent Grove,
With pensive Pleasure listen'd wakeful *Love*.
Half-dreaming *Fancy* form'd an Angel's Tongue,   645
And *Pain* forgot to groan, so sweet she sung.
The *Night-Crone*, with the Melody alarm'd,
Now paus'd, now listen'd, and awhile was charm'd;
But like the Man, whose frequent-stubborn Will
Resists what kind, seraphic Sounds instill;   650
Her heart the Love-inspiring Voice repell'd,
Her Breast with agitating Mischief swell'd;
Which clos'd her Ear, and tempted to destroy
The tuneful Life, that charms with vertuous Joy.
        Now fast we measure back the trackless Way;   655
No friendly Stars directive Beams display.
But, lo!—a thousand Lights shoot instant Rays!
Yon kindling Rock reflects the startling Blaze.
I stand astonish'd—thus the Hermit cries,
Fear not, but listen with enlarg'd Surprize!   660

Still, muſt these Hours our mutual Converse claim,
And cease to echo ſtill *Olympia*'s Name?
Grots, Riv'lets, Groves *Olympia*'s Name forget,
Olympia now no sighing Winds repeat.
Can I be mortal, and those Hours no more,   665
Those am'rous Hours, that plaintive Echoes bore?
Am I the same? Ah no!—Behold a Mind,
Unruffl'd, firm, exalted, and refin'd!
Late Months, that made the vernal Season gay,
Saw my Health languish off in pale Decay.   670
No racking Pain yet gave Disease a Date;
No sad, presageful Thought preluded Fate:
Yet number'd were my Days—My deſtin'd End
Near, and more near—Nay, ev'ry Fear suspend!
I pass'd a weary, ling'ring, sleepless Night;   675
Then rose, to walk in Morning's earlieſt Light:
But few my Steps—A faint, and chearless few!
Refreshment from my flagging Spirits flew.
When, lo! retir'd beneath a Cypress Shade,
My Limbs upon a flow'ry Bank I laid.   680
Soon by soft-creeping, murm'ring Winds compos'd,
A Slumber press'd my languid Eyes—they clos'd:
But clos'd not long,—methought *Olympia* spoke;
Thrice loud she call'd, and thrice the Slumber broke.
I wak'd. Forth-gliding from a neighb'ring Wood,   685
Full in my View the shad'wy Charmer ſtood.
Rapt'rous I ſtarted up to clasp the Shade;
But ſtagger'd, fell, and found my Vitals fade.
A mantling Chilness o'er my Bosom spread,
As if that Inſtant number'd with the Dead.   690
Her Voice now sent a far, imperfeƈt Sound,
When in a swimming Trance my Pangs were drown'd.
Still farther off she call'd—with soft Surprize,
I turn'd, —but void of Strength, and Aid to rise;
Short, shorter, shorter yet, my Breath I drew: 695
Then up my ſtruggling Soul unburthen'd flew.
Thus from a State, where Sin, and Grief abide,

Heav'n summon'd me to Mercy—thus I died.
　　　He said. Th' Astonishment, with which I start,
Like bolted Ice runs shiv'ring through my Heart.　　700
Art thou not mortal then? (I cried) But lo!
His Raiment lightens, and his Features glow!
In shady Ringlets falls a length of Hair;
Embloom'd his Aspect shines, enlarg'd his Air.
Mild from his Eyes enliv'ning Glories beam;　　705
Mild on his Brow sits Majesty supreme.
Bright Plumes of ev'ry Die, that round him flow,
Vest, Robe, and Wings in varied Lustre show.
He looks, and forward steps with Mien Divine;
A Grace celestial gives him all to shine.　　710
He speaks—Nature is ravish'd at the Sound,
The Forests move, and Streams stand list'ning round!
　　　Thus He. As Incorruption I assum'd,
As instant in immortal Youth I bloom'd!
Renew'd, and chang'd, I felt my vital Springs,　　715
With diff'rent Lights discern'd the Form of Things;
To Earth my Passions fell like Mists away,
And Reason open'd in eternal Day.
Swifter than Thought from World to World I flew,
Celestial Knowledge shone in ev'ry View.　　720
My Food was Truth—what Transport cou'd I miss?
My Prospect all Infinitude of Bliss.
Olympia met me first, and, smiling Gay,
Onward to Mercy led the shining Way;
As far transcendant to her wonted Air,　　725
As her dear, wonted self to many a Fair!
In Voice, and Form, Beauty more beauteous shows,
And Harmony still more harmonious grows.
She points out Souls, who taught me Friendship's Charms,
They gaze, they glow, they spring into my Arms!　　730
Well-pleas'd, high Ancestors my View command;
Patrons, and Patriots all; a glorious Band!
Horatio too, by well-borne Fate refin'd,
Shone out white-rob'd with Saints, a spotless Mind!

What once, below, Ambition made him miss,   735
Humility here gain'd, a Life of Bliss!
Though late, let Sinners then from Sin depart!
Heav'n never yet despis'd the contrite Heart.
Last shone, with sweet, exalted Lustre grac'd,
The *SERAPH-BARD*, in highest Order plac'd!   740
Seers, Lovers, Legislators, Prelates, Kings,
All raptur'd listen, as he raptur'd sings.
Sweetness, and Strength his Look, and Lays employ,
Greet Smiles with Smiles, and ev'ry Joy with Joy:
Charmful he rose; his ever-charmful Tongue   745
Joy to our second Hymeneals sung;
Still as we pass'd, the bright, celestial Throng
Hail'd us in social *Love*, and heav'nly Song.
         Of that no more! my deathless Friendship see!
I come an Angel to the *Muse* and *Thee*.   750
These Lights, that vibrate, and promiscuous shine,
Are Emanations all of Forms Divine,
And here the *Muse*, though melted from thy Gaze,
Stands among Spirits, mingling Rays with Rays.
If thou would'st Peace attain, my Words attend,   755
The last, fond Words of thy departed Friend!
True Joy's a Seraph, that to Heav'n aspires,
Unhurt it triumphs mid celestial Quires.
But shou'd no Cares a mortal State molest,
Life were a State of Ignorance at best.   760
Know then, if Ills oblige thee to retire,
Those Ills Solemnity of Thought inspire.
Did not the Soul abroad for Objects roam,
Whence cou'd she learn to call Ideas home?
Justly to know thy self, peruse Mankind!   765
To know thy God, paint Nature on thy Mind!
Without such Science of the worldly Scene,
What is Retirement? empty Pride, or Spleen:
But with it Wisdom. There shall Cares refine,
Render'd by *Contemplation* half-divine.   770
Trust not the frantick, or mysterious Guide,

Nor stoop a Captive to the Schoolman's Pride.
On Nature's Wonders fix alone thy Zeal!
They dim not Reason, when they Truth reveal;
So shall Religion in thy Heart endure,   775
From all traditionary Falshood pure;
So Life make Death familiar to thy Eye;
So shalt thou live, as thou may'st learn to die;
And, though thou view'st thy worst Oppressor thrive,
From transient Woe, immortal Bliss derive.   780
Farewell—Nay stop the parting Tear!—I go!
But leave the *Muse* thy Comforter below.
He said. Instant his Pinions upward soar,
He less'ning as they rise, till seen no more.
   While *Contemplation* weigh'd the mystic View,   785
The Lights all vanish'd, and the Vision flew.

EPITAPH *on a young* LADY.

TEXTS: (1) *The Weekly Medley*, 11 October 1729: 'EPITAPH on a Lady
lately dead.'
   (2) *Grub-street Journal*, 3 January 1734: 'EPITAPH *on a young Lady.*'
   (3) LM, 34, 38.
   (4) *GM, 37, 373.

The identity of the young lady is unknown.

CLos'd are those eyes, that beam'd seraphic fire;
   Cold is that breast, which gave the world desire;
Mute is the voice, where winning softness warm'd,
Where music melted, and where wisdom charm'd,
And lively wit, which, decently confin'd,   5
No prude e'er thought impure, no friend unkind.
   Cou'd modest knowledge, fair untrifling youth,
Persuasive reason and endearing truth,
Cou'd honour, shewn in friendships most refin'd,
And sense, that shields th'attempted virtuous mind,   10
The social temper never known to strife,

The height'ning graces that embellish life;
Cou'd these have e'er the darts of death defied,
Never, ah! never had *Melinda* died;
Nor can she die—ev'n now survives her name,   15
Immortaliz'd by friendship, love and fame.

The Triumph of HEALTH and MIRTH.

VERSES, Occasion'd by The Right Honourable the Lady Viscountess *Tyrconnel*'s RECOVERY at *BATH*.

TEXTS: (1) *VERSES, Occasion'd by the Right Honourable the Lady
Viscountess *Tyrconnel*'s RECOVERY at *BATH*....M.DCC.XXX.
(2) *GM*, 37, 243: 'The Triumph of HEALTH and MIRTH, a Poem
occasion'd by the Recovery of BELINDA, a Lady of Quality, at BATH.

This poem must have been written during either the spring or early
summer of 1730. On 6 August the *Grub-street Journal* reported that
Lady Tyrconnel's physicians had given her over, and she died on 11
September. The poem must then refer to an earlier attack. Johnson
believed that this was one of RS's best poems. 'This performance is
remarkable,' he wrote, 'not only for the gaiety of the ideas and the
melody of the numbers, but for the agreeable fiction upon which it is
formed' (*Account*, p. 370). When RS quarrelled with Lord Tyrconnel
he blotted his name out of copies of the *Wanderer* and his lady's name
out of this poem, replacing it in ll. 28 and 32 with 'Belinda'. *Various
Poems* (1761), going back to the text of 1730, restored 'Tyrconnel'
in ll. 28 and 32, but for some obscure reason in l. 85 it introduced
the name 'Saphira'. This was copied from it into RS's *Works* (1775
and 1777) and the volume of his poems in the *Works of the English Poets*
(1779).

WHERE *Thames* with pride beholds *Augusta*'s charms,
 And either *India* pours into her arms;
Where Liberty bids honeſt arts abound,
And Pleasures dance in one eternal round;
High-thron'd appears the Laughter-loving Dame,   5
Goddess of mirth! *Euphrosinè* her name.
Her smile more chearful than a vernal morn;

All life! all bloom! of *Youth* and *Fancy* born.
Touch'd into joy, what hearts to her submit!
She looks her *Sire*, and speaks her *Mother*'s wit.   10
    O'ER the gay world the sweet Inspirer reigns;
Spleen flies, and Elegance her pomp suſtains.
Thee Goddess! thee! the Fair and Young obey;
Wealth, Wit, Love, Music, all confess thy sway.
In the bleak wild even Want by thee is bless'd,   15
And pamper'd Pride without thee pines for reſt.
The Rich grow richer, while in thee they find
The matchless treasure of a smiling mind.
Science by thee flows soft in social ease,
And Vertue, losing rigour, learns to Please.   20
    THE Goddess summons each illuſtrious name,
Bids the Gay talk, and forms th'amusive game.
She, whose fair throne is fix'd in human souls,
From joy to joy her eye delighted rolls.
But where (she cry'd) is she, my fav'rite! she,   25
Of all my race, the deareſt far to me!
Whose life's the life of each refin'd delight?
She said—But no *Tyrconnel* glads her sight.
Swift sunk her laughing eyes in languid fear;
Swift rose the swelling sigh, and trembling tear.   30
In kind, low murmurs all the loss deplore;
Tyrconnel droops, and pleasure is no more.
    THE Goddess silent, paus'd in museful air;
But *Mirth*, like *Vertue*, cannot long despair.
Cœleſtial-hinted thoughts gay hope inspir'd,   35
Smiling she rose, and all with hope were fir'd.
Straight wafted on the tepid breeze she flies,
Where *Bath*'s ascending turrets meet her eyes;
She flies, her elder siſter *Health* to find;
She finds her on the mountain-brow reclin'd.   40
Around her birds in earlieſt consort sing;
Her cheek the semblance of the kindling spring;

---

28 *Tyrconnel*] BELINDA *GM*, 37.   32 *Tyrconnel*] BELINDA *GM*, 37.

Fresh-tinctur'd like a summer-evening sky,
And a mild sun sits smiling in her eye.
Loose to the wind her verdant vestments flow;   45
Her limbs yet-recent from the springs below;
There oft she bathes, then peaceful sits secure,
Where every gale is fragrant, fresh, and pure;
Where flowers and herbs their cordial odours blend,
And soul-reviving vertues fast ascend.   50
    HAIL sister, hail! (the kindred Goddess cries)
No common suppliant stands before your eyes.
You, with whose living breath the morn is fraught,
Flush the fair cheek, and point the chearful thought!
Strength, Vigour, Wit, without thee all decline!   55
Each finer sense, that forms delight, is thine!
Bright suns by thee diffuse a brighter blaze,
And the fresh green a fresher green displays!
Without thee pleasures die, or dully cloy,
And life with thee, howe'er depress'd, is joy.   60
Such thy vast power!—The Deity replies,
Mirth never asks a boon, which *Health* denies.
Our mingled gifts transcend imperial wealth;
Health strengthens mirth, and mirth inspirits health.
These gales, yon springs, herbs, flowers, and sun are
      mine;   65
Thine is their smile! be then their influence thine.
    Euphrosynè rejoins—Thy friendship prove!
See the dear, sickening object of my love!
Shall that warm heart, so chearful even in pain,
So form'd to please, unpleas'd itself remain?   70
Sister! in her my smile anew display,
And all the social world shall bless thy sway.
    SWIFT, as she speaks, *Health* spreads the purple
      wing,
Soars in the colour'd clouds, and sheds the spring;

---

55 without thee all decline!] depriv'd of thee decline! *GM*, 37.
66 then] all *GM*, 37.

Now bland and sweet she floats along in air;   *75*
Air feels, and softening owns th'ethereal Fair!
In ſtill descent she melts on opening flowers,
And plants impregnates deep with genial showers.
The genial showers, new-rising to the ray,
Exhale in roseat clouds, and glad the day.   *80*
Now in a Zephir's borrow'd voice she sings,
Sweeps the fresh dews, and shakes them from her wings,
Shakes them embalm'd; or, in a gentle kiss,
Breathes the sure earneſt of awakening bliss.
The Patient feels it, with a soft surprize,   *85*
Glide through her veins, and quicken in her eyes!
    INSTANT in her own form the Goddess glows,
Where, bubbling warm, the mineral water flows;
Then plunging, to the flood new virtue gives;
Steeps ev'ry charm; and, as she bathes, it lives!   *90*
As from her locks she sheds the vital shower,
'Tis done! (she cries) These springs possess my power!
Let these immediate to thy darling roll
Health, vigour, life, and gay-returning soul.
    THOU smil'ſt *Euphrosinè*; and conscious see,   *95*
Prompt to thy smile, how nature joys with thee!
All is green life! all beauty rosy-bright!
Full harmony, young love, and dear delight!
See vernal Hours lead circling Joys along!
All sun, all bloom, all fragrance, and all song!   *100*
    RECEIVE thy care! Now *Mirth* and *Health* combine.
Each heart shall gladden, and each vertue shine.
Quick to *Auguſta* bear thy prize away;
There let her smile, and bid a world be gay.

---

78 plants impregnates deep] deep impregnates plants *GM*, 37.

A POEM
TO THE MEMORY OF Mrs. *OLDFIELD*.
INSCRIB'D TO *The Honourable Brigadier*
CHURCHILL.

TEXTS: (1) *A POEM TO THE MEMORY OF Mrs. OLD-FIELD*....MDCCXXX. [Anon.]
   (2) AUTHENTICK MEMOIRS OF THE LIFE Of...Mrs. *ANN OLDFIELD*...London & Dublin, 1730. [Anon.]

Mrs Oldfield died on Friday, 23 October 1730, and was buried on Tuesday the 27th. RS's poem was published probably no later than the day of the funeral, because the editor of the *Authentick Memoirs*, in which it was reprinted, remarks in a footnote dated the day afterwards (28 October): 'We have just now seen a POEM advertized in Memory of Mrs *OLDFIELD*, which inciting in us a Curiosity to peruse it, we found it to be exactly the same with one we have had in our Hands ever since Monday last [26 October], and which we have above inserted.' RS may have prepared two copies of his poem, both of which got into the hands of publishers. There are no substantial differences between the texts, and I have reprinted the first, because it is the more likely to have been authorized.

The reason for anonymity is not apparent. RS, as I have suggested in *AB*, p. 48, may not have wished to revive memories of his unsuccessful career in the theatre by associating his name with that of Mrs Oldfield, and he may also have feared scandal. Moreover, Lord Tyrconnel, with whom he was now living, may not have approved. In any case, being anonymous, it was not included in the *Works* of 1775, 1777, or 1779. But it is most likely by RS. W. R. Chetwood (*General History of the Stage*, Dublin, 1749, p. 206) states that it was written by RS, and RS's explicit denial of authorship to Johnson (*Account*, pp. 336–7) is highly suspicious.

Brigadier Churchill, to whom the poem was dedicated, was a brother of the Duke of Marlborough, and had taken Mrs Oldfield into keeping after the death of her former keeper, Arthur Maynwaring. Her son by him was one of the beneficiaries of her will.

> *Quis desiderio sit pudor, aut modus*
> *Tam Chari Capitis?*   Horat.

> *Tho' to her Share some Female Faults may fall,*
> *Think of her Charms, and you'll forget them all.*
>   POPE's Rape of the Lock.

Motto: Horace, *Odes*, I, 24, 1–2.

O LDFIELD's no more!—And can the Muse forbear
O'er *Oldfield*'s Grave to shed a grateful Tear?
Shall She, the Glory of the *British* Stage,
Pride of her Sex, and Wonder of the Age;
Shall She, who living charm'd th'admiring Throng,   5
Die undistinguish'd, and not claim a Song?
No. Feeble as it is, I'll boldly raise ⎫
My willing Voice to celebrate her Praise, ⎬
And with her Name immortalize my Lays. ⎭

    Had but my Muse her Art to touch the Soul,   10
Charm ev'ry Sense, and ev'ry Pow'r controul,
I'd paint her as she was—the Form divine,
Where ev'ry lovely Grace united shine;
A Mien, majestick as the Wife of *Jove*;
An Air, as winning as the Queen of *Love*;   15
In every Feature rival Charms should rise,
And *Cupid* hold his Empire in her Eyes.

    O! she was more than Numbers can express:
Creation's Darling in her fairest Dress.
A Form so charming, with such Beauties fraught,   20
As might have nigh excus'd the Want of Thought;
And yet a Mind with such Perfections stock'd,
As made the Beauties of her Form o'erlook'd.
A Soul with ev'ry Elegance refin'd,
By Nature, and the Converse of Mankind.   25
Wit, which could strike assuming Folly dead;
And Sense—which temper'd every thing she said;
Judgment, which ev'ry little Fault could spy;
But Candor, which would pass a thousand by.
That native Force—that Energy of Mind,   30
Which left the Toiling Pedant far behind.
Such finish'd Breeding, so Polite a Taste,
Her Fancy always for the Fashion past:
So sweetly serious, so discreetly gay,
None went unpleas'd, or unimprov'd, away.   35
And yet so negligent She seem'd of Fame,

36 She] *Omitted in Authentick Memoirs.*

165

As if She thought Applause beneath her Aim.
Disdaining Flattery She was still sincere;
Warm to approve, and modestly severe.
Whilst every Social Virtue fir'd her Breast,   40
To help the Needy; succour the Distrest;
A Friend to all in Misery she stood,
And her chief Pride was plac'd, in doing Good.
    But say, ye few, ye happy few, who e'er
Enjoy'd the private Friendship of the Fair;   45
Who saw the Charmer in a nearer Light,
All open, free, and unreserv'dly bright;
Who felt the Raptures which her Smiles bestow'd,
And prov'd the Joys which from her Converse flow'd:
Oh speak her friendly, affable, and mild,   50
Brave, generous, firm, by no false Shows beguil'd.
With ev'ry Art, and Talent form'd to please,
The Scholar's Learning, and the Lady's Ease;
The Gay, the Grave, the Florid, and Serene,
Mix'd in her Soul, and sparkling in her Mien.   55
    Thrice happy *Churchill*! who her Love could gain,
For whom so many Thousands sigh'd in vain;
Whose wondrous Charms made every one her Slave:
Dear to the Wise, the Witty, and the Brave.
And justly did She judge to place her Name   60
With Thine, the greatest in the Books of Fame.
Thus join'd, Advantages to each accrue,
Renown to her, Beauty and Wit to you.
Renown should ever on the Fair one wait,
And Beauty be the Portion of the Great.   65
From such a Pair we well may hope to see
Another *Marlbrô*, *Charles*, appear in thee.
    But now, my Muse, the arduous Task engage,
And show the Charming Figure on the Stage,
Describe her Look, her Action, Voice, and Mien,   70
The gay Coquette, soft Maid, or haughty Queen.

---

53 Lady's] Ladies *1730* and *Authentick Memoirs*.
67 *Charles*. Her son by Brigadier Churchill.

So bright She shone in every different Part,
She gain'd despotick Empire o'er the Heart;
Knew how each various Motion to controul,
Sooth every Passion, and subdue the Soul: 75
As She or gay, or sorrowful appears,
She claims our Mirth, or triumphs in our Tears:
Whilst from her Eyes delusive Sorrows flow,
Our Breasts are touch'd with undissembl'd Woe;
Or if Ambition calls her forth to Arms,   80
The Thirst of Glory every Bosom warms;
No Soul so senseless but what felt her Flame,
Nor Breast so savage but her Art could tame.
Ev'n the Pert Templer, and the City Prig,
Who come to Plays to show their Wit—or Wigg, 85
The snarling Critick, and the sneering Beau,
Who neither Sense of Worth, or Manners know,
Aw'd by her Looks their Brutish Din forbear,
And for a while a little Human are.
So *Orpheus* charm'd the Savages of old,   90
And all Hell's Furies with his Harp controul'd.
  Painters may sketch the Image of a Face,
And Sculptors Form and Attitude express;
Poets the Graces of the Mind relate,
And History tell the Actions of the Great.   95
Still each wants something to compleat the whole,
The Poet wants a Form, the Painter Soul.
But *Oldfield* all the Heroine display'd,
Show'd how she look'd, she mov'd, she wept, she pray'd,
And was her self the Character she play'd.   100
When *Cleopatra*'s Form she chose to wear,
We saw the Monarch's Mien, the Beauty's Air;
Charm'd with the Sight, her Cause we straight approve,
And, like her Lover, give up all for Love;
Antony's Fate, instead of *Cæsar*'s, chuse,   105
And wish for her we had a World—to lose.

---

95 tell] tells *Authentick Memoirs.*
101 Cleopatra. Cf. *Epistle to Mrs Oldfield.*

But when a more familiar Part did please,
Letitia's Artifice, or *Townley*'s Ease,
Each Beauty in the finest Light she plac'd,
Improv'd each Charm, and every Action grac'd.　　　110
Nay, so enchanting was her lovely Frame,
She spoilt against her Will the Poet's Aim;
Making those Follies which we should despise,
When seen in her, seem Virtues in our Eyes.
So, when with *Cytherea*'s Girdle bound,　　　　　115
The homliest Hag, a shining Fair is found.
　　But now the gay delightful Scene is o'er,
And that sweet Form must glad the World no more;
Relentless Death has stop'd the tuneful Tongue,
And clos'd those Eyes, for all but Death too strong;　120
Blasted that Face where every Beauty bloom'd.
And to eternal Rest the graceful Mover doom'd.
　　Calm and serene she met the fatal Hour,
Smil'd at Death's Terrors, and contemn'd its Power.
Sustain'd unmov'd the cruel Scourge of Pain,　　　125
Whilst blund'ring Doctors try'd their Art in vain;
(Those lawful Executioners, whose Skill
Is shown not when they cure—but when they kill.)
She only griev'd to see her *Churchill* grieve,
And for his sake alone desir'd to live;　　　　　　130
Her long-imprison'd Soul rejoic'd to see
The wish'd-for Moment come to set it free;
Then bravely strugling leapt its Bounds of Day,
And to the Place from whence it came, impetuous wing'd
　　　　its Way.
　　Thus subterranean Fire in *Etna* pent,　　　　135
Which long in vain has labour'd for a Vent,
(When once some weaker part begins to yield
Its long resisted Enemy the Field)
Grows more enrag'd, with double Fury plays,
And once got Air, it mounts into a Blaze.　　　　　140

---

108 Letitia is a character in Congreve's *Old Batchelor* and Lady Townley in Cibber's
Provoked Husband.

O'ercharg'd with Sorrow at the Thought—the Muse
Drooping—no more her airy Flight pursues;
With *Oldfield* all her flattering Hopes are fled,
In her the Muses' dearest Friend is dead:
For lo! the sinking Stage attends her Fall,   *145*
Whilst Opera, Farce, and Trick prevail o'er all;
Wilks, Nature's Master, soon, by years opprest,
And tir'd with Bus'ness, must retire to Rest;
And *Cibber*, baulk'd by the ungrateful Town,
Will lay th'unprofitable Burthen down.   *150*
Mourn then, ye Muses! all your Sorrows vent,
Your Shafts are useless, and your Bows unbent.
Now weep, ye Forests; droop, ye shady Bowers;
Be dry, ye Fountains; sicken, all ye Flowers;
The Night of universal Ign'rance comes,   *155*
In Darkness ev'ry pleasing Scene entombs;
With *Oldfield* the last glympse of Light is fled,
Wit, Nature, Sense, with her their Exits made:
The Goddess *Dulness* lifts her cloudy Head,
And smiles to see her dark Dominion spread;   *160*
Chaos o'er all his Leaden Scepter rears,
And not one Beam throughout the Gloom appears.

---

145 ff. These lines are an obvious imitation of *Dunciad*, IV, 627–56. Robert Wilks
and Colley Cibber were two veterans, both near the end of their careers on the stage.

THE VOLUNTEER LAUREAT.
A POEM.
Most humbly Address'd to HER MAJESTY
ON HER BIRTH-DAY.

TEXTS: (1) *THE VOLUNTEER LAUREAT, etc., MDCCXXXII.
(Published 1 March 1732, according to *GM*, 32, 636.)
(2) *GM*, 38, 210: '*The* VOLUNTEER LAUREAT. No. I. *A* POEM
On the Queen's Birth-Day, 1731–2: *Humbly address'd to her* MAJESTY.'

A longer version of this poem is to be found in the posthumously
published *Dramatic Works of Aaron Hill* (1760), where its authorship
is claimed for Hill by the editor, I.K. But Hill himself made no such

claim, and it was not one of RS's faults to claim the credit for a poem he had not written. I.K.'s version is perhaps a first draught, by RS, but possibly in Hill's handwriting (which I.K. must have known). It was not possible here to include variants from it, without reprinting the whole.

The text given in *GM*, 38 is a mere reprint of that printed here from the edition of 1732, except that it is introduced by the following letter.

'Mr URBAN,

'*IN your* Magazine *for* February *you publish'd the last* Volunteer Laureat *written on a very melancholy occasion, viz. the death of the royal patroness of arts and literature in general, and of the author of that poem in particular; I now send you the first that Mr* Savage *wrote under that Title.—This Gentleman, notwithstanding a very considerable interest, being, on the death of Mr* Eusden, 5 *disappointed of the Laureat's place, wrote the following verses; which were no sooner publish'd, but the late queen sent to a Bookseller for them; the author had not at that time a friend either to get him introduced, or his poem presented at Court, yet such was the unspeakable goodness of that Princess, that, notwithstanding this act of ceremony was wanting, in a few days after publication, Mr* 10 Savage *receiv'd a bank bill of fifty pounds, and a gracious message from her majesty, by the lord* North *and* Guilford, *to this effect: 'That her majesty was highly pleased with the verses; that she took particularly kind his lines there relating to the king; that he had permission to write annually on the same subject, and that he should yearly receive the like present, till something better* 15 (*which was her majesty's intention*) *could be done for him!—After this he was permitted to present one of his annual poems to her majesty, had the honour of kissing her hand, and met with the most gracious reception.*

Yours,
T.B.'

Johnson states that RS himself wrote the above letter, in spite of its signature (*Account*, p. 382). But more likely the author was Thomas Birch, through whom RS often transmitted copy to *GM*, even though it may have been based on information provided by RS, and may incorporate much of the latter's language. The motive for reprinting the poem in 1738, after the death of Queen Caroline, was that RS's name had been struck out of the list of the pensioners of the Queen, even though all her other benefactions were continued at his majesty's command. RS and his friend Birch were attempting to regain lost favour by reminding the King of the fine things RS had said about him in 1732.

TWICE twenty tedious Moons have roll'd away,
  Since Hope, kind Flatt'rer! tun'd my pensive Lay,
Whisp'ring, that You, who rais'd me from Despair,

Meant, by Your Smiles, to make Life worth my Care;
With pitying Hand an Orphan's Tears to screen,   5
And o'er the *Motherless* extend the *Queen*.
    'Twill be—the Prophet guides the Poet's Strain!
Grief never touch'd a Heart like Yours in vain:
Heav'n gave You Pow'r, because You love to bless,
And Pity, when you feel it, is Redress.   10
    Two Fathers join'd to rob my Claim of *One*!
My *Mother* too thought fit to have *no Son*!
The *Senate* next, whose Aid the Helpless own,
Forgot *my* Infant Wrongs, and mine alone!
Yet Parents pitiless, nor Peers unkind,   15
Nor Titles lost, nor Woes mysterious join'd,
Strip me of Hope—by Heav'n thus lowly laid,
To find a PHARAOH'S DAUGHTER in the Shade.
    You cannot hear unmov'd, when Wrongs implore,
Your Heart is *Woman*, though Your Mind be *more*;   20
Kind, like the Pow'r who gave You to our Pray'rs,
You would not lengthen Life to sharpen Cares;
They, who a *barren Leave* to live bestow,
Snatch but from Death to sacrifice to Woe.
    Hated by Her, from whom my Life I drew,   25
Whence should I hope, if not from Heav'n and You?
Nor dare I groan beneath Affliction's Rod,
My QUEEN my Mother, and my Father GOD.
    The pitying MUSES saw me Wit pursue,
A BASTARD-SON, alas! on that Side too   30
Did not Your Eyes exalt the Poet's Fire,
And what the *Muse* denies, the *Queen* inspire,
While rising thus Your heav'nly Soul to view,
I learn, how Angels think, by copying You.
    Great Princess! 'Tis *decreed*—once ev'ry Year   35
I march uncall'd, Your LAUREAT VOLUNTEER;
Thus shall Your Poet his low Genius raise,

1–6 RS is reminding the Queen that she has done nothing for him since his pardon,
in spite of a hint made then that she would find him an appointment of some sort.
See *The Bastard*, especially the latter part.

And charm the World with Truths too va&t for Praise.
    Nor need I dwell on Glories all Your Own,
Since surer Means to tempt Your Smiles are known,   *40*
Your Poet shall allot Your Lord his Part,
And paint Him in his noble&t Throne, your Heart.
    Is there a Greatness that adorns Him be&t,
A rising Wish, that ripens in his Brea&t?
Has He foremeant some di&tant Age to bless,   *45*
Disarm Oppression, or expel Di&tress?
Plans He some Scheme to reconcile Mankind,
People the Seas, and busy ev'ry Wind?
Would He by *Pity* the *Deceiv'd* reclaim,
And smile contending Fa&ctions into Shame?   *50*
Would his Example lend his Laws a Weight,
And breathe his own soft Morals o'er his State?
The Muse shall find it all, shall make it seen,
And teach the World His Praise, to charm his Queen.
    Such be the Annual Truths my Verse imparts,   *55*
Nor frown, fair FAV'RITE of a People's Hearts!
Happy, if plac'd, perchance, beneath Your Eye,
My Muse *unpension'd* might her Pinions try,
Fearless to fail, whil&t You indulge her Flame,
And bid me proudly boa&t *Your Laureat*'s Name;   *60*
Renobled thus by Wreaths my QUEEN be&tows,
I lose all Memory of Wrongs and Woes!

RELIGION AND LIBERTY:
AN EPISTLE TO THE Right Honourable Sir *ROBERT WALPOLE*, KNIGHT
of the Mo&t Noble Order of the Garter.

TEXTS: (1) *AN EPISTLE, etc....MDCCXXXII. (Published in August. See *GM*, 32, 22 (September number).)
(2) [RELIGION AND LIBERTY: An Epistle, etc. as advertised on the title-page of *Volunteer Laureat* II (1733), and *Volunteer Laureat* IV (1735). I have not seen a copy.]

The pro-Walpole bias of this poem is in keeping with the political line adopted by RS in his *Poem sacred to King George*, and reflects his gratitude for the royal pardon granted him, and for Walpole's promise of a government job (cf. l. 26). RS's interest in public works and public welfare recalls *The Picture* and a passage in *The Wanderer* (i, ll. 270 ff.), and looks forward to *Of Public Spirit in Regard to Public Works*. Donald Greene describes this poem as 'an uneven, derivative, confusedly organized, but always intelligent piece of writing' (*The Politics of Samuel Johnson* (New Haven, 1960), p. 85). He notices that RS had stressed the following political principles: the security of property, the freedom of investigation, the rights of individuals, and the natural equality of men—all of them virtues dear to the middle class.

STILL let low Wits, who Sense nor Honour prize,
Sneer at all Gratitude, all Truth disguise;
At living Worth, because alive, exclaim,
Insult the Exil'd, and the Dead defame!
Such paint what Pity veils in private Woes,　　　　　5
And what we see with Grief, with Mirth expose;
Studious to urge—(whom will mean Authors spare?)
The Child's, the Parent's, and the Consort's Tear:
Unconscious of what Pangs the Heart may rend,
To lose what they have ne'er deserv'd—a Friend.　　10
Such, ignorant of Facts, invent, relate,
Expos'd persist, and answer'd still debate:
Such, but by Foils, the clearest Lustre see,
And deem aspersing Others, praising Thee.

　　FAR from these Tracks my honest Lays aspire,　　15
And greet a gen'rous Heart with gen'rous Fire.
Truth be my Guide! Truth, which thy Virtue claims!
This, nor the Poet, nor the Patron shames:
When Party-Minds shall lose contracted Views,
And Hist'ry question the recording Muse;　　　　　20
'Tis this alone to After-Times must shine,
And stamp the Poet and his Theme divine.

　　LONG has my Muse, from many a mournful Cause,
Sung with small Pow'r, nor sought sublime Applause;
From that great Point she now shall urge her Scope;　25

On that fair Promise rest her future Hope;
Where Policy, from State Illusion clear,
Can through an open Aspect shine sincere;
Where Science, Law, and Liberty depend,
And own the Patron, Patriot, and the Friend;   30
(That Breast to feel, that Eye on Worth to gaze,
That Smile to cherish, and that Hand to raise!)
Whose best of Hearts her best of Thoughts inflame,
Whose Joy is Bounty, and whose Gift is Fame.
    WHERE, for Relief, flies Innocence distrest?   35
To you, who chase Oppression from th'Opprest:
Who, when Complaint to you alone belongs,
Forgive your own, though not a People's Wrongs:
Who still make publick Property your Care,
And thence bid private Grief no more despair.   40
    ASK they what State your shelt'ring Care shall own?
'Tis Youth, 'tis Age, the Cottage, and the Throne:
Nor can the Prison 'scape your searching Eye,
Your Ear still opening to the Captive's Cry.
Nor less was promis'd from thy early Skill,   45
Ere Power enforc'd Benevolence of Will!
To Friends refin'd, thy private Life adher'd
By thee improving, ere by thee prefer'd.
Well hadst thou weigh'd what Truth such Friends afford,
With thee resigning, and with thee restor'd.   50
Thou taught'st them All *extensive* Love to bear,
And now Mankind with thee their Friendships share.
    AS the rich Cloud by due Degrees expands,
And showers down Plenty thick on sundry Lands,
Thy spreading Worth in various Bounty fell,   55
Made Genius flourish, and made Art excell.
    HOW many, yet deceiv'd, all Power oppose?

---

26 That fair Promise. According to Johnson, some of RS's friends 'solicited Sir
Robert Walpole in his favour, with so much earnestness, that they obtained a promise
of the next place that should become vacant, not exceeding two hundred pounds
a year' (*Account*, p. 391).
43-4 Walpole saved RS's life in 1727 by means of a royal pardon.

Their Fears increasing, as decrease their Woes;
Jealous of Bondage, while they Freedom gain,
And moſt oblig'd moſt eager to complain.   60

But well we count our Bliss, if well we view,
When Power Oppression, not Protection grew;
View present Ills that punish diſtant Climes;
Or bleed in Mem'ry here from ancient Times.

Mark firſt the Robe abus'd *Religion* wore,   65
Storied with Griefs, and ſtain'd with human Gore!
What various Tortures, Engines, Fires, reveal,
Study'd, empower'd, and sanctify'd by Zeal!

Stop here my Muse!—Peculiar Woes descry!
Bid 'em in sad Succession ſtrike thy Eye!   70
Lo, to her Eye the sad Succession springs!
She looks, she weeps, and, as she weeps, she sings.

See the doom'd *Hebrew* of his Stores bereft!
See holy Murder juſtify the Theft!
His ravag'd Gold some useless Shrine shall raise!   75
His Gems on superſtitious Idols blaze!
His Wife, his Babe, deny'd their little Home,
Stripp'd, ſtarv'd, unfriended, and unpity'd roam.

Lo, the Prieſt's Hand the *Wafer-God* supplies!
A King by consecrated Poison dies!   80

See *Learning* range yon broad Etherial Plain,
From World to World, and God-like Science gain!
Ah! what avails the curious Search suſtain'd,
The finish'd Toil, the God-like Science gain'd?
Sentenc'd to Flames th'expansive Wisdom fell,   85
And Truth from Heav'n was Sorcery from Hell.

See *Reason* bid each myſtic Wile retire,
Strike out new Light! and Mark!—the Wise admire!
Zeal shall such Heresy, like *Learning*, hate;
The same their Glory, and the same their Fate.   90

Lo, from sought Mercy, one his Life receives!
Life, worse than Death, that cruel Mercy gives:
The Man, perchance, who Wealth and Honours bore,
Slaves in the Mine, or ceaseless ſtrains the Oar.

So doom'd are these, and such perhaps, our Doom, 95
Own'd we a Prince (avert it Heaven!) from *Rome*.
    NOR private Worth alone false Zeal assails;
Whole Nations bleed when Bigotry prevails.
What are sworn Friendships? What are Kindred Ties?
What's Faith with Heresy? (the Zealot cries.)   100
See, when War sinks the thund'ring Cannon's Roar;
When Wounds, and Death, and Discord are no more;
When Musick bids undreading Joys advance,
Swell the soft Hour, and turn the swimming Dance:
When, to crown these, the social Sparkling Bowl   105
Lifts the chear'd Sense, and pours out all the Soul;
Sudden he sends red Massacre abroad;
Faithless to Man, to prove his Faith to God.
What pure persuasive Eloquence denies,
All-drunk with Blood, the arguing Sword supplies;   110
The Sword, which to th'Assassin's Hand is given!
Th'Assassin's Hand!—pronounc'd the Hand of Heaven!
Sex bleeds with Sex, and Infancy with Age;
No Rank, no Place, no Virtue stops his Rage.
Shall Sword, and Flame, and Devastation cease,   115
To please with Zeal (wild Zeal!) the *God* of *Peace*?
    NOR less Abuse has scourg'd the Civil State,
When a King's Will became a Nation's Fate.
Enormous Pow'r! Nor noble, nor serene;
Now fierce and cruel; now but wild and mean.   120
See Titles sold, to raise th'unjust Supply!
Compell'd the Purchase! or be fin'd, or buy!
No public Spirit, guarded well by Laws,
Uncensur'd censures in his Country's Cause.
See from the Merchant forc'd th'unwilling Loan!   125
Who dares deny, or deem his Wealth his own?
Denying, See! where Dungeon-Damps arise,
Diseas'd he pines, and unassisted dies.
Far more than Massacre that Fate accurst!
As of all Deaths the ling'ring is the worst.   130
    NEW Courts of Censure griev'd with new Offence,

176

Tax'd without Power, and fin'd without Pretence;
Explain'd, at Will, each Statute's wrested Aim,
'Till Marks of Merit were the Marks of Shame;
So monstrous!—Life was the severest Grief,   135
And the worst Death seem'd welcome for Relief.

In vain the Subject sought Redress from Law,
No Senate liv'd the partial Judge to awe:
Senates were void, and Senators confin'd
For the great Cause of Nature and Mankind;   140
Who Kings superiour to the People own;
Yet prove the Law superiour to the Throne.

Who can review, without a gen'rous Tear,
A Church, a State, so impious, so severe;
A Land uncultur'd through Polemic Jars,   145
Rich!—but with Carnage from intestine Wars;
The Hand of Industry employ'd no more,
And Commerce flying to some safer Shore;
All Property reduc'd, to Pow'r a Prey,
And Sense and Learning chas'd by Zeal away?   150
Who honours not each dear departed Ghost,
That strove for Liberty so won, so lost:
So well regain'd when God-like *William* rose,
And first entail'd the Blessing *George* bestows?
May *Walpole* still the growing Triumph raise,   155
And bid These emulate *Eliza*'s Days;
Still serve a Prince, who, o'er his People Great,
As far transcends in Virtue, as in State!

The Muse pursues thee to thy rural Seat;
Ev'n there shall Liberty inspire Retreat.   160
When solemn Cares in flowing Wit are drown'd,
And sportive Chat and social Laughs go round:
Ev'n then, when pausing Mirth begins to fail,
The Converse varies to the serious Tale.
The Tale pathetic speaks some Wretch that owes   165

---

159 Walpole's 'rural seat' at Houghton had been under fire in the papers for some
time.

To some deficient Law reliefless Woes.
What instant Pity warms thy gen'rous Breast!
How all the Legislator stands confess'd!
Now springs the Hint! 'tis now improv'd to Thought!
Now ripe! and now to public Welfare brought!   *170*
New Bills, which regulating Means bestow,
Justice preserve, yet soft'ning Mercy know:
Justice shall low vexatious Wiles decline,
And still thrive most, when Lawyers most repine.
Justice from Jargon shall refin'd appear,   *175*
To Knowledge through our native Language clear.
Hence may we learn, no more deceiv'd by Law,
Whence Wealth and Life their best Assurance draw.

     T H E freed *Insolvent*, with industrious Hand,
Strives yet to satisfy the just Demand: *180*
Thus ruthless Men, who wou'd his Pow'rs restrain,
Oft what Severity would lose obtain.

     T H E S E, and a thousand Gifts, thy Thought acquires,
Which Liberty benevolent inspires.
From Liberty the Fruits of Law increase,   *185*
Plenty, and Joy, and all the Arts of Peace.
Abroad the Merchant, while the Tempests rave,
Advent'rous sails, nor fears the Wind and Wave;
At Home untir'd we find th'auspicious Hand
With Flocks, and Herds, and Harvests, bless the
         Land: *190*
While there, the Peasant glads the grateful Soil,
Here mark the Ship-Wright, there the Mason toil,
Hew, square, and rear magnificent the Stone,
And give our Oaks a Glory not their own!
What Life demands by this obeys her Call,   *195*
And added Elegance consummates all.
Thus stately Cities statelier Navies rise,
And spread our Grandeur under distant Skies.
From Liberty each nobler Science sprung,
A *Bacon* brighten'd, and a *Spenser* sung;   *200*
A *Clarke* and *Locke* new Tracks of Truth explore,

And *Newton* reaches Heights unreach'd before.
    WHAT Trade sees Property that Wealth maintain,
Which Industry no longer dreads to gain;
What tender Conscience kneels with Fears resign'd,   *205*
Enjoys her Worship, and avows her Mind;
What Genius now from Want to Fortune climbs,
And to *safe* Science ev'ry Thought sublimes;
What Royal Pow'r, from his superiour State,
Sees public Happiness his own create;   *210*
But kens those Patriot-Souls, to which he owes
Of Old each Source, whence now each Blessing flows?
And if such Spirits from their Heav'n descend,
And blended flame, to point one glorious End;
Flame from one Breast, and thence on *Britain* shine,   *215*
What Love, what Praise, O *Walpole*, then is thine?

THE Volunteer-Laureat.
Most humbly inscribed to Her MAJESTY,
ON HER *BIRTH-DAY*.
NUMBER II. For the YEAR 1733.
To be continued Annually.

TEXT: *THE Volunteer-Laureat, etc. M.DCC.XXXIII.

'GREAT Princess, 'tis decreed!—once ev'ry Year,
  'I march uncall'd, your Laureat-Volunteer.'
So sung the Muse; nor sung the Muse in vain:
My Queen accepts, the Year renews the Strain.
Ere first your Influence shone with heav'nly Aid,   *5*
Each Thought was Terror; for each View was Shade.
Fortune to Life each flow'ry Path deny'd;
No Science learn'd to bloom, no Lay to glide.
Instead of hallow'd Hill, or vocal Vale,
Or Stream, Sweet-echoing to the tuneful Tale;   *10*

1–2 Quoted from *Volunteer Laureat*, no. 1, ll. 35–6.

Damp Dens confin'd, or barren Desarts spread,
Which Spectres haunted, and the Muses fled;
Ruins in pensive Emblem seem'd to rise,
And all was dark, or wild, to Fancy's Eyes.

     BUT hark! a glad'ning Voice all Nature chears!   *15*
Disperse ye Glooms! a Day of Joy appears!
Hail, happy Day!—'Twas on thy glorious Morn,
The First, the Fairest of her Sex was born!
How swift the Change? Cold, wintry Sorrows fly;
Where-e'er she looks, Delight surrounds the Eye!   *20*
Mild shines the Sun, the Woodlands warble round,
The Vales sweet echo, sweet the Rocks resound!
In cordial Air soft Fragrance floats along;
Each Scene is Verdure, and each Voice is Song!

     SHOOT from yon Orb divine, ye quick'ning Rays!   *25*
Boundless, like her Benevolence, ye blaze!
Soft Emblems of her Bounty, fall ye Showers!
And Sweet ascend, and Fair unfold ye Flowers!
Ye Roses, Lillies, you we earliest claim,
In Whiteness, and in Fragrance, match her Fame!   *30*
'Tis yours to fade, to Fame like Hers is due
Undying Sweets, and Bloom for ever new.
Ye Blossoms, that one varied Landscape rise,
And send your scentful Tribute to the Skies;
Diffusive like yon *Royal Branches* smile,   *35*
Grace the young Year, and glad the grateful Isle!
Attend ye Muses! mark the feather'd Quires!
Those the Spring wakes, as you the Queen inspires.
O let her Praise for ever swell your Song!
Sweet let your sacred Streams the Notes prolong,   *40*
Clear, and more clear, through all my Lays refine;
And there let Heav'n and Her reflected shine!

     As when chill Blights from vernal Suns retire,
Chearful the vegitative World aspire,
Put forth unfolding Blooms, and waving try   *45*

---

35 *Royal Branches*. Possibly the rose of York and Lancaster, which has a branching stem and was later used as a royal emblem. The Queen was an enthusiastic gardener.

Th'enlivening Influence of a milder Sky;
So gives her Birth, (like yon approaching Spring,)
The Land to flourish, and the Muse to sing.
    'Twas thus, *Zenobia*, on *Palmyra*'s Throne,
In Learning, Beauty, and in Virtue shone;   *50*
Beneath her rose, *Longinus*, in thy Name,
The Poet's, Critick's, and the Patriot's Fame!
Is there (so high be you, great Princess, prais'd!)
A Woe unpitied, or a Worth unrais'd?
Art learns to soar by your sweet Influence taught;   *55*
In Life well cherish'd; nor in Death forgot:
In Death, as Life, the Learn'd your Goodness tell!
Witness the sacred Busts of *Richmond*'s Cell!
Sages, who in unfading Light will shine;
Who grasp'd at Science, like your own, divine!   *60*
    The Muse, who hails with Song this glorious Morn,
Now looks through Days, through Months, through Years
        unborn;
All white they rise, and in their Course exprest
A *King* by *Kings* rever'd, by Subjects blest!
A *Queen*, where-e'er true Greatness spreads in Fame;   *65*
Where Learning tow'rs beyond her Sex's Aim;
Where pure Religion no Extream can touch,
Of Faith too Little, nor of Zeal too much;
Where these behold, as on this bless'd of Morns,
What Love protects 'em, and what Worth adorns;   *70*
Where-e'er diffusive Goodnes smiles, a Queen
Still prais'd with Rapture, as with Wonder seen!
    See Nations round, of ev'ry Wish possest!
Life in each Eye, and Joy in ev'ry Breast!
Shall I, on what I lightly touch, explain?   *75*
Shall I (vain Thought!) attempt the finish'd Strain?
No!—Let the *Poet* stop unequal Lays,
And to the just *Historian* yield your Praise.

---

58 The Queen's lodge at Richmond. Cf. *Volunteer Laureat*, no. 4, l. 96.

EPIGRAM ON JOHN DENNIS

TEXT: *Grub-street Journal, 27 December 1733. [Anon.]

In *The Daily Journal* for 22 December 1733 the following short poem appeared:

To Mr THOMSON,

on Occasion of the Part which That Gentleman took,
in the Concern for Mr DENNIS's late Benefit.

While I reflect thee o'er, methinks, I find
Thy various SEASONS, in their Author's Mind!
Spring, in thy flow'ry *Fancy*, spreads her Hues;
And, like thy soft Compassion, sheds her Dews.
Summer's hot Strength, in thy *Expression*, glows;
And, o'er thy Page, a beamy Ripeness throws.
Autumn's rich *Fruits*, th'instructed Reader gains;
Who tastes the meaning *Purpose* of thy Strains.
Winter—But *That*—no Semblance takes, from *Thee*!
That hoary Season's Type was drawn from ME.—
Shatter'd, by Time's bleak Storms, I, With'ring, lay:
Leafless, and whit'ning, in a cold Decay.
Yet, shall my propless *Ivy*,—pale, and bent,
Bless the short Sunshine which thy Pity lent.

J.D. [= John Dennis]

The only early reference to the authorship of these lines occurs in the anonymous *Life of Mr John Dennis*, 'not written by Mr Curll', published in 1734, after Dennis's death. The author of this work says that they were written by a gentleman 'in Mr *Dennis*'s Name', and reports that when they were read aloud to Dennis, who was then blind, he swore, 'by G——, they could be no one but that Fool S——'s' (p. 57). Nevertheless the evidence that the above poem was not written by Dennis but by a gentleman in his name is not reliable, and it is more than likely that what aroused the ire of the old man was a couplet added to the poem when it was reprinted a few days later in the *Grub-street Journal*. This may very well have been by Savage.

I'm glad to find my brother's grateful lay,
Like medlar fruit, delicious in decay.

I have not found a copy of this poem, though it was published in March 1734 (*GM*, 34, 167) and was still being advertised for sale in *Volunteer Laureat, No. 4* (1735). The first edition of RS's *Works* in 1775 contained only four of the seven *Volunteer Laureats*, and the second edition in 1777 contained six. The missing one, number 3, was not in either of these, and does not seem to have found its way into any of the newspapers. It was undoubtedly one of the poems of which RS 'had himself so low an opinion that he intended to omit them in the collection of poems, for which he printed proposals and solicited subscriptions' (*Account*, p. 384).

The GENIUS of LIBERTY.
A POEM.
Occasion'd by the Departure of the Prince and Princess of Orange, written in the Year 1734.

TEXTS: (1) ON THE DEPARTURE OF THE Prince and Princess of Orange. A POEM....1734. (Published July 1734 according to *GM*, 34, 395 and *LM*, 34, 392.)
    (2) **GM*, 38, 315: 'The GENIUS of LIBERTY', etc.

According to *LM*, 34, 151, 'the Nuptials between his Serene Highness the Prince of *Orange* and the Princess Royal were solemnized in a most magnificent and grand Manner, in the *French-Chapel* at St. *James's*' on Thursday, 14 March 1734. The bridal couple left on Monday, 22 April, for Holland, where they arrived on Friday morning, the 26th. Johnson quotes RS has having said that he wrote this poem only 'because it was expected of him', and that no attention was paid to it at court (*Account*, p. 385).

    The text given here is the revised one published in *GM*. But I have restored the original dedication, omitted in 1738 because of the Queen's death.

To the QUEEN.

MADAM,

I AM afraid the following Poem may be thought too inconsiderable to merit the Distinction of your Majesty's Patronage: But the Subject of it is extreamly interesting to the Nation in general, to 5 *the whole Royal Family, and to your Majesty in particular. On that Consideration, I humbly beg leave to lay it at your Feet.*

Had I not been prevented by an ill State of Health, and a Train of Misfortunes, which I have been struggling through almost from my Birth, this Poem had been published sooner, in Acknowledgment 10 of your Majesty's great and undeserved Goodness to its Author. I hope however it is not too late to express, in this public Manner, my Gratitude to the best of Queens, and my inviolable Attachment to his Majesty's Person and Government.

That the illustrious House of HANOVER *may ever flourish, in 15 all its Branches, to guide and adorn these Nations, is the daily and zealous Prayer of,*

MADAM,

Your Majesty's most Obedient,

Dutiful, and Devoted Servant,   20

R. Savage.

MILD rose the morn, the face of nature bright
    Wore one extensive smile of calm and light;
Wide, o'er the land, did hov'ring silence reign,
Wide o'er the blue diffusion of the main;
When lo! before me, on the *Southern* shore,   5
Stood forth the POW'R, whom ALBION's sons adore;
Blest LIBERTY, whose charge is ALBION's isle;
Whom *Reason* gives to bloom, and *Truth* to smile;
Gives *Peace* to gladden, shelt'ring *Law* to spread,
Learning to lift aloft her laurel'd head,   10
Rich *Industry* to view, with pleasing eyes,
Her fleets, her cities, and her harvests rise.
In curious emblems ev'ry *art*, exprest,
Glow'd from the loom, and brighten'd on his vest.
Science in various lights attention won,   15
Wav'd on his robe, and glitter'd in the sun.

---

6 ALBION's sons adore;] free-born Souls adore! *1734.*
8] Who gives ev'n Youth to bloom, and Health to smile; *1734.*
9 Gives *Peace*] Kind *Peace 1734.*   10 *Learning*] *Science 1734.*
11 Rich] And *1734.*
14 Glow'd...brighten'd] Glows...brightens *1734.*
15–16] Gay, o'er his Robe, a Chase of Colours run; / And varying wave, and glitter on the Sun. *1734.*

My words (he cry'd) my words observance claim:
Resound ye Muses, and receive 'em Fame!
Here was my ſtation, when, o'er ocean wide,
The great, third *William* ſtretch'd his naval pride: 20
I, with my sacred influence, swell'd his soul;
Th'enslav'd to free, th'enslaver to controul.
In vain did waves disperse, and winds detain:
He came, he sav'd; in *his* was seen *my* reign.
How juſt, how great, the plan his soul design'd,   25
To humble tyrants, and secure mankind!
Next *Marlbro'* in his ſteps successful trod:
This, godlike, plann'd; that finish'd, like a god!
And, while *Oppression* fled to realms unknown,
Europe was free, and *Britain* glorious shone.   30

Where *Nassau*'s Race, extensive growth, display'd;
There *Freedom* ever found a shelt'ring shade.
Still heav'n is kind!—see, from the princely root,
Millions to bless, the BRANCH auspicious shoot!
He lives, he flourishes, his honours spread;   35
Fair virtues blooming on his youthful head;
Nurse him ye heav'nly dews, ye sunny rays,
Into firm health, fair fame, and length of days!

He paus'd, and, caſting o'er the deep his eye;
Where the laſt billow swells into the sky;   40
Where, in gay vision, round th'horizon's line,
The moving clouds with various beauty shine;
As drooping from their bosom, ting'd with gold,

---

17 observance] Attention *1734*.

20–6 The reference is to the arrival of William III in 1688.

22] The Good to succour, and the Bad controul. *1734*.

24] He came, restor'd, confirm'd my tott'ring Reign. / For me he conquer'd, bade
my Rights extend, / Liv'd my Asserter, and expir'd my Friend. *1734*.

27–30 Compare the satire on Marlborough in *An Ironical Panagerick*, ll. 13–16.

31 *Nassau*'s Race. The family name of William III was Orange-Nassau. The
'branch' of Nassau's race was the Prince of Orange, whose family name was Nassau-
Dietz, and who married the Princess Anne. Cf. *Volunteer Laureat*, ii, l. 35.

32] *After this line occur the four following in 1734:* How late, how low, Fate's threaten
ing Tempest hung / O'er this their last of Hopes, auspicious sprung! / From them
I fear'd; and, in their Fate agen [*sic*], / I fear'd, and trembl'd for the Sons of Men.

33 Still] But *1734*.   34 auspicious] reviving *1734*.

Shoots forth a sail, amusive to behold!
Lo! while its light the glowing wave returns,   45
Broad like a *sun* the bark approaching burns.
Near, and more near, great *Nassau* soon he spy'd,
And beauteous *Anna*, *Britain*'s eldest pride!
Thus spoke the *Genius*, as advanc'd the sail,
Hail blooming heroe! high-born princess hail!   50
Thy charms thy *Mother*'s love of truth display,
Her light of virtue, and her beauty's ray;
Her dignity; which, copying the divine,
Soften'd, through condenscension, learns to shine.
Greatness of thought, with prudence for its guide;   55
Knowledge, from nature and from art supply'd;
To noblest objects pointed various ways;
Pointed by judgment's clear, unerring rays.
    What manly virtues in her mind excel!
Yet on her heart what tender passions dwell!   60
For ah! what pangs did late her peace destroy,
To part with thee, so wont to give her joy!
How heav'd her breast! how sadden'd was her mien!
All in the *Mother* then was lost the *Queen*.
The swelling tear then dim'd her parting view,   65
The struggling sigh stopp'd short her last adieu:

---

45 Lo!] And, *1734*.

46] Th'approaching Bark, one sunny Radiance, burns. *1734*.

49 Thus spoke] Resum'd *1734*.

50] Hail high-born Princess! blooming Heroe, hail! *1734*. *After this line occur the following in 1734:* Sea, prize this Bark! more high the Charge it brings; / Than num'rous Navies which Ambition wings, / 'Tis *Britain*'s Heart-felt Joy!—What then is He, / From whom this Union glads the *Land*, and *Me*? / O *Britain!* Heaven's distinguish'd, fav'rite Isle! / Thou, in thy *Sov'reign*, seest a *Parent* smile; / A *Sov'reign*, form'd to rule a People free; / His Wish, but to secure all Bliss to thee. / How *Europe* waits the mighty *Monarch*'s Nod, / Who holds the Ballance, and who waves the Rod; / The Senate speeds his naval Pow'r away; / The Wind shall waft it, and the World obey. / And thou, bright *Anna*, too (said he) art mine! / Thou Hope and Joy of Nations, born to shine! / Yes, thou art mine; fair, elegant, and wise: / Born to love Truth, and Liberty to prize. / In thee thy *Mother*'s Graces we survey.

59–60] In public Scenes what Dignity of Mind! / In private Life, what Tenderness refin'd! *1734*.

66 The struggling sigh] And the swift Sigh *1734*. *After this line occur the following in 1734:* Or was the gen'rous Anguish inward pent, / (Kind Struggle!) thine to soften, or prevent?

Ev'n now thy fancied perils fill her mind;
The secret rock, rough wave, and rising wind;
The shoal, so treach'rous, near the tempting land:
Th'ingulphing whirlpool, and the swallowing sand: 70
These fancied perils all, by day, by night,
In thoughts alarm her, and in dreams affright!
For thee her heart unceasing love declares,
In doubts, in hopes, in wishes, and in pray'rs!
Her pray'rs are heard!—from me, 'tis thine to brave   75
The sand, the shoal, rock, whirlpool, wind, and wave:
Kind safety waits, to waft thee gently o'er,
And joy to greet thee on the *Belgic* shore.
　　May future times, when their fond praise would tell
How most their fav'rite characters excell;   80
How blest! how great!—then may their songs declare,
So great! so blest!—such *Anne* and *Nassau* were.

78] *After this line occur the following in 1734:* Hail, happy Pair! connubial Bliss descend! /
Such may auspicious Fruitfulness attend, / Unfading Love through life each Blessing
raise, / And Glory crown you with her *clearest* Blaze!
79 May] Then *1734*.
81 may] shall *1734*.

Verses occasioned by the *Vice-principal* of *St. Mary hall, Oxford*, being presented by the honourable Mrs. *Knight*, to the *living* of *Gosfield* in *Essex*.

TEXTS: (1) *Grub-street Journal*, 6 February 1735.
　(2) *LM*, 35, 91.
　(3) *GM* 37, 178.

Walter Harte was commended by Johnson for his *History of Gustavus Adolphus*, and described as 'a man of the most companionable talents he had ever known' (Boswell, II, 120). He was presented to the living of Gosfield in December 1734 (*LM*, 34, 667). Notice in the opening lines an allusion to *The Progress of a Divine*, which must have already been written.

While by mean arts, and meaner patrons rise
    Priests, whom the learned, and the good despise;
This sees fair KNIGHT, in whose transcendant mind,
Are wisdom, purity, and truth enshrin'd.
As modest merit now she plans to lift,   5
Thy living, *Gosfield*, falls her instant gift.
'Let me (she said) reward alone the wise,
And make the church revenue virtue's prize.'
    She sought the man of honest, candid breast,
In faith, in works of goodness, full exprest;   10
Though young, yet tut'ring academic youth
To science, moral, and religious truth.
She sought where the disinterested friend,
The scholar sage, and free companion blend;
The pleasing poet, and the deep divine: 15
She sought, she found, and HARTE, the prize was thine.

---

12 science, moral] science moral *GM*, 37; *LM*, 37.

CHARACTER OF THE REV.
JAMES FOSTER

TEXTS: (1) **LM*, 35, 152 (March): '*An Extract from an Epistle not yet publish'd.*'
    (2) *GM*, 35, 213 (April): '*An Extract from an Epistle not yet publish'd.*'

The *Gentleman's Magazine* described the *Character of the Rev. James Foster* as an 'extract' from RS's *Progress of a Divine* (*GM*, 35, 222). But it is not a part of any text of the *Progress* which I have seen or on which I have been able to get a report.

These lines must have been written in the summer of 1734. In a letter to Thomas Birch, undated but related in content to other letters dated in that year, RS wrote: 'I have now, as I think, compleated my Lines on my Favourite M'r Foster' (MS Sloane 4318, f. 53 (British Museum)).

Pope praised Foster in the *Epilogue to the Satires*—

    'Let modest *Foster*, if he will, excell
      Ten Metropolitans in preaching well'—   [1, 131–2]

and was snubbed by Bishop Warburton. *Works of Alexander Pope* (1751), IV, 312: 'This confirms an observation which Mr Hobbes made long ago, *That there be very few Bishops that act a sermon so well, as divers Presbyterians and fanatic Preachers can do.*' Thomas Evans, editor and publisher of RS's *Works* in 1775, answered him in a note: 'In this Character of the Rev. James Foster, truth guided the pen of the muse.... The character and writings of Foster will be admired and read, when the works of the bitter Controversialist are forgotten.'

RS seems to have anticipated Foster's controversy with Rev. Henry Stebbing on the subject of heresy, which broke out in the early summer of 1735 and which brought him sharply into collision with the formidable Bishop of London, Edmund Gibson, known as 'Dr Codex'. No doubt the quarrel was simmering as early as 1734.

FROM *Codex* hear, ye ecclesiastick men,
This past'ral charge to *W—bs—r, S—bb—g, V——n*;
Attend ye emblems of your *P——*'s mind!
Mark *faith*, mark *hope*, mark *charity*, defin'd;
On terms, whence no ideas ye can draw,   5
Pin well your *faith*, and then pronounce it *law*;
First wealth, a crosier next, your *hope* enflame;
And next church power;—a power o'er conscience claim;
In modes of worship *right* of *choice* deny;
Say, to convert, all means are fair;—add, why?   10
'Tis *charitable*—let your power decree,
That *persecution* then is *charity*;
Call reason error; *forms*, not *things*, display;
Let *moral* doctrine to *abstruse* give way;
Sink demonstration; myst'ry preach alone;   15
Be thus *religion*'s friend, and thus your *own*!
    But *Foster* well this honest truth extends;
Where *mystery* begins, *religion* ends.
In him (great modern miracle) we see
A priest, from av'rice, and ambition free;   20
One, whom no persecuting spirit fires;
Whose heart and tongue benevolence inspires;

---

2 *W—bs—r.* William Webster. *S—bb—g.* Henry Stebbing. *V——n.* Richard Venn. The latter had deposed to Bishop Gibson that Rundle had expressed heretical views on the sacrifice of Isaac. Cf. *Progress of a Divine*, l. 336.

3 *P——.* Prelate.

18 See Foster's sermon 'Of Mysteries'. *Sermons*, 3rd ed. (1736), p. 171: 'Where the *mystery* begins, religion *ends.*'

Learn'd, not assuming; eloquent, yet plain;
Meek, though not tim'rous; conscious, though not vain;
Without craft, reverend; holy, without cant;   25
Zealous for truth, without enthusiast rant.
His *faith*, where no credulity is seen,
'Twixt infidel, and bigot, marks the mean;
His *hope*, no mitre militant on earth,
'Tis that bright crown, which heav'n reserves for worth;   30
A priest, in *charity* with all mankind;
His love to virtue, not to sect confin'd;
Truth his delight; from him it flames abroad,
From him, who fears no being, but his God:
In him from christian, moral light can shine;   35
Not mad with myst'ry, but a sound divine!
He wins the wise, and good, with reason's lore;
Then strikes their passions with pathetick power;
Where vice erects her head, rebukes the page;
Mix'd with rebuke, persuasive charms engage;   40
Charms, which th'unthinking must to thought excite;
Lo! vice less vicious! virtue more upright:
Him copy, *Codex*, that the good, and wise,
Who so abhor thy heart, and head despise,
May see thee now, though late, redeem thy name,   45
And glorify what else is damn'd to fame.
      But should some *churchman*, aping wit severe,
The poet's sure turn'd *baptist* say, and sneer?
Shame on that narrow mind so often known,
Which in one mode of faith, owns worth alone;   50
Sneer on, rail, wrangle!—nought this truth repels;
Virtue is *virtue*, wheresoe'er she dwells;
And sure, where learning gives her light to shine,
Hers is all praise; if hers, 'tis, *Foster*, thine.
Thee boast dissenters; we with pride may own   55
Our *Tillotson*; and *Rome*, her *Fenelon*.

THE PROGRESS OF A DIVINE.
A SATIRE.

TEXT: *THE PROGRESS OF A DIVINE. A SATIRE....
MDCCXXXV. (Advertised in *GM*, 35, 222 (April), but said in *GM*,
84, 175 to have been published in July.)

Johnson informs us that the occasion of this poem was the 'dispute
between the Bishop of London and the Chancellor' (*Account*, pp. 386 ff.).
This occurred over the proposal to elevate Dr Rundle, RS's friend, to the
see of Gloucester. The Bishop of London, Gibson, was high church
and strictly orthodox, while Rundle was a latitudinarian of the school
of Dr Samuel Clarke, and a friend of Rev. James Foster, a dissenter.
The result of the dispute was a draw. In December 1734 Rundle found
himself exiled to Ireland, but given the lucrative see of Derry, and his
supporter, Benson, the see of Gloucester.

RS's poem is not primarily an attack on Gibson, even though he is
mentioned as aiding a corrupt divine on his road to the high places in
the Church. But the main content of the poem is a satirical sketch, in
the style of Vanbrugh, of an imaginary churchman, worldly, corrupt,
and ignorant; avid of power; and unscrupulous of the means which he
adopts to achieve his ends. In spite of its sensationalism, the satire in
many parts of this poem is effective.

ALL Priests are not the same, be understood!
  Priests are, like other Folks, some bad, some good.
What's Vice, or Virtue sure admits no Doubt;
Then Clergy, with church Mission, or without;
When Good, or Bad, annex we, to your Name,   5
The greater Honour, or the greater Shame.
    Mark how a country Curate once cou'd rise;
Though neither learn'd, nor witty, good, nor wise!
Of *Inkeeper*, or *Butcher*, if begot,
At *Cam*, or *Isis* bred, imports it not.   10
A *Servitor* he was—'Of *Hall*, or *College*?'
Ask not—to neither Credit is his Knowledge.
    Four Years, through foggy Ale, yet made him see,

---

4 Perhaps this line means: Just as there is a clear distinction between virtue and
vice, so is there one between clergymen with a vocation for the church and those
without one.

Juſt his *neck Verse* to read, and *take Degree*.
A Gown, with added Sleeves, he now may wear;   15
While his round Cap transforms into a Square.
Him, quite unsconc'd, the butt'ry Book shall own;
At Pray'rs, though ne'er devout, so conſtant known.
Let *Teſtimonials* then his Worth disclose!
He gains a Cassock, Beaver, and a Rose.   20
A *Curate* now, his *Furniture* review!
A few old Sermons, and a Bottle-screw.
'A *Curate?*—*Where?* His Name (cries one) recite!
'Or tell me this—Is *Pudding* his Delight?
'Why, *Our's* loves *Pudding*'—Does he so?—''tis *He*!   25
'A *Servitor*;'—Sure *Curll* will find a *Key*.
His *Alma Mater* now he quite forsakes;
She gave him *one Degree*, and *two* he takes.
He now the *Hood* and *Sleeve* of *Maſter* wears;
'*Doctor*!' (quoth they)—and lo, a *Scarf* he bears!   30
A swelling, russling, glossy *Scarf*!—yet he,
By *Peer* unqualify'd, as by *Degree*.
This Curate learns *church Dues*, and *Law* to teize,
When Time shall serve, for *Tythes*, and *surplice Fees*;
When 'scapes some portion'd Girl from Guardian's Pow'r   35
He the snug Licence gets for nuptial Hour;
And, rend'ring vain her Parent's prudent Cares,
To Sharper weds her, and with Sharper shares.
Let Babes of Poverty convulsive lie;
No Bottle waits, though Babes unsprinkled die.   40
Half Office serves the Fun'ral, if it bring
No Hope of Scarf, of Hatband, Gloves, or Ring.
Does any wealthy Fair desponding lye,

---

14 A '*neck Verse*' was a Latin verse set before one claiming benefit of clergy by
reading which he might save his neck.

17 Unsconc'd. Not fined for missing chapel. Such fines would have been entered
in the college Buttery Book.

20 Beaver. A fur hat. Rose. The rosette worn on the headdress of a clergyman.

26 One of Edmund Curll's most lucrative projects was the publication of keys to
satires that had aroused wide interest, like the *Dunciad*, in which the persons
mentioned were identified, not always correctly.

With scrup'lous Conscience, though she knows not why?
Would cordial Counsel make the Patient well?   45
Our Priest shall raise the Vapours, not dispel.
His Cant some *Orphan*'s piteous Case shall bring;
He bids her *give the Widow's Heart to sing*:
He pleads for *Age* in *Want*; and, while she lingers,
Thus snares her Charity with bird-lime Fingers.   50
      Now in the Patron's Mansion see the Wight,
Factious for Power—a *Son* of *Levi* right!
Servile to 'Squires, to Vassals proud his Mien,
As *Codex* to *inferior Clergy* seen.
He flatters till you blush; but, when withdrawn,   55
'Tis his to slander, as 'twas his to fawn.
He pumps for Secrets, pries o'er Servants' Ways,
And, like a meddling Priest, can Mischief raise;
And from such Mischief thus can plead Desert:
''Tis all my Patron's Int'rest at my Heart.'   60
Deep in his Mind all Wrongs from others live;
None more need Pardon, and none less forgive.
      At what does next his Erudition aim?
To kill the footed and the feather'd Game:
Then this *Apostle*, for a daintier Dish,   65
With Line, or Net, shall plot the Fate of Fish.
In *Kitchen* what the *Cookmaid* calls a *Cot*;
In *Cellar*, with the *Butler* brother *Sot*.
Here too he corks, in *Brewhouse* hops the Beer;
Bright in the *Hall*, his Parts at *Whisk* appear;   70
Dext'rous to *pack*; yet at all Cheats exclaiming:
The Priest has Av'rice, Av'rice Itch of Gaming,
And Gaming Fraud:—But *fair* he strikes the *Ball*,
And at the *Plain* of *Billiard* pockets all.
At *Tables* now!—But oh, if *gammon'd* there,   75
The *startling Echoes* learn, like *him*, to *swear*!
Though ne'er at *Authors*, in the *Study*, seen,
At *Bowls*, sagacious *Master* of the *Green*.
A *Connoisseur*, as cunning as a Fox,
To bet on Racers, or on battling Cocks;   80

To preach o'er Beer, in *Burroughs*, to procure
Voters, to make the 'Squire's Election sure:
For this, where Clowns stare, gape, and grin, and baul,
Free to buffoon his Function to 'em all.
When the clod Justice some Horse-laugh wou'd raise,   85
Foremost the dullest of dull Jokes to praise;
To say, or unsay, at his Patron's Nod;
To do the *Will* of *All*—save that of *God*.

His Int'rest the most servile Part he deems;
Yet much he sways, where much to serve he seems: 90
He sways his Patron, rules the Lady most,
And, as he rules the Lady, *rules the Roast*.

Old Tradesmen must give Way to new—his Aim
Extorted *Poundage*, once the *Steward*'s Claim.
Tenants are rais'd; or, as his Pow'r encreases,   95
Unless they fine to Him, renew no Leases.
Thus Tradesmen, Servants, Tenants, none are free;
Their Loss and Murmur are his Gain and Glee.

Lux'ry he loves; but, like a Priest of Sense,
Ev'n Lux'ry, loves not at his own Expence.   100
Though harlot Passions wanton with his Will,
Yet Av'rice is his wedded Passion still.

See him with *Napkin*, o'er his *Band*, tuck'd in,
While the rich Grease hangs glist'ning on his Chin;
Or, as the *Dew* from *Aaron*'s Beard declines,   105
Ev'n to his garment Hem, soft-trickling shines!
He feeds, and feeds, swills Soop, and sucks up Marrow;
Swills, sucks, and feeds, 'till leach'rous as a Sparrow.
Thy Pleasure, *Onan*, now no more delights;
The lone Amusement of his chaster Nights.   110
He boasts—(let Ladies put him to the Test!)
Strong Back, broad Shoulders, and a well-built Chest.
With stiff'ning Nerves, now steals he sly away;
Alert, warm, chuckling, ripe for am'rous Play;
Ripe, to caress the Lass; he once thought meet,   115
At Church to chide, when pennanc'd in a Sheet.
He pants, the titillating Joy to prove;

194

The fierce, short Sallies of luxurious Love.
Not fair *Cadiere* and *Confessor*, than they,
In straining Transport, more lascivious lay.   120
  Conceives her Womb, while Each so melts, and thrills?
He plies her now with Love, and now with Pills.
No more falls *Pennance*, cloath'd in Shame, upon her;
These kill her *Embrio*, and preserve her *Honour*.
  Riches, Love, Pow'r, his Passions then we own;   125
Can he court Pow'r, and pant not for Renown?
Fool, Wise, Good, Wicked,—All desire a Name:
Than Him, young Heroes burn not more for Fame.
While, about *Ways* of *Heav'n*, the Schoolmen jar;
(The Church re-echoing to the wordy War)   130
The *Ways* of *Earth*, He (on his Horse a-stride)
Can with big Words contest, with Blows decide;
He dares some *Carrier*, charg'd with *cumb'rous Load*,
Disputes, dismounts, and *boxes* for the *Road*.
  Ye hooting Boys, *Oh, well-play'd Parson*, cry!   135
Oh, well-play'd Parson, hooting Vales reply!
Winds waft it to *CATHEDRAL DOMES* around!
CATHEDRAL DOMES, from *inmost Quires*
   resound!
  The Man has many, meritorious Ways:
He'll *smoke* his *Pipe*, and *London*'s *Prelate* praise.   140
His *publick Prayers*, his *Oaths* for *George* declare;
Yet mental Reservation may forswear;
For, safe with Friends, He now, in loyal Stealth,
Hiccups, and, stagg'ring, cries—'*King Jemmy*'s Health.'
God's *Word* He preaches now, and now profanes;   145
Now *swallows Camels*, and *at Gnats* now *strains*.
He pities Men; who, in unrighteous Days,
Read, or what's worse, write *Poetry*, and *Plays*.

---

119 Catherine Cadière, a remarkably beautiful French girl much given to reading
mystical books, became the penitent and mistress of a jesuit, J.-B. Girard. Becoming
pregnant, she was about to be sent to a nunnery when the authorities interfered and
a complicated legal battle ensued, which received wide publicity and was finally
settled in 1731.

He readeth not what any Author saith;
The more his Merit in implicit Faith.   150
Those, who a Jot from *Mother Church* receed,
He *damns*, like any *Athanasian Creed*.
He rails at *Hoadley*; so can Zeal possess him,
He's *Orthodox*, as G—*bs—n*'s self—*God bless him.*

    Satan, whom yet, for once, he pays *Thanksgiving*,   155
Sweeps off th'*Incumbent* now of *Fat-goose Living.*
He seeks his Patron's Lady, finds the Fair,
And for her Int'reſt firſt prefers his Prayer.
'You pose me not (said she) though hard the Task;
'Though Husbands seldom give what Wives will ask.   160
'*My Dearee* does not yet to think encline,
'How oft your Neſt you feather Prieſt from mine.
'This Pin-money, though short, has not betray'd;
'Nor Jewels pawn'd, nor Tradesmen's Bills unpay'd;
'Mine is the female, fashionable Skill,   165
'To win my Wants, by cheating at *Quadrille.*
'You bid me, with prim Look, the World delude;
'Nor sins my Prieſt demurer than his Prude.
'Leaſt thinks, my Lord, you plant the secret Horn;
'That yours his hopeful Heir, so newly born.   170
''Tis mine, to teize him firſt, with jealous Fears,
'And thunder all my *Virtue* in his Ears:
'My *Virtue* rules *unqueſtion'd*—Where's the Cue
'For that, which governs him, to govern you?
'I gave you Pow'r, the Family complain;   175
'I gave you Love; but all your Love is Gain.
'My Int'reſt, Wealth; for these alone you burn;
'With these you leave me, and with these return:
'Then, as no Truant wants Excuse for Play,
''Twas *Duty—Duty* call'd you far away;   180
'The *Sick* to *visit*—some Miles off to *preach*:
'—You come not, but to suck one like a Leach.'

---

156 Parson Bull in Vanbrugh's *The Relapse* was the prototype of RS's divine. He performs hasty private weddings, does not shrink from bigamous ones, and rises in the Church by means of corruption. He is bribed with Fatgoose living (act v, scene iii).

Thus, *Lady-like*, she wanders from the Case,
Keeps to no Point; but runs a *wild-goose Chase.*
She talks, and talks—to him her Words are Wind; *185*
For *fat-goose Living* fills alone his Mind.
　　He leaves her, to his Patron warm applies:
'But Parson, mark the Terms! (his Patron cries)
'Yon Door you held for *Me*, and hand-maid *Nell*:
'The Girl now *sickens*, and she soon will *swell.* *190*
'My Spouse has yet no jealous, odd Conjecture:
'Oh, shield my *morning Rest* from *curtain Lecture!*
'Parson, take breeding *Nelly* quick to *Wife*,
'And *fat-goose Living* then is yours for Life!'
　　Patron and Spouse thus mutually beguil'd, *195*
Patron and Priest thus own each other's Child.
Smock Simony agreed—thus Curate rise;
Though neither learn'd, nor witty, good, nor wise.
　　Vicars, (poor Wights!) for lost Impropriation,
Rue, though good Protestants, the *Reformation.* *200*
Prefer'd from Curate, see our Soul's Protector
No murm'ring Vicar; but rejoicing Rector;
Not hir'd by Laymen, nor by Laymen shown
Church Lands now theirs, and Tythes no more his own!
　　His Patron can't revoke; but may repent; *205*
To bully now, not please, our Parson's bent.
When from Dependance freed, (such priesty Will!)
Priests soon treat all, but first their Patrons, ill.
　　Vestries he rules—Ye Lawyers hither draw!
He snacks—His People deep are plung'd in Law! *210*
Now these plague those, this Parish now sues that,
For burying, or maintaining foundling Brat.
Now with *Churchwardens* cribs the *rev'rend Thief*,

188–94 Horace Walpole told a correspondent that his father once offered a benefice
to a clergyman on condition that he marry a bastard of his (*Letters of Horace Walpole*,
ed. Mrs P. Toynbee (1903), III, 138).

199 To impropriate a benefice is to divert its revenues into lay hands.

210 To go snacks is to divide the proceeds, usually of a swindle. The divine is in
confederacy with the lawyers.

From workhouse Pittance, and collection Brief;
Nay *sacramental* Alms purloins as sure,   215
And ev'n at *Altars* thus defrauds the Poor.
  Poor Folks he'll shun; but *pray* by Rich, if ill,
And *watch, and watch*—to *slide* into their *Will*;
Then *pop*, perchance, in *consecrated Wine*,
What *speeds* the Soul, he fits for Realms divine.   220
  Why cou'd not *London*, this good Parson, gain?
Before him *Sepulchres* had *rent in twain*.
Then had he learn'd, with Sextons, to invade,
And strip with sacrilegious Hands the Dead;
To tear off Rings, ere yet the Finger rots;   225
To *part 'em*, for the *vesture* Shroud *cast Lots*;
Had made dead Sculls for Coin the Chymist's Share,
The Female Corpse the Surgeon's purchas'd Ware;
And peering view'd, when for Dissection laid,
That secret Place, which Love has sacred made.   230
  Grudge Heroes not your Heads in Stills enclos'd!
Grudge not, ye Fair, your *Parts* ripp'd up, expos'd!
As strikes the choice Anatomy our Eyes;
As here dead Sculls, in quick'ning Cordials, rise;
From *Egypt* thus a rival Traffic springs: 235
Her vended *Mummies* thus were once her *Kings*;
The *Line* of *Ninus* now in *Drugs* is roll'd,
And *Ptolemy's* himself for *Balsam* sold.
  Volumes, *unread*, his *Library*, compose;
Gay shine their gilded Backs in letter'd Rows.   240
Cheap he collects—His Friends the Dupes are known;
They buy, he borrows, and each Book's his own,
  Poor Neighbors earn his *Ale*; but earn it dear;
His *Ale* he trafficks for a nobler Cheer.
For *Mugs* of *Ale*, some poach—No Game they spare;   245

---

214 Collection Brief. A letter patent issued by the Sovereign as head of the Church authorizing a collection for a specified purpose.

235-8 Mummy was a medicinal preparation actually made from mummies ground to powder.

Nor Pheasant, Patridge, Woodcock, Snipe, nor Hare.
Some plunder Fishponds; Others (Ven'son Thieves)
The Forreſt ravage, and the Prieſt receives.
Let *Plenty*, at his *Board*, then *Lacquey* serve!
No,—though with Plenty, Penury will ſtarve.　　250
He deals with *London* Fishmongers—His Books
Swell in Accompts with Poult'rers and with Cooks.
　　　Wide, and more wide, his swelling Fortune flows;
Narrower, and narrower ſtill, his Spirit grows.
　　　His *Servants*—Hard has Fate their Lot decreed:　255
They toil like Horses, like Camelions feed.
Sunday, no Sabbath, is in *Labour* spent,
And *Chriſtmas* renders 'em as lean as *Lent*.
Him, long, nor faithful Services engage;
See 'em *dismiss'd* in *Sickness*, or in *Age*!　　260
　　　His *Wife*, poor *Nelly*, leads a Life of Dread;
Now beat, now pinch'd on Arms, and now in Bread.
If decent Powder deck th'adjuſted Hair;
If modish Silk, for once, improve her Air;
Her with paſt Faults, thus shocks his cruel Tone;　265
(Faults; though from thence her Dow'ry, now his own)
'Thus shall my Purse your carnal Joys procure?
'All Dress is nothing, but a *Harlot*'s Lure.
'Sackcloth alone your Sin shou'd, pennanc'd, wear;
'Your Locks, uncomb'd, with Ashes sprinkled ſtare.　270
'Spare Diet thins the Blood—if more you crave,
''Tis mine my Viands, and your Soul to save.
'Blood muſt be drawn, not swell'd—then ſtrip, and
　　　dread
'This waving Horse-whip, circling o'er my Head!
'Be yours the blubb'ring Lip, and whimp'ring Eye!　275
'Frequent this Lash shall righteous Stripes supply.
'What squal you? Call no Kindred to your Aid!
'You wedded, when no Widow; yet no Maid.

---

246 Patridge. RS probably wrote Partridge, but as Patridge is a dialect form,
I have not altered it.
256 Chameleons were supposed to live on air.

'Did *Law Mosaic now in Force remain,
'Say to what Father durst you then complain?   *280*
'What had your Virtue witness'd? Well I know,
'No *bridal Sheets* cou'd *Virgin Tokens* show;
'*Elders* had sought; but miss'd the *signing Red*,
'And *Law*, then Harlot, straight had *ston'd* you *dead*.'
    Nor former Vice alone her Pain ensures;   *285*
Nelly, for present Virtue, much endures;
For lo, she charms some wealthy, am'rous Squire!
Her Spouse wou'd lett her, like his Mare, for Hire.
'Twere thus no Sin, shou'd Love her Limbs employ:
Be his the Profit, and be hers the Joy!   *290*
This, when her Chastity, or Pride denies;
His Words reproach her, and his Kicks chastise.
    At length, in Childbed, she, with broken Heart,
Tips off—poor Soul!—Let her in Peace depart!
He mourns her Death, who did her Life destroy;   *295*
He weeps, and weeps—Oh, how he weeps—for Joy!
Then cries, with seeming Grief, 'Is *Nelly* dead?
'No More with Woman *creak* my *Couch*, or *Bed*!'
'Tis true; he, Spouse nor Doxy, more enjoys;
Women farewell! He *lusts* not—but for *Boys*.   *300*
    This Priest ye Clergy not fictitious call;
Think him not form'd, to represent ye all.
Shou'd Satire Quirks of vile Attornies draw;
Say, wou'd that mean to ridicule all Law?
Describe some murd'ring Quack with Want of
          Knowledge,   *305*
Wou'd true Physicians cry—you mean the College?
Blest be your *Cloth*!—But, if in *him*, 'tis *curst*,
'Tis as best Things, corrupted, are the worst.
    But lest, with Keys, the guiltless, *Curll* defame,
Be publish'd here—*Melchisedeck* his Name!   *310*

---

* For a particular Account of this Law, we refer to *Deuteronomy*, Chap. xxii. Ver.
13, 14, 15, 16, 17, 18, 19, 20, 21. [RS]

---

309 Cf. l. 26.

Of *OXFORD* too; but her *strict Terms* have *dropp'd*
   him:
And *CAMBRIDGE, ad eundem,* shall *adopt* him.
  Of *Arts* now *Master* him the *Hood* confirms;
'Scap'd are his *Exercises, 'scap'd* his *Terms.*
See the *Degree* of *Doctor* next excite!   *315*
The *Scarf,* he once usurp'd, becomes his Right.
A *Doctor?* cou'd he *Disputants* refute?
Not so—first *compromis'd* was the *Dispute.*
  At *fat-goose Living* seldom he resides;
A curate there, small Pittance well provides.   *320*
See him at *London,* studiously profound,
With Bags of Gold, not Books, encompass'd round!
He, from the *Broker,* how to *job* discerns;
He, from the *Scriv'ner, Art* of *Usury* learns;
How to let Int'rest run on Int'rest knows,   *325*
And how to draw the Mortgage, how foreclose.
Tenants and Buroughs, bought with monstrous Treasure,
Elections turn obedient to his Pleasure.
Like *St—bb—ng,* Let him *countrey Mobs* support,
And then, like *St—bb—ng,* crave a Grace at *Court!* *330*
He sues, he teizes, and he perseveres:
Not blushless *Henley* less abash'd appears.
His Impudence, of Proof in ev'ry Tryal,
Kens no polite, and heeds no plain Denial.
A *Spy,* he aims, by others' Fall to rise;   *335*
Vile as *Iscariot V——n,* betrays; belies;
And say, what better recommends than this?
Lo, *CODEX greets* him with, a *holy Kiss;*
Him thus instructs in controversial Stuff;
Him, who ne'er argu'd, but with *Kick* and *Cuff!* *340*
  '*My Weekly Miscellany* be your Lore;

* The worthy Orator. [RS]

---

329 St—bb—ng. Stebbing.   *336 Iscariot V——n.* Richard Venn.
338 CODEX. Gibson, Bishop of London.
341 The Weekly Miscellany ran from 1732 to 1741 under the editorship of Webster.
A poem violently attacking RS appeared in it.

'Thence rise, at once, the Champion of Church Power!
'The Trick of jumbling Contradictions know;
'In Church be high, in Politicks seem low;
'Seek some Antagonist, then wound his Name;   345
'The better still his Life, the more defame;
'Quote him unfair; and, in Expression quaint,
'Force him to father Meanings, never meant!
'Learn but mere Names, resistless is your Page;
'For these enchant the Vulgar, those enrage.   350
'Name *CHURCH*, that *mystic Spell* shall *Mobs* command;
'Let *Heretic*, each *reas'ning Christian*, brand;
'Cry *Schismatick*, let *Men* of *Conscience* shrink!
'Cry *Infidel*, and *Who* shall dare to *think*?
'Invoke the *civil Pow'r*, not *Sense*, for Aid;   355
'Assert, not argue; menace, not persuade;
'Shew, *Discord*, and her *Fiends* wou'd save the Nation;
'But *Her* call *Peace*, her *Fiends* a *CONVOCATION*!
    'By *Me*, and *Webster*, finish'd thus at School,
'Last, for the *Pulpit*, learn this *golden Rule!*   360
'Detach the Sense, and pother o'er the Text,
'And puzzle first yourself, your Audience next;
'Ne'er let your Doctrine, ethic Truth, impart;
'Be *That* as free from *Morals*, as your *Heart*!
'Say Faith, without one Virtue, shall do well;   365
'But, without Faith, all Virtues doom to Hell!
'What is this Faith? Not what (as Scripture shows)
'Appeals to Reason, when 'twou'd Truth disclose;
'This, *against Reason*, dare we recommend;
'Faith may be true; yet not on Truth depend.   370
''Tis mystic Light—A Light, which shall conceal;
'A Revelation, which shall not reveal.
'If Faith is Faith, 'tis orthodox—in brief,
'Belief, not orthodox, is not Belief;

---

344 Gibson, though personally a high-churchman, was tied up with the low-church
group, which, as nominees of the Whig government, was in control of the administration of the Church. This inconsistency in his position was mainly responsible for
his failure in the quarrel over Bishop Rundle.

'And who has not Belief, pronounce him plain   375
'No *Christian*—*Codex* bids you *this* maintain.'
  Thus with much wealth, some jargon, and no grace,
To *Seat episcopal* our *Doctor* trace!
Codex, deceiving the superior Ear,
Procures the *Congé* (much miscall'd) *D'Elire*.   380
(Let this the Force of our fine Precept tell;
That Faith, without one Virtue, shall do well.)
The *Dean* and *Chapter*, daring not t'enquire,
Elect him—Why?—to shun a *Præmunire*.
Within, without, be Tidings roll'd around;   385
Organs within, and Bells without resound.
Lawn-sleev'd, and mitred, stand he now confest:
See *Codex* consecrate!—A solemn Jest!
The Wicked's Pray'rs prevail not—pardon me,
Who, for your *Lordship's Blessing*, bend—no Knee.   390
  Like other Priests, when to small *Sees* you send 'em,
Let Ours hold *fat-goose Living* in *Commendam*!
An *Officer*, who ne'er his King rever'd;
For trait'rous Toasts, and Cowardice cashier'd;
A broken *'Pothecary*, once renown'd   395
For Drugs, that poison'd half the Country round;
From whom warm Girls, if pregnant ere they marry,
Take Physick, and for *Honour*'s Sake miscarry:
A *Lawyer*, fam'd for length'ning Bills of Cost;
While much he plagu'd Mankind, his Clients most,   400
To lick up ev'ry Neighbour's Fortune known,
And then let Lux'ry lick up all his own;
A *Cambridge Soph*, who, once for Wit, was held

---

380 Congé D'Elire is royal permission to a cathedral chapter to fill a vacant see by
election, usually accompanied by Letters Missive nominating the person to be elected.
The Whig government was using this method for filling vacancies on the bench with
its own nominees.

384 A *Præmunire* is a writ charging the sheriff to summon a person accused.
According to Tindal's *Rights of the Christian Church* (1706), bishops are 'under a
præmunire oblig'd to confirm and consecrate the person nam'd in the Congé d'Elire'.
Quoted in *OED*.

392 A benefice is held *in commendam* if it is held along with another preferment.
397 Cf. *The Authors of the Town*, ll. 125–6.

Esteem'd; but vicious, and for Vice expell'd;
With Parts, his Lordship's lame ones to support,   *405*
In well-tim'd *Sermons*, fit to cant at *Court*;
Or accurately pen (a Talent better!)
His Lordship's *senate Speech*, and *past'ral Letter*:
These *Four*, to purify from sinful Stains,
This *Bishop* first absolves, and then ordains.   *410*
His *Chaplains these*; and each of rising knows
Those righteous Arts: by which their *Patron* rose.
    See him LORD SPIRITUAL, *dead-voting* seated!
He soon, though ne'er to *Heav'n*, shall be *translated*.
Wou'd now the *Mitre* circle *Rundle*'s Crest?   *415*
See *him*, with *Codex*, ready to *protest*!
Thus holy, holy, holy *Bishop* rise;
Though neither learn'd, nor witty, good, nor wise!
    Think not these Lays, the *Clergy*, wou'd abuse;
Thus, when these Lays commenc'd, premis'd the Muse. *420*
'All Priests are not the same, be understood!
'Priests are, like other Folks, some bad, some good.'
The Good no Sanction give the Wicked's Fame;
Nor, with the Wicked, share the good in Shame.
Then wise *Free-thinkers* cry not smartly thus—   *425*
'Is the Priest work'd?—The Poet's one of us.'
Free-thinkers, Bigots are alike to me;
For these misdeem half-thinking thinking free;
Those, speculative without Speculation,
Call Myst'ry, and Credulity Salvation.   *430*
Let us believe with Reason, and, in chief,
Let our good Works demonstrate our Belief;
Faith, without Virtue, never shall do well;
And never Virtue without Faith excell.

---

413 Possibly, since he remained seated, he was abstaining.

THE Volunteer-Laureat.
Most humbly inscribed to Her MAJESTY,
ON HER *BIRTH-DAY.*
NUMBER IV. For the YEAR 1735.

TEXT: *THE Volunteer-Laureat, etc....M.DCC.XXX.V.

IN Youth no Parent nurs'd my infant Songs,
'Twas mine to be inspir'd alone by Wrongs;
Wrongs, that with Life their fierce Attack began,
Drank Infant Tears, and still pursue the Man.
Life scarce is Life—Dejection all is mine;   5
The Power, that loves in lonely Shades to pine;
Of faded Cheek, of unelated Views;
Whose weaken'd Eyes the Rays of Hope refuse.
'Tis mine the mean, inhuman Pride to find;
Who shuns th'oppress'd, to Fortune only kind;   10
Whose Pity's Insult, and whose cold Respect
Is keen as Scorn, ungen'rous as Neglect.
Void of benevolent, obliging Grace,
Ev'n dubious Friendship half averts his Face:
Thus sunk in Sickness, thus with Woes opprest,   15
How shall the Fire awake within my Breast?
How shall the Muse her flagging Pinions raise?
How tune her Voice to *Carolina's* Praise?
From jarring Thought no tuneful Raptures flow;
These with fair Days, and gentle Seasons glow: 20
Such give alone sweet *Philomel* to sing,
And *Philomel's* the Poet of the Spring.
      But soft my Soul! see yon celestial Light!
Before whose lambent Lustre breaks the Night.
It glads me like the Morning clad in Dews,   25
And beams reviving from the *vernal Muse*:
Inspiring joyous Peace, 'tis *She*! 'tis *She*!
A Stranger long to *Misery* and *Me*.
      Her verdant Mantle gracefully declines,
And, flow'r-embroidered, as it varies, shines.   30

To form her Garland, *Zephir*, from his Wing,
Throws the first Flow'rs and Foliage of the Spring.
Her Looks how lovely! Health and Joy have lent
Bloom to her Cheek, and to her Brow Content.
Behold, sweet-beaming, her etherial Eyes!   35
Soft as the *Pleiads* o'er the dewy Skies.
She blunts the Point of Care, alleviates Woes,
And pours the Balm of Comfort and Repose;
Bids the Heart yield to Virtue's silent call,
And shews Ambition's Sons mere Children all;   40
Who hunt for Toys, which please with tinsel Shine;
For which they squabble, and for which they pine.
Oh! hear her Voice, more mellow than the Gale,
That breath'd through Shepherd's Pipe, enchants the Vale!
Hark! she invites from city Smoke and Noise,   45
Vapours impure, and from impurer Joys;
From various Evils, that, with Rage combin'd,
Untune the Body, and pollute the Mind:
From Crowds, to whom no social Faith belongs,
Who tread one Circle of Deceit and Wrongs;   50
With whom Politeness is but civil Guile,
And Laws oppress, exerted by the vile.
        To this oppos'd, the Muse presents the Scene;
Where Sylvan Pleasures ever smile Serene;
Pleasures, that emulate the Blest above,   55
Health, Innocence, and Peace, the Muse, and Love;
Pleasures that ravish, while alternate wrought
By friendly Converse, and abstracted Thought.
These sooth my throbbing Breast. No Loss I mourn;
Though both from Riches and from Grandeur torn.   60
Weep I a *cruel Mother?* No—I've seen,
From Heaven, a pitying, a *maternal Queen.*
One gave me Life; but would no Comfort grant;
She more than Life resum'd by giving Want.
Would she the Being which she gave destroy?   65
My Queen gives Life, and bids me hope for Joy.
Honour and Wealth I chearfully resign;

If Competence, if learned Ease be mine!
If I by mental, heartfelt Joys be fired,
And in the Vale by all the Muse inspired! 70
  Here cease my Plaint—See yon enlivening Scenes!
Child of the Spring! Behold the *Best* of *Queens!*
Softness and Beauty rose this heav'nly Morn,
Dawn'd Wisdom, and Benevolence was born.
Joy, o'er a People, in her Influence rose; 75
Like that which Spring o'er rural Nature throws.
War to the peaceful Pipe resigns his Roar,
And breaks his Billows on some distant Shore.
Domestick Discord sinks beneath her Smile,
And Arts, and Trade, and Plenty glad the Isle. 80
Lo! Industry surveys, with feasted Eyes,
His due Reward, a plenteous Harvest rise!
Nor (taught by Commerce) joys in that alone;
But sees the Harvest of a World his own.
Hence thy just Praise, thou mild, majestic *Thames!* 85
Rich River! Richer than *Pactolus'* Streams!
Than those renowned, of Yore, by Poets roll'd
O'er intermingled Pearls, and Sands of Gold.
How glorious thou, when, from old Ocean's Urn,
Loaded with *India's* Wealth thy Waves return! 90
Alive thy Banks! along each bordering Line,
High Culture blooms, inviting Villas shine;
And while around ten thousand Beauties glow,
These still o'er those redoubling Lustre throw.
  'Come then (so whisper'd the indulgent *Muse*) 95
'Come then, in *Richmond* Groves thy Sorrows lose!
'Come then, and hymn this Day!—The pleasing Scene
'Shews, in each View, the Genius of thy *Queen.*
'Hear Nature whispering in the Breeze her Song!

---

96 During the summer of 1735 Queen Caroline was busy building Merlin's Cave
at Richmond, and establishing a library there. RS may have wished to be appointed
its custodian. Cf. *Volunteer Laureat,* no. 2, l. 58. But on 21 August, Stephen Duck
was made 'Cave and Library Keeper, and his Wife Necessary Woman there'
(*GM,* 35, 498.)

'Hear her Sweet-Warbling through the feather'd
        Throng!   _100_
'Come! with the warbling World thy Notes unite,
'And with the vegitative Smile delight!
'Sure such a Scene and Song will soon restore
'Lost Quiet, and give Bliss unknown before;
'Receive it grateful, and adore, when given,   _105_
'The Goodness of thy Parent _Queen_, and _Heaven_!
    'With me each private Virtue lifts the Voice;
'While public Spirit bids a Land rejoice:
'O'er all thy _Queen_'s Benevolence descends,
'And wide o'er all her vital Light extends.   _110_
'As Winter softens into Spring, to _You_
'Blooms Fortune's Season, through her smile, anew.
'Still, for past Bounty, let new Lays impart
'The sweet Effusions of a grateful Heart!
'Cast through the Telescope of Hope your Eye!   _115_
'There Goodness infinite, supreme descry!
'From Him that Ray of Virtue stream'd on Earth,
'Which kindled _Caroline_'s bright Soul to Birth.
'Behold! he spreads one universal Spring!
'Mortals, transform'd to Angels, then shall sing: _120_
'Oppression then shall fly with Want and Shame,
'And Blessing and Existence be the same!'

THE VOLUNTEER LAUREAT.
A POEM.
ON HER MAJESTY's BIRTH-DAY.
For the YEAR 1736.
[Number V.]

TEXTS: (1) *THE VOLUNTEER LAUREAT, etc. . . . M.DCC.XXXVI.
    (2) _GM_, 36, 100.
    (3) _LM_, 36, 87.

The three editions must have appeared almost simultaneously, since
the Queen's birthday was 1 March, and the magazines were usually

published during the first week of the month. The separate edition was required for presentation, and would have been published on the first.

L O! the mild Sun salutes the opening Spring,
 And glad'ning Nature calls the Muse to sing!
Gay chirp the Birds, the bloomy Sweets exhale,
And Health, and Song, and Fragrance fill the Gale:
Yet mildeſt Suns, to *Me*, are Pain severe,   5
And Music's self is Discord to *my* Ear.
I, jocund Spring, unsympathizing, see,
And Health, that comes to All, comes not to Me.
Dear Health once fled, what Spirits can I find?
What Solace meet, when fled my Peace of Mind?   10
From absent Books, what ſtudious Hint devise?
From absent Friends, what Aid to Thought can rise?
      A *Genius* whisper'd in my Ear, 'Go seek
'Some *Man* of *State*! the *Muse* your *Wrongs* may speak.'
But will *such* liſten to the plaintive Strain?   15
The Happy seldom heed th'Unhappy's Pain.
To Wealth, to Honours, wherefore was I born?
Why left to Poverty, Repulse, and Scorn?
Why was I form'd of elegant Desires?
Thought, which beyond a vulgar Flight aspires?   20
Why, by the *Proud*, and *Wicked*, crush'd to Earth?
Better the Day of Death, than Day of Birth!
      Thus I exclaim'd—A little *Cherub* smil'd:
'H O P E I am call'd (said He) a Heav'n-born Child!
'Wrongs sure you have, complain you juſtly may;   25
'But let wild Sorrow whirl not Thought away!
'No—truſt to H O N O U R! That you ne'er will ſtain
'From Peerage Blood, which fires your filial Vein!
'Truſt more to P R O V I D E N C E!—from *Me* ne'er swerve!
'Once to diſtruſt, is never to deserve.   30
'Did not *this Day* a C A R O L I N E disclose?
'I promis'd at her Birth, and Blessing rose!
'Blessing, o'er all the *letter'd World* to shine,

'In Knowledge clear, Beneficence divine.
''Tis *Hers*, as *Mine*, to chase away Despair;   35
'Woe undeserv'd is her peculiar Care:
'Her bright Benevolence sends me to Grief,
'On Want sheds Bounty, and on Wrongs Relief.'
        Then calm-ey'd PATIENCE, born of *Angel-Kind*,
Open'd a *Dawn* of *Comfort* on my *Mind*:   40
With HER came FORTITUDE, of *Godlike* Air!
These arm to conquer Ills; at leaſt to bear.
Arm'd thus, my QUEEN, while Wayward Fates ordain,
My Life to lengthen, but to lengthen Pain,
Your Bard, his Sorrows, with a Smile, endures;   45
Since to be wretched is to be made *Yours*.

---

38 Wrongs] Wrong *GM, 36.*

To Miss M.H. *sent with Mr* POPE's *Works.*

TEXTS: (1) **GM, 36, 348.*
      (2) *LM, 36, 328.*

There is no evidence that RS left the London area between 1715 and
1739, but he writes in this poem as if he had been to Burford and spent
some time there with Miss M.H. It is not impossible that he had visited
Bath with Lord Tyrconnel, whose lady was taken ill there in 1730, and
that they took in Burford on the way. I do not know who Miss M.H.
was, unless she was a daughter of George Hart, who was one of the
town bailiffs in 1731, 1733, and 1736. R. H. Gretton, *The Burford
Records* (Oxford, 1920).

SEE female vice and female folly here,
  Rallied with wit polite, or lash'd severe!
Let *Pope* present such objeĉts to our view!
Such are, my fair, the full reverse of you.
Rapt when, to *Loddon*'s ſtream* from *Windsor*'s shades,   5
He sings the modeſt charms of sylvan maids;
Dear *Burford's* hills in mem'ry's eye appear,
And *Luddal*'s spring† ſtill murmurs in my ear:

  * *Alluding to the beautiful Episode of* Loddona *in* Windsor Forest. [RS]
  † *A Spring near* Burford. [RS]

But when you cease to bless my longing eyes,
Dumb is the spring, the joyless prospect dies: 10
Come then, my charmer come! here transport reigns!
New health, new youth inspirits all my veins.
Each hour let intercourse of hearts employ!
Thou life of loveliness! thou soul of joy!
Love wakes the birds—oh hear each melting lay!   15
Love warms the world—come charmer, come away!
But hark!—immortal *Pope* resumes the lyre!
Diviner airs, diviner flights, inspire:
Hark where an angel's language tunes the line!
See where the thoughts and looks of angels shine!   20
Here he pour'd all the music of your tongue,
And all your looks and thoughts, unconscious sung.

An EPISTLE to DAMON and DELIA.

TEXTS: (1) *GM, 36, 348.
    (2) LM, 36, 328.

HEAR *Damon*, *Delia* hear, in candid lays,
Truth without anger, without flattr'y praise!
  A bookish mind, with pedantry unfraught,
Oft a sedate, yet never gloomy thought:
Prompt to rejoice when others pleasure know,   5
And prompt to feel the pang for others' woe;
To soften faults, to which a foe is prone,
And, in a friend's perfections praise your own:
A will sincere, unknown to selfish views;
A heart of love, of gallantry a muse;   10
A delicate, yet not a jealous mind;
A passion ever fond, yet never blind;
Glowing, with am'rous, yet with guiltless fires,
In ever eager, never gross desires;
A modest honour, sacred to contain   15
From tatling vanity, when smiles you gain;
Constant, most pleas'd when beauty most you please:

Damon! your picture's shown in tints like these.
　　Say, *Delia*, must I chide you or commend?
Say, must I be your flatt'rer or your friend?　　　　*20*
　　To praise no graces in a rival fair,
Nor your own foibles in a sister spare,
Each lover's billet, bant'ring, to reveal,
And never known one secret to conceal:
Young, fickle, fair, a levity inborn,　　　　*25*
To treat all sighing slaves with flippant scorn;
An eye expressive of a wand'ring mind;
Nor this to read, nor that to think inclin'd;
Or, when a book, or thought from whim retards,
Intent on songs or novels, dress or cards;　　　　*30*
Choice to select the party of delight,
To kill time, thought and fame in frolic flight;
To flutter here, to flurry there on wing;
To talk, to teaze, to simper or to sing;
To prude it, to coquet it—him to trust,　　　　*35*
Whose vain, loose life shou'd caution or disgust;
Him to dislike, whose modest worth shou'd please.
Say, is your picture shown in tints like these?
Yours? you deny it—hear the point then tried!
Let judgment, truth, the muse and love decide!　　　　*40*
What yours?—nay, fairest trifler, frown not so!
Is it? the muse will doubt, love answer *no*:
You smile—is't not? again the question try!—
Yes judgment thinks, and truth will yes reply.

27 eye *LM*, 36] eye; *GM*, 36.
42 will doubt *LM*, 36] with doubt *GM*, 36.
　answer *LM*, 36] answers *GM*, 36.

A POET's *Dependance on a* STATESMAN.

TEXTS: (1) *GM*, 36, 225.
　　(2) *LM*, 36, 210.

RS sent the manuscript of this poem to Thomas Birch on 8 April 1736 to
be transmitted 'without loss of Time, to M'r Cave', editor and publisher

of the *Gentleman's Magazine* (MS Sloane 4318, f. 43 (British Museum)). It was printed in the April number, which came out in the first week of May. How, like other poems of this period of his life, it also got into the *London Magazine* is not clear, but it is likely that RS sent a duplicate manuscript. There are no variants of any importance.

RS's thoughts on the plight of a government hireling and on the sort of work to which hackney poets were put reflect his continued disappointment over a place in the government.

SOme seem to hint, and others proof will bring,
That, from neglect, my num'rous hardships spring.
'Seek the *great man*'! they cry—'tis then decreed,
In *him* if I court *fortune*, I succeed.
What friends to second? who, for *me*, shou'd sue,   5
Have int'rests, partial to *themselves*, in view.
They own my matchless fate compassion draws;
They all wish well, lament; but drop my cause.
There are who ask no pension, want no place,
No title wish, and wou'd accept no grace.   10
(Can I entreat, they should for *me* obtain
The least, who greatest for *themselves* disdain?)
A *statesman*, knowing this, unkind, will cry,
'Those love him: let those serve him!—why shou'd I?'
Say, shall I turn where *Lucre* points my views;   15
At first desert my friends, at length abuse?
But, on less terms, in *promise* he complies:
Years bury years, and hopes on hopes arise;
I trust, am trusted on my fairy gain;
And woes on woes attend, an endless train.   20
        Be posts dispos'd at will!—I have, for these,
No gold to plead, no impudence to teize.
All *secret service* from my *soul* I hate;
All dark intrigues of pleasure, or of state.
I have no pow'r, election votes to gain;   25
No will to hackney out polemic strain;
To shape, as time shall serve, my verse, or prose;
To flatter thence, nor slur a *courtier*'s foes;

---

11 should] wou'd *LM*, 36.

Nor *him* to daub with praise, if I prevail;
Nor shock'd by *him*, with *libels* to assail.   *30*
Where *these* are not, what claim to *me* belongs;
Though *mine* the *muse* and *virtue*, *birth* and *wrongs*?
Where lives the *statesman*, so in *honour* clear,
To give where he has nought to hope, nor fear?
No!—there to seek, is but to find fresh pain: *35*
The promise broke, renew'd and broke again;
To be, as humour deigns, receiv'd, refus'd;
By turns affronted, and by turns amus'd;
To lose that time, which worthier thoughts require;
To lose that health, which shou'd those thoughts inspire; *40*
To starve on hope; or, like *camelions*, fare
On *ministerial faith*, which means but *air*.

    But still, undrooping, I the *crew* disdain,
Who, or by *jobs*, or *libels*, wealth obtain.
Ne'er let me be, through *those*, from want exempt;   *45*
In *one man*'s favour, in the *world*'s contempt;
Worse in *my own*!—through *those*, to posts who rise,
Themselves, in secret, must themselves despise;
Vile, and more vile; till they at length disclaim
Not sense alone of glory, but of shame.   *50*

    What! though I hourly see the servile herd,
For meanness honour'd, and for guilt prefer'd;
See selfish passion, public virtue, seem;
And public virtue an enthusiast dream;
See favour'd falshood, innocence belied,   *55*
Meekness depress'd, and pow'r-elated pride;
A scene *will* shew (all-righteous vision haste!)
The meek exalted, and the proud debas'd!—
Oh, to be there!—to tread that friendly shore;
Where *falshood*, *pride*, and *statesmen* are no more!   *60*

    But ere indulg'd—ere fate my breath shall claim,
A poet still is anxious after fame.
What future fame, wou'd my ambition crave?
This were my wish—cou'd ought my mem'ry save.—
Say, when in death my sorrows lie repos'd,   *65*

That my past life, no venal view, disclos'd!
Say, I well knew, while in a state obscure,
Without the being base, the being poor!
Say I had parts, too mod'rate to transcend;
Yet sense to mean, and virtue not t'offend!⠀⠀⠀⠀⠀⠀70
My heart supplying what my head denied.
Say, that by POPE esteem'd, I liv'd and died;
Whose writings the best rules to write could give;
Whose life the nobler science how to live.

THE FRIEND.
An EPISTLE to AARON HILL, Esq;
[Second version]

TEXTS: (1) *GM, 36, 673.
⠀⠀⠀⠀(2) LM, 36, 633-4.
(For the text of the first version see pp. 59-60).

Though RS's intimacy with Aaron Hill was cooling in the years preceding the revision of this poem in 1736, there had not been an estrange-
ment. The two men were in correspondence over RS's poem to the
Prince of Wales (1736), which turned into *Of Public Spirit* (1737).
Cf. Hill's letter to RS in the *Works of Aaron Hill* (2nd ed. 1754), I,
323-8, and his letter to Thomson, 20 May 1736, *ibid.* pp. 317-18.
RS attempted to renew the friendship. He rewrote *The Picture*, altering
his statement of opinion on aristocracy in order to conform more nearly
to Hill's views, and he rewrote *The Friend*.

O My lov'd HILL! O thou, by heav'n design'd,
⠀⠀To charm, to mend, and to adorn mankind!
To thee my hopes, fears, joys and sorrows tend,
Thou brother, father, nearer yet!—thou *friend*!
⠀⠀⠀⠀If worldly friendships oft cement, divide,⠀⠀⠀⠀⠀5
As interests vary, or as whims preside;
If leagues of lux'ry borrow friendship's light;
Or leagues, subversive of all social right:
Oh! say, my HILL, in what propitious sphere,
Gain we the *friend*, pure, knowing and sincere?⠀⠀⠀10

'Tis where the worthy, and the wise retire;
There wealth may learn its use, may love inspire;
There may young worth, the noblest end obtain,
In want may friends, in friends may knowledge gain;
In knowledge bliss; for wisdom virtue finds,   15
And brightens mortal to immortal minds.
Kind then my wrongs, if *love*, like *yours*, succeed!
For *you*, like *virtue*, are a *friend indeed*.

    Oft when you saw my youth, wild error, know,
Reproof, *soft-hinted*, taught the blush to glow.   20
Young and unform'd, you first my genius rais'd,
Just smil'd when faulty, and when mod'rate prais'd.
Me shun'd, me ruin'd (such a *mother*'s rage!)
You sung, 'till pity wept o'er ev'ry page.
You call'd my lays and wrongs to early fame;   25
Yet, yet th'*obdurate mother* felt no *shame*.
Pierc'd as I was! your counsel soften'd care,
To ease turn'd anguish, and to hope despair.
The man who never wound afflictive feels;
He never felt the balmy worth, that heals.   30
Welcome the wound, when blest with such relief!
For *deep* is felt the *friend*, when felt in *grief*.

    From you shall never, but with life, remove
Aspiring genius, condescending love.
When some, with cold, superior looks, redress,   35
Relief seems insult, and *confirms* distress;
You, when you view the man, with wrongs, besieg'd;
While warm you act th'obliger, seem th'oblig'd.

    All winning-mild to each of lowly state;
To equals free, unservile to the great;   40
Greatness you honour, when, by worth, acquir'd;
Worth is by worth in ev'ry rank admir'd.
Greatness you scorn, when titles insult speak;
Proud to vain pride, to honour'd meekness meek.

23–5 RS refers here to Hill's writing on his behalf in the *Plain Dealer*, especially
a poem which was sent to Mrs Brett. Cf. *AB*, pp. 71–4.
35 looks] look *LM*, 36.

That worthless bliss, which others court, you fly;   45
That worthy woe, they shun, attracts your eye.
    But shall the *muse* resound alone *your* praise?
No—let the *publick friend* exalt her lays!
Oh trace *that friend* with me!—he's yours!—he's mine!—
The world's!—beneficent behold him shine!   50
    Is *wealth* his *sphere?* if *riches*, like a tide,
From *either India*, pour their golden pride;
Rich in good works, him others' wants employ;
He gives the widow's heart to sing for joy.
To orphans, prisoners, shall his bounty flow;   55
The weeping family of want and woe.
    Is *knowledge* his? benevolently great,
In leisure active, and in care sedate;
What aid, his *little wealth* perchance denies,
In each *hard instance* his *advice* supplies.   60
With modest truth he sets the wand'ring right,
And gives *religion* pure, primæval light;
In love diffusive, as in light refin'd,
The lib'ral emblem of his maker's mind.
    Is *pow'r* his *orb?* he then like *pow'r divine*,   65
On all, though with a varied ray, will shine.
Ere pow'r was his, the man, he once caress'd,
Meets the same faithful smile, and mutual breast;
But asks his friend some dignity of state;
His friend, unequal to th'incumbent weight?   70
Asks it a stranger, one whom parts inspire
With all a people's welfare would require?
His choice admits no pause; his gift will prove
All private well absorb'd in publick love.
He shields *his country*, when, for aid she calls;   75
Or, should she fall, with her he greatly falls;
But (as proud *Rome*, with guilty conquest crown'd,
Spread slav'ry, death and desolation round)
Shou'd e'er *his country*, for *dominion's* prize,
Against the *sons* of *men* a *faction* rise,   80
Glory, in hers, is in his eye disgrace;

The *friend* of *truth*; the *friend* of *human race*.
Thus to no *one*, no *sect*, no *clime* confin'd,
His boundless love embraces *all mankind*;
And all their virtues in his life are known;   85
And all their joys and sorrows are his own.
These are the lights, where ſtands *that friend* confeſt;
This, this the spirit, which informs thy breaſt.
Through fortune's cloud thy genuine worth can shine;
What wou'dſt thou not, were wealth and greatness thine?   90

THE VOLUNTEER LAUREAT.
AN ODE
ON HER MAJESTY's BIRTH-DAY
NUMB. VI. for the YEAR 1737.
Continued annually by PERMISSION.

TEXTS: (1) *THE VOLUNTEER LAUREAT, etc.... [N.D.] (Printed on a
single folded half-sheet, without place or publisher's name.)
    (2) GM, 37, 114: 'The VOLUNTEER LAUREAT: *An ODE on
her* MAJESTY'S BIRTH-DAY', etc.

I

YE Guardian Pow'rs! that *Ether* rove;
    That breathe the vernal Soul of Love;
Bid Health descend in balmy Dews,
    And Life in ev'ry Gale diffuse;
That give the Flow'rs to shine, the Birds to sing;   5
Oh glad this Natal Day, the Prime of Spring!

II

The Virgin *Snow-drop* firſt appears;
Her Golden Head the *Crocus* rears.
The flow'ry Tribe, Profuse and Gay,
Spread to the soft, inviting Ray.   10
So Arts shall bloom by CAROLINA's Smile.
So shall her Fame waft Fragrance o'er the Isle.

---

1 YE Guardian Pow'rs!] YE *Spirits* bright, *GM*, 37.

III

The Warblers various, sweet and clear,
From bloomy Sprays, salute the Year.
O Muse, awake! ascend and sing!   15
Hail the fair Rival of the Spring!
To Woodland Honours Woodland Hymns belong;
To HER, the *Pride* of *Arts*! the Muse's Song.

IV

Kind, as of late her clement Sway,
The Season sheds a tepid Ray.   20
The Storms of Winter are no more;
The Storms of Faction cease to roar.
At vernal Suns as wint'ry Tempests cease,
SHE, lovely Pow'r! smiles Faction into Peace.

21 Winter are] *Boreas* rave *GM*, 37.

OF PUBLIC SPIRIT IN REGARD TO
PUBLIC WORKS. A POEM.
To His Royal Highness
FREDERICK, Prince of *WALES*.

TEXTS: First version: (1) *A POEM ON THE BIRTH-DAY OF THE Prince of *WALES*. Humbly Inscribed to HIS ROYAL HIGHNESS....[N.D.] (Published in January 1736, according to *LM*, 36, 52.)
Second version: (2) OF PUBLIC SPIRIT, etc., An EPISTLE, etc. ...M.DCC.XXXVII. (Published in June 1737, according to *GM*, 37, 374.)
(3) *OF PUBLIC SPIRIT..., A POEM,...The SECOND EDITION. M.DCC.XXXIX.

'I am sorry to hear,' wrote Aaron Hill in June 1736, 'that your poem, (for which I return you my thanks) has not yet found its way to *his* hands, in whose honour it was written; But possibly, it may be better (as you design it) under a different title, and a new publication since, the P——e might, perhaps, have look'd for more, on the subject, profess'd in the present title-page; whereas the world will be more immediately concern'd in, and pleas'd with those ideas of *public spirit*, and *magnificent*

219

purposes, which you have touch'd with great force, in that poem' (*Works of the late Aaron Hill* (2nd ed. 1754), I, 324). RS accordingly revised his poem and, a year later, published it under the new title. Only seventy-two copies of it were sold (*Account*, p. 397). Nevertheless a 'second edition' appeared in 1739, called into existence primarily for the purpose of restoring some lines on the Queen's gardens (ll. 79–86) that the author had cut out at the last minute. He also took the opportunity of making other revisions. These, however, are confined to the earlier part of the poem, because, of the six sheets comprising the book, only the first two needed to be reprinted, the remaining four evidently being taken from the unsold stock.

RS had long been interested in public works. Compare the lines on Industry in *Wanderer* I (ll. 270 ff.). Notice also that Horatio, one of the three rebels described in *Wanderer* V (ll. 541 ff.), sinned through excessive zeal for public welfare. Cf. C. A. Moore, 'Whig Panegyric Verse', *PMLA*, XLI (1926), 375–6, 394, and A. D. McKillop, *The Background of Thomson's 'Liberty'* (Houston, Texas, 1951).

[First Version]

CONTENTS

The Splendor of the Court, on this Occasion, just mentioned and declined. The Happiness of Liberty shewn by Industry and Peace (A Subject more worthy the Day) Their Works touch'd upon: In Gardening and Agriculture: In making Roads in Emulation of the old Romans: *In Reservoirs, and their Use: In draining Fens, and building Bridges, repairing Harbours, and stopping Inundations: In making Rivers Navigable: In planting for the noblest Uses: In Commerce: In publick Buildings. All the Labours of low Life, viz. Hospitals, Churches, and Colleges. The Variety of Worthies produc'd by the last. Thence a Transition to Persons in* Middle *and* High Life, *worthy the Honour of conversing with a* young Prince. *A short Remark on his late Majesty. The Conclusion, a View of the Expected Marriage of His Royal Highness.*

AWAKE, my Muse! awake! expand thy Wing!
Prompt as the Lark, awake, ascend, and sing!
Let some the Colours of the Ball unfold;

1–14 Compare second version, ll. 1–12.

Paint figur'd Silks, and Velvets stiff with Gold;
Of Spangles, Gems, and Stars, reflect the Rays;   5
Or to soft Minuets form their dancing Lays!
Sing thou of Liberty the Works and Worth!
A Theme, not foreign to a Prince's Birth.
Then view, great Sir! (to count what Muse can cease?)
The Works of Freedom, Industry, and Peace!   10
To count, what Time so just! What more serene,
Or strong to glance 'em, than the Sylvan Scene?
These, when O Muse, you see, or hope to see,
Praise where they *are*, and point where they *will* be.

    Unlike, where Tyranny the Rod maintains   15
O'er Turfless, Leafless, and Uncultur'd Plains;
Here Gardens call up Woods, and healthful Roots,
And, in due Season, give nectareous Fruits.
Along the Furrows yellow plenty shines;
On verdant Lawns, the Steed, or Ox, reclines;   20
Wild frisk the Flocks; which Fate has pleas'd to doom
Our Feast of Health, and Profits of the Loom.

    Who digs the Mine, or Quarry, digs with Glee;
No Slave!—His Option, and his Gain are free.
Him the same Laws, the same Protection yield,   25
Who ploughs the Furrow, as who owns the Field.

    Rough, honest, Industry, and smiling Peace,
Thus plant, thus build, and give the Land Encrease.
From peasant Hands, Imperial Works arise;
And *British* hence with *Roman* Grandeur vies.   30
Roads, yet unknown, through Rocks, shall winding tend,
And the safe Causeway, o'er the Clays, ascend.
From Reservoirs, the nether Pipe here owns
New, ductile Streams, to visit distant Towns.
There vanish Fens; whence Vapours rise no more;   35
Whose aguish Influence tainted Heav'n before.

15–22 *Compare second version,* ll. 49–56.
23–6 *Compare second version,* ll. 46–8.
27–32 *Compare second version,* ll. 91–108.
33–6 *Compare second version,* ll. 17–22.

Where Waters deep'ning glide, and wide extend,
From Road to Road, the Bridge her Arch shall bend.
Where Ports were choak'd; where Mounds, in vain, arose;
There Harbours open, and there Breaches close.   40
Rivers are taught a new, commercive Flow;
And young Plantations, future Navies, grow;
(Navies, which to invasive Foes explain,
Heav'n throws not round us Rocks and Seas in vain.)
The Sail of Commerce, in each Sky, aspires;   45
And Property assures what Toil acquires.
          See worthy Crafts, which low-born Life, divide,
Give Towns their Opulence, and Courts their Pride!
See Structures, rising from the healthy Soil,
For Sickness, Want, and Age, worn out with Toil!   50
Stupendous Piles (which useful Pomp compleats)
Here shine Religion's, and there Learning's Seats;
Where moral Truth, and mystic Science, spring;
The Sage to tutor, and the Bard to sing;
Where some draw Health from Herbs, and min'ral Veins; 55
And some form Systems from etherial Plains:
Where some from Hist'ry, call past Times to View;
And others trace old Laws, and sketch out new.
Hence saving Rights, by Legislators plann'd;
And Guardian Patriots hence inspire the Land;   60
These praise the Hour when your great Sire was born.
And these inflame to hail your natal Morn.
          When in familiar Scenes, you pleas'd appear,
The Modest and the Candid gain your Ear.
These, Sir, salute you from Life's middle State;   65
Rich without Gold, and without Titles great.
Knowledge of Books and Men exalts their Thought;
In Wit accomplish'd, though in Wiles untaught;
Careless of Whispers, meant to wound their Name;

37–40 Compare second version, ll. 23–32.
41–6 Compare second version, ll. 27–30, 39–44.
47–8 Compare second version, ll. 123–4.   49–50 Compare second version, ll. 111–14.
51–60 Compare second version, ll. 161–70.   65–88 Compare second version, ll. 320–38.

Nor sneer'd, nor brib'd, from Virtue into Shame.   *70*
In Letters elegant, in Honour bright;
They come, they catch, and they reflect Delight.

    Mixing with these, a *Few* of *Rank* are found;
For Councils, Embassies, and Camps, renown'd.
Vers'd in gay Life, in honest Maxims read;   *75*
And ever warm of Heart; yet cool of Head.
One, various Gallantry of Courts, relates;
And *One* the various Interests of States.
These tell of Characters grotesque and new;
And *Those* call *publick Spirit* full in View.   *80*
From intermingling Veins of Humour bright,
Flows Knowledge, soft'ning into Ease polite.

    Happy the Men, who such a Prince can please!
Happy the Prince, rever'd by Men, like these!
His Condescensions Dignity display;   *85*
Grave with the Wise, and with the Witty gay.
From these, the circling Glass gives Wit to shine;
The Bright grows brighter, and ev'n Courts refine.
In Scenes like these, shone the first GEORGE confest:
His smiling Grandeur, social Grace, express'd.   *90*
Look'd He on Foes? there loyal Love wou'd spring;
And still, when least assum'd, shone most the KING.

    Candour is yours, and yours transparent Truth:
Beauty will next attract accomplish'd Youth.
Oh!—Mark the White, Propitious Hour on Wing;   *95*
Which gives the Muse prophetick Strains to sing.
Blooming, she sees the *Fair* from *Princes* sprung;
Friends to *pure Faith*, when *Faith reform'd* was young!
A semblant *Progeny*, she next descries!
In them new Lights; to us new Joys arise;   *100*
But abler Bards, whom Zeal, like mine, shall fire,
Sublime shall sing, what humbler I admire.

93–102 These lines were not imitated in the second version. After many delays,
George II was finally persuaded to arrange a marriage for the Prince of Wales, whom
he detested. The bride was the Princess Augusta of Saxe Gotha, a Protestant, and
the wedding took place in September 1736.

[Second Version]

CONTENTS.

OF Reservoirs and their Use; Of draining Fens and building Bridges, cutting Canals, repairing Harbours and stopping Inundations, making Rivers navigable, building Light-Houses; Of Agriculture, Gardening; and planting for the noblest Uses; Of Commerce; Of public Roads; of public Buildings, *viz*. Squares, Streets, Mansions, Palaces, Courts of Justice, Senate-Houses, Theatres, Hospitals, Churches, Colleges; The variety of Worthies produced by the Latter; Of Colonies. The Slave Trade censured, *&c*.

GREAT *HOPE* of *BRITAIN*!—Here the *Muse* essays
A Theme, which, to attempt alone, is Praise.
Be *Hers* a Zeal of *Public Spirit* known!
A *Princely* Zeal!—a Spirit all your *Own*!
Where never Science beam'd a friendly Ray,   5
Where one vast Blank neglected Nature lay;
From *Public Spirit*, ceaseless there employ'd,
Creation varying glads the chearless Void.
The Arts, whence Safety, Treasure and Delight,
Bless Land and Sea, these Arts, O Muse, recite;   10
Once more to View the long-lost Wonders raise,
Display their Dignity, diffuse their Praise.
Let Those of Luxury, with These to vie,
Magnificently useless strike the Eye!
What though no Streams, in fruitless Pomp display'd,   15
Rise a proud Column, fall a grand Cascade;
Through secret Pipes, which nobler Use renowns,

7] From *Publick Spirit* there, by Arts employ'd, *1737*.
9–12 Hail Arts, where Safety, Treasure and Delight, / On Land, on Wave, in wond'rous Works unite! / Those wond'rous Works, O Muse, successive, raise, / And point their Worth, their Dignity and Praise! *1737*.
13–14] *Added 1739. Cf. ll. 99–102.*
15 in fruitless Pomp display'd] magnificently play'd *1737*
17 secret] nether *1737*

Here ductile Riv'lets visit distant Towns.
On Fens, where Pestilence, with poison'd Breath,
Tainted the Gale, and fill'd the Land with Death,   20
Now drain'd, the Grove ascends, the Harvest springs,
The Heifer grazes, and the Linnet sings.
Now, where the Flood deep rolls, or wide extends,
From Road to Road the Bridge connective bends;
O'er the broad Arch the Cars of Commerce go,   25
And fearless hear the Billows rage below.
Now the firm *Isthmus* sinks a wat'ry Space,
And wonders, in new State, at naval Grace;
While Commerce, check'd by Nature's Bars no more,
Steers, through the Land, a Course unknown before.   30
Now Harbours open, and, where Mounds were vain,
The bulwark Mole repels the boist'rous Main.
When the sunk Sun, no homeward Sail, befriends,
On the Rock's Brow the *Light-House* kind ascends,
And from the shoaly, o'er the gulphy Way,   35
Points to the Pilot's Eye the warning Ray.
    Count still, my Muse (to count what Muse can cease?)
The Works of *Public Spirit*, Freedom, Peace!
By them shall Plants, in Forests, reach the Skies;
Then lose their leafy Pride, and, Navies, rise: 40
Navies, which to invasive Foes explain,
Heav'n throws not round us Rocks and Seas in vain.
The Sail of Commerce, in each Sky, aspires,
And Property assures what Toil acquires.
    Who digs the Mine or Quarry, digs with Glee;   45

---

18 Here] Lo! *1737.*

19–32] Now vanish Fens, whence Vapours rise no more; / Whose aguish Influence
tainted Heav'n before. / The solid *Isthmus* sinks a watry Space, / And wonders, in
new State, at naval Grace. / Where the Flood, deep'ning, rolls, or wide extends, /
From Road to Road yon Arch, connective, bends. / Where Ports were choak'd; where
Mounds, in vain, arose; / There Harbours open, and there Breaches close. / To Keels,
obedient, spreads each liquid Plain, / And bulwark Moles repel the boist'rous Main.
1737.   *28* Cf. *The Wanderer*, 1, 288 and n.

34 The Eddystone lighthouse had been destroyed in a storm and rebuilt at the
beginning of the eighteenth century.

41–2] *Enclosed in parentheses 1737.*

Lord of himself, his Choice and Gain are free:
Him the same Laws, the same Protection, yield,
Who plows the Furrow, as who owns the Field.
     Unlike where Tyranny, the Rod, maintains
O'er turfless, leafless and uncultur'd Plains,   50
Here Herbs of Food and Physic, Plenty showers,
Gives Fruits to blush, and colours various Flowers.
Where Sands or stony Wilds once starv'd the Year,
Laughs the green Lawn, and nods the golden Ear.
White shine the fleecy Race, which Fate shall doom   55
The Feast of Life, the Treasure of the Loom.
     On Plains, now bare, shall Gardens wave their
               Groves,
While settling Songsters woo their feather'd Loves.
Where pathless Woods, no grateful Openings, knew,
Walks tempt the Step, and Vistoes court the View.   60
See the Parterre confess expansive Day!
The Grot, elusive of the noon-tide Ray!
Up yon green Slope a Length of Terras lies;
Whence gradual Landscapes fade in distant Skies.
Now the blue Lake, reflected Heav'n, displays;   65
Now darkens, regularly wild, the Maze.
Urns, Obelisks, Fanes, Statues intervene;
Now center, now commence or end the Scene.
Lo proud Alcoves! lo soft sequester'd Bowers!
Retreats of social, or of studious Hours!   70
Rank above Rank, here shapely Greens ascend;
There others, natively grotesque, depend.
The Rude, the Delicate immingled tell
How Art wou'd Nature, Nature Art excell,
And how, while these their rival Charms impart,   75
Art brightens Nature, Nature brightens Art;
Thus blends the various yet harmonious Space,
And All is Symmetry, and Force, and Grace.

46] No Slave!—His Option and his Gain are free: *1737*.
77–8] Thus in the various, yet harmonious, Space, / Blend Order, Symmetry, and
Force, and Grace. *1737*.

But what the flow'ring Pride of Gardens rare,
However royal, or however fair?   *80*
If Doors, which to Access should ſtill give Way,
Ope but like *Peter*'s Paradise for Pay;
If perquisited Varlets frequent ſtand
And each new Walk muſt a new Tax demand,
What foreign Eye but with Contempt surveys?   *85*
What Muse shall from Oblivion snatch their Praise?
    When these from *Public Spirit* smile, we see
Free-opening Gates, and bow'ry Pleasures free;
For sure great Souls, one Truth, can never miss;
Bliss not communicated is not Bliss.   *90*
    Thus *Public Spirit*, Liberty and Peace
Carve, build, and plant, and give the Land Increase;
From peasant Hands imperial Works arise,
And *British* hence with *Roman* Grandeur vies;
Not Grandeur, that in pompous Whim appears;   *95*
That levels Hills; that Vales to Mountains rears;
That alters Nature's regulated Grace;
Meaning to deck, but deſtin'd to deface.
Here let no Forts some native Tyrant aid,
To awe the Free!—should foreign Foes invade;   *100*
How useless these, where Rocks a Barrier lend,
Where Seas encircle, and where Fleets defend[!]
Here let no Arch of Triumph be assign'd
To laurel'd Pride, whose Sword has thin'd Mankind;
Though no vaſt Wall extend from Coaſt to Coaſt,   *105*
No Pyramid aspire, sublimely loſt;
Yet the safe Road through Rocks shall, winding, tend,
And the firm Cause-way o'er the Clays ascend;
Here ſtately Streets, here ample Squares invite

79–86] *These lines were omitted in 1737. See headnote.*
99–102] Though no proud *Gates*, with *China*'s taught to vie, / Magnificently useless,
strike the Eye; / (Useless, where Rocks a surer Barrier lend, / Where Seas encircle,
and where Fleets defend) *1737. Cf. l. 14.*
103] What though no *Arch* of *Triumph* is assign'd *1737.*
105 extend] extends *1737.*   *106* aspire] aspires *1737.*
109 Here...here] Lo!...lo! *1737.*

The salutary Gale, that breath[e]s Delight.   *110*
Here Structures mark the charitable Soil,
For casual Ill; maim'd Valour; feeble Toil,
Worn out with Care, Infirmity and Age;
The Life here ent'ring, quitting there the Stage:
The Babe of lawless Birth, condemn'd to moan;   *115*
To starve, or bleed, for Errors not his own!
Let the frail Mother scape the Fame defil'd,
If from the murd'ring Mother scape the Child!
Oh, guard his Youth from Sin's alluring Voice;
From Deeds of dire Necessity, not Choice!   *120*
His grateful Hand, thus never harmful known,
Shall, on the public Welfare, build his own.

      Thus worthy Crafts which low-born Life divide,
Give Towns their Opulence, and Courts their Pride.
Sacred to Pleasure Structures rise elate;   *125*
To That still worthy of the Wise and Great.
Sacred to Pleasure then shall Piles ascend?
They shall—When Pleasure and Instruction blend.
Let *Theatres*, from *Publick Spirit*, shine!
Such *Theatres*, as, *Athens*, once were thine!   *130*
See! the *gay Muse*, of pointed Wit possest,
Who wakes the virtuous Laugh, the decent Jest:
What, though she mock? she mocks with honest Aim,
And laughs each fav'rite Folly into Shame.
With lib'ral Light the *Tragic* charms the Age: *135*
In solemn-training Robes she fills the Stage;
There human Nature, mark'd in diff'rent Lines,
Alive, in Character, distinctly shines.
Quick Passions change, alternate, on her Face;
Her Diction, Music; as her Action, Grace.   *140*
Instant we catch her *Terror-giving* Cares,
Pathetic Sighs, and *Pity-moving* Tears;

---

111 Here] Lo! *1737.*   115 condemn'd] doom'd else *1737.*
135–44 In his Advertisement to *Sir Thomas Overbury* (1724), RS said that he had
intended prefixing an essay on tragedy. These lines possibly give the substance of
what he would have written then.

Instant we catch her gen'rous Glow of Soul,
'Till one great striking Moral crowns the Whole.
   Hence in warm Youth, by Scenes of Virtue taught,   *145*
Honour exalts, and Love expands the Thought;
Hence Pity, to peculiar Grief assign'd,
Grows wide Benevolence to all Mankind.
   Where various *Edifice*, the Land, renowns,
There *Publick Spirit* plans, exalts and crowns.   *150*
She chears the *Mansion* with the spacious *Hall*;
Bids Painting live along the storied Wall;
Seated, she, smiling, eyes th' unclosing Door,
And much she welcomes all, but most the Poor.
She turns the *Pillar*, or the *Arch* she bends;   *155*
The *Quire* she lengthens, or the *Quire* extends;
She rears the *Tow'r*, whose Height the Heav'ns admire;
She rears, she rounds, she points the less'ning *Spire*;
At her Command the *College-roofs* ascend;
For *Publick Spirit* still is *Learning*'s Friend.   *160*
Stupendous Piles, which useful Pomp compleats,
Thus rise *Religion*'s, and thus *Learning*'s Seats:
There moral Truth and holy Science spring,
And give the Sage to teach, the Bard to sing.
There some draw Health from Herbs and min'ral Veins,   *165*
Some search the Systems of the heavenly Plains;
Some call from History past Times to View,
And Others trace old Laws, and sketch out new;
Thence saving Rights, by Legislators, plann'd,
And guardian Patriots thence inspire the Land.   *170*
   Now grant, ye Pow'rs, one great, one fond Desire,
And, granting, bid a new *White-Hall* aspire!
Far let it lead, by well pleas'd *Thames* survey'd,
The swelling Arch and stately Colonnade;
Bid Courts of Justice, Senate-chambers join,   *175*
Till various All in one proud Work combine!
   But now be all the *gen'rous Goddess* seen,
When most diffus'd she shines, and most benign!
Ye sons of Misery attract her View!

Ye sallow, hollow-ey'd and meagre Crew!   *180*
Such high Perfection have our Arts attain'd,
That now few Sons of Toil our Arts demand?
Then to the Publick, to it self, we fear,
Ev'n willing Industry grows useless here.
Are we too populous at length confess'd,   *185*
From confluent Strangers refug'd and redress'd?
Has War so long withdrawn his barb'rous Train,
That Peace o'erstocks us with the Sons of Men?
So long has Plague left pure the ambient Air,
That Want must prey on those, Disease wou'd spare? *190*
Hence beauteous Wretches, (Beauty's foul Disgrace!)
Though born the Pride, the Shame of human Race;
Fair Wretches hence, who nightly Streets annoy,
Live but themselves and others to destroy.
Hence Robbers rise, to Theft, to Murder prone,   *195*
First driv'n by Want, from Habit desp'rate grown;
Hence for ow'd Trifles oft our Jayls contain
(Torn from Mankind) a miserable Train;
Torn from, in spite of Nature's tend'rest Cries,
Parental, filial and connubial Ties;   *200*
The Trader, when on ev'ry Side distrest,
Hence flies to what Expedient Frauds suggest;
To prop his question'd Credit's tott'ring State,
Others he first involves, to share his Fate;
Then for mean Refuge must, self-exil'd, roam;   *205*
Never to hope a Friend, nor find a Home.
    This *Publick Spirit* sees, she sees and feels!
Her Breast the Throb, her Eye the Tear reveals;
(The Patriot Throb that beats, the Tear that flows
For others' Welfare, and for others' Woes).   *210*
'And what can I (she said) to cure their Grief?
'Shall I or point out Death, or point Relief?
'Forth shall I lead 'em to some happier Soil,
'To Conquest lead 'em, and enrich with Spoil?
'Bid 'em convulse a World, make Nature groan,   *215*
'And spill in shedding others' Blood their own?

'No, no—such Wars do thou, *Ambition*, wage!
'Go sterilize the Fertile with thy Rage!
'Whole Nations to depopulate is thine;
'To people, culture and protect, be mine!   220
'Then range the World, *Discov'ry*!' Strait He goes
O'er Seas, o'er *Libya*'s Sands and *Zembla*'s Snows;
He settles where kind Rays till now have smil'd
(Vain Smile!) on some luxuriant houseless Wild.
How many Sons of Want might here enjoy   225
What Nature gives for Age but to destroy?
'Blush, blush, O *Sun* (she cries) here vainly found,
'To rise, to set, to roll the Seasons round!
'Shall Heav'n distill in Dews, descend in Rain,
'From Earth gush Fountains, Rivers flow in vain?   230
'There shall the *watry Lives* in Myriads stray,
'And be, to be alone each other's Prey?
'Unsought shall here the teeming Quarries own
'The various Species of mechanic Stone?
'From Structure This, from Sculpture That confine?   235
'Shall Rocks forbid the latent Gem to shine?
'Shall Mines, obedient, aid no Artist's Care,
'Nor give the martial Sword and peaceful Share?
'Ah! shall they never precious Ore unfold,
'To smile in Silver, or to flame in Gold?   240
'Shall here the vegetable World alone,
'For Joys, for various Virtues rest unknown?
'While Food and Physick, Plants and Herbs supply,
'Here must they shoot alone to bloom and die?
'Shall Fruits, which none, but brutal Eyes, survey,   245
'Untouch'd grow ripe, untasted drop away?
'Shall here th'irrational, the salvage Kind
'Lord it o'er Stores by Heav'n for Man design'd,
'And trample what mild Suns benignly raise,
'While Man must lose the Use, and Heav'n the Praise?   250
'Shall it then be?' (Indignant here she rose,
Indignant, yet humane her Bosom glows)
'No! By each honour'd *Grecian Roman* Name,

231

'By Men for Virtue deified by Fame,
'Who peopled Lands, who model'd infant State,   255
'And then bade Empire be maturely Great,
'By *These* I swear (be witness Earth and Skies!)
'Fair Order here shall from Confusion rise.
'Rapt I a future Colony survey!
'Come then, ye Sons of Mis'ry! come away!   260
'Let Those, whose Sorrows from Neglect are known,
'(Here taught[,] compell'd[,] empower'd) Neglect atone!
'Let Those enjoy, who never merit Woes,
'In Youth th'industrious Wish, in Age Repose!
'Allotted Acres (no reluctant Soil)   265
'Shall prompt their Industry, and pay their Toil.
'Let Families, long Strangers to Delight,
'Whom wayward Fate dispers'd, by Me unite;
'Here live enjoying Life, see Plenty, Peace;
'Their Lands encreasing as their Sons encrease!   270
'As Nature yet is found in leafy Glades
'To intermix the Walks with Lights and Shades;
'Or as with Good and Ill, in chequer'd Strife,
'Various the Goddess colours human Life;
'So in this fertile Clime if yet are seen   275
'Moors, Marshes, Cliffs by turns to intervene;
'Where Cliffs, Moors, Marshes desolate the View,
'Where haunts the Bittern, and where screams the Mew;
'Where prowls the Wolf, where roll'd the Serpent lies,
'Shall solemn Fanes and Halls of Justice rise,   280
'And Towns shall open (all of Structure fair!)
'To bright'ning Prospects, and to purest Air,
'Frequented Ports and Vineyards green succeed,
'And Flocks encreasing whiten all the Mead,
'On Science Science, Arts on Arts refine;   285
'On these from high all Heav'n shall smiling shine,
'And *Publick Spirit* here a People show,
'Free[,] num'rous[,] pleas'd and busy all below.

---

259 Johnson praised the originality and worth of this passage on colonization
(*Account*, p. 393).

'Learn future Natives of this promis'd Land
'What your Forefathers ow'd my saving Hand!   *290*
'Learn when *Despair* such sudden Bliss shall see,
'Such Bliss must shine from *OGLETHORPE* or *ME*!
'Do You the neighb'ring blameless *Indian* aid,
'Culture what he neglects, not His invade;
'Dare not, oh dare not, with ambitious View,   *295*
'Force or demand Subjection, never due.
'Let by *My* specious Name no *Tyrants* rise,
'And cry, while they enslave, they civilize!
'Know *LIBERTY* and *I* are still the *same*,
'Congenial!—ever mingling Flame with Flame!   *300*
'Why must I *Afric*'s sable Children see
'Vended for Slaves, though form'd by Nature free,
'The nameless Tortures cruel Minds invent,
'Those to subject, whom Nature equal meant?
'If these you dare, albeit unjust Success   *305*
'Empow'rs you now unpunish'd to oppress,
'Revolving Empire you and yours may doom,
'(*Rome* all subdued, yet *Vandals* vanquish'd *Rome*)
'Yes, Empire may revolve, give Them the Day,
'And Yoke may Yoke, and Blood may Blood repay.'   *310*
      Thus (Ah! how far unequal'd by *my* Lays,
Unskill'd the Heart to melt or Mind to raise.)
Sublime[,] benevolent[,] deep[,] sweetly clear,
Worthy a Thomson's Muse, a Fred'rick's Ear,
Thus spoke the *Goddess*. Thus I faintly tell   *315*
In what lov'd Works Heav'n gives her to excell.
But who her Sons, that to her Int'rest true,
Conversant lead her to a Prince like you?
These, Sir, salute you from Life's *middle* State,
Rich without Gold and without Titles great: *320*
Knowledge of Books and Men exalts their Thought,
In Wit accomplish'd though in Wiles untaught,

301–10 According to C. A. Moore (p. 394), this is the first protest made in verse against negro slavery, except for a brief allusion in Thomson's *Summer*.
314 James Thomson's *Liberty* was also dedicated to the Prince of Wales.

Careless of Whispers meant to wound their Name,
Nor sneer'd nor brib'd from Virtue into Shame;
In Letters elegant, in Honour bright,   *325*
They come[,] they catch[,] and they reflect Delight.
        Mixing with these a *few* of *Rank* are found,
For Councils, Embassies and Camps renown'd.
Vers'd in gay Life, in honest Maxims read;
And ever warm of Heart, yet cool of Head.   *330*
From these the circling Glass gives Wit to shine,
The Bright grow brighter, and ev'n Courts refine;
From These so gifted[,] candid and upright,
Flows Knowledge soft'ning into Ease polite.
        Happy the Men, who such a Prince can please!   *335*
Happy the Prince rever'd by Men like These!
His Condescensions Dignity display,
Grave with the Wise and with the Witty gay;
For Him fine Marble in the Quarry lies,
Which in due Statues to his Fame shall rise,   *340*
Ever shall *Publick Spirit* beam his Praise,
And the *Muse* swell it in immortal Lays.

VOLUNTEER LAUREAT,
NUMBER VII. For the First of *March*, 1738.
A POEM Sacred to the Memory of the late QUEEN.
Humbly address'd to his MAJESTY.

TEXTS: (1) *VOLUNTEER LAUREAT, etc.... MDCCXXXVIII.
  (2) *Old Whig: Or, the Consistent Protestant*, no. 157, 9 March 1738.
  (3) *GM*, 38, 154.

Queen Caroline died 20 November 1737, but RS did not learn that
his pension was to be discontinued until late in the following summer,
when he wrote to Thomas Birch on 1 September 1738 as follows: 'I
take this opportunity of letting you know y't I am struck out (& am
y'e only Person struck out) of y'e Late Queen's List of Pensions'
(MS Sloane 4318, f. 46 (British Museum)). *The Volunteer Laureat*, No. 7,
was a part of a campaign to appeal to the king for the restoration of his

pension. It was followed up in the next number of the *Gentleman's Magazine* (April) by a reprinting of the text of *Volunteer Laureat, No. 1*, with a prefatory note making another pointed appeal to the king. See headnote to *Volunteer Laureat, No. 1*.

OFT has the MUSE, on this distinguish'd Day,
  Tun'd to glad Harmony the vernal Lay;
But, O lamented Change! the Lay must flow
From grateful Rapture now to grateful Woe.
She, to this Day who joyous Lustre gave,   5
Descends for ever to the silent Grave.
She born at once to charm us and to mend;
Of human Race the Pattern and the Friend.
To be or fondly or severely kind,
To check the rash or prompt the better Mind,   10
Parents shall learn from HER, and thus shall draw
From filial Love alone a filial Awe.
Who seek in Av'rice Wisdom's Art to save;
Who often squander, yet who never gave;
From Her These know the righteous *Mean* to find;   15
And the mild Virtue stole on half Mankind.
The Lavish now caught frugal Wisdom's Lore;
Yet still, the more they sav'd, bestow'd the more.
Now Misers learn'd at others' Woes to melt,
And saw and wonder'd at the Change they felt.   20
The Gen'rous, when on HER they turn'd their View,
The Gen'rous ev'n themselves more gen'rous grew,
Learn'd the shun'd Haunts of shame-fac'd Want to
      trace;
To Goodness Delicacy adding Grace.
The conscious Cheek no rising Blush confess'd,   25
Nor dwelt one Thought to pain the modest Breast;
Kind and more kind did thus her Bounty shower,
And knew no Limit, but a bounded Power.
This Truth the Widow's Sighs, alas! proclaim;
For this the Orphan's Tears embalm her Fame.   30
The Wise beheld Her Learning's Summit gain;
Yet never giddy grow, nor ever vain;

But on one Science point a stedfast Eye;
That Science, how to live and how to die.
     SAY, MEMORY, while to thy grateful Sight   *35*
Arise her Virtues in unfading Light,
What Joys were ours, what Sorrows now remain:
Ah! how sublime the Bliss! how deep the Pain!
     AND, Thou, bright PRINCESS, seated now on
       High,
Next One, the fairest Daughter of the Sky,   *40*
Whose warm-felt Love is to all Beings known,
Thy Sister CHARITY! next Her thy Throne;
See at thy Tomb the Virtues weeping lye!
There in dumb Sorrow seem the Arts to die.
So were the SUN o'er other Orbs to blaze,   *45*
And from our World, like Thee, withdraw his Rays,
No more to visit where he warm'd before,
All Life must cease, and Nature be no more.
Yet shall the MUSE a heav'nly Height essay
Beyond the Weakness mix'd with mortal Clay;   *50*
Beyond the Loss, which, though she bleeds to see,
Though ne'er to be redeem'd, the Loss of Thee;
Beyond ev'n This, she hails with joyous Lay,
Thy better Birth, thy first true Natal Day;
A Day, that sees Thee born, beyond the Tomb,   *55*
To endless Health, to Youth's eternal Bloom;
Born to the mighty Dead, the Souls sublime
Of ev'ry famous Age, and ev'ry Clime;
To Goodness fix'd by Truth's unvarying Laws;
To Bliss that knows no Period, knows no Pause—   *60*
Save when thine Eye, from yonder pure Serene,
Sheds a soft Ray on this our gloomy Scene.
     WITH Me now Liberty and Learning mourn,
From all Relief, like thy lov'd CONSORT, torn;
For where can PRINCE or PEOPLE hope Relief,   *65*
When each contend to be supreme in GRIEF?
So vy'd thy Virtues, that could point the Way,
So well to govern; yet so well obey.

DEIGN one Look more! Ah! see thy CONSORT dear
Wishing all Hearts, except his OWN, to chear.   *70*
Lo! ſtill he bids thy wonted Bounty flow
To weeping Families of Worth and Woe.
He ſtops all Tears, however faſt they rise,
Save Those, that ſtill muſt fall from grateful Eyes,
And spite of Griefs, that so usurp his Mind,   *75*
Still watches o'er the Welfare of Mankind.
    FATHER of Those, whose Rights thy Care defends,
Still moſt their own, when moſt their Sovereign's
      Friends;
Then chiefly brave, from Bondage chiefly free,
When moſt they truſt, when moſt they copy Thee;   *80*
Ah! let the loweſt of thy SUBJECTS pay
His honeſt heart-felt tributary Lay;
In Anguish happy, if permitted here,
One Sigh to vent, to drop one virtuous TEAR;
Happier, if pardon'd, should HE wildly moan,   *85*
And with a Monarch's Sorrow *mix his* Own.

71–2 George II ordered that all of Queen Caroline's pensions and other charitable
contributions be continued after her death. RS was the only one deprived.

75 Griefs, that so usurp] Grief, that so usurps *Old Whig*.

E Græco RUF.

TEXTS: (1) *GM*, 40, 567.
    (2) *LM*, 41, 565.

These lines are a fantasia composed on a theme by George Buchanan,
who was in turn translating the Greek of the obscure Byzantine poet
Rufinus. Buchanan's poem is no. 30 in his *Liber Primus Epigrammatum*.
That of Rufinus is no. 94 in *Epigrammatum Anthologia Palatina*.

> *Qui te videt beatus eſt,*
> *Beatior qui te audiet,*
> *Qui basiat semideus eſt,*
> *Qui te potitur eſt Deus.*   BUCHANAN

> *The foregoing Lines paraphras'd.*

I

H Appy the Man; who, in thy sparkling eyes
His am'rous wishes, sees, reflecting, play;
Sees little laughing *Cupids*, glancing, rise,
And, in soft-swimming languor, die away.

II

Still happier he! to whom thy meanings roll   5
In sounds; which love, harmonious love, inspire;
On his charm'd ear sits, rapt, his list'ning soul;
'Till admiration form intense desire.

III

Half deity is he who warm may press
Thy lip, soft-swelling to the kindling kiss;   10
Ah, may that lip, assentive warmth, express;
'Till love draw willing love to ardent bliss!

IV

Circling thy waiſt, and circled in thy arms;
Who, melting on thy mutual-melting breaſt,
Entranc'd enjoys love's whole luxurious charms,   15
Is all a God!—Is of all *Heav'n* posseſt.

On FALSE HISTORIANS.
A SATIRE.

TEXTS: (1) *GM*, 41, 491–2.
  (2) *LM*, 41, 510–11.

The germ of *On False Historians* is contained in *The Authors of the Town*
(1725), from which the author borrowed several lines. According to
Johnson, it is a fragment of an 'Epistle upon Authors', of which
only one other part—*A Character*—was published. The 'Epistle', in
fact, may have been only a rewritten and enlarged *Authors of the Town*,
and the revision must have been made about 1735, shortly after the
Progress of a Divine, because *A Character* alludes to the prosecution for

obscenity which resulted from the publication of that poem. Moreover, the tribute to Lord Bolingbroke in *On False Historians* connects the poem in time with RS's persistent support of his Lordship about 1735 (*Account*, pp. 385, 392).

Originally the poem also contained a tribute to RS's friend, Thomas Birch, to whom he dispatched the whole MS of the 'Epistles upon Authors' to be forwarded for publication to the *Gentleman's Magazine* (Sloane MS 4318, f. 49—undated, perhaps 1738–9 (British Museum)). This is the last contact that we know of between RS and Birch, and they may have quarrelled over this poem:

'But of all plagues, wth which dull prose is curst,
Sure from y'e false Historian comes y'e worst.
Is there of genius one ne'er partial seen,
Thrô Fancy, thrô Affection, or thrô Spleen;
Whose aim quite honest, whose discernment clear,
To Truth can, twixt contending parties, steer;
Nor splits [strikes] on this, or that, in state, or Church?
Lives such a Man? There does—read candid *Birch*!
      While worthy pens, like his, &c.'

Cf. headnote to *The Authors of the Town*.

In this edition the text found in the *London Magazine* has been given, mainly because of the reading of line 100. Otherwise there are no variants worth recording.

S URE, of all plagues with which dull prose is curst,
  Scandals from *false historians* spot the worst:
In quest of *these* the *Muse* shall first advance,
Bold to explore the *regions* of *romance*:
Romance call'd *hist'ry*.—Lo! at once she skims   5
The visionary world of monkish whims;
Where fallacy in legends wildly shines,
And vengeance glares from violated shrines;
Where saints perform all tricks, and startle thought
With many a miracle, that ne'er was wrought;   10
Saints that ne'er liv'd, or such as justice paints
Jugglers, on superstition palm'd for saints.
Here *canoniz'd*, let *creed-mongers* be shown
Red-letter'd saints, and *red assassins* known;
While those they martyr'd, such as angels rose!   15

---

8 Cf. *The Authors of the Town*, l. 64.

All, black-enroll'd among religion's foes,
Snatch'd by sulphureous clouds, a *lye* proclaims,
Number'd with fiends, and plung'd in endless flames.
    Hiſt'ry from air or deep draws many a *ſprite*,
Such as from *nurse* or *prieſt* might *boys* affright;   20
Or such as but o'er fev'rish slumbers fly,
And fix in melancholy *frenzy*'s eye.
Now meteors make enthusiaſt *wonder* ſtare,
And image wild portentous wars in air!
Seers fall intranc'd! Some *wizard*'s lawless skill   25
Now whirls, now fetters nature's works at will!
Thus *hiſt'ry* by *machine* mock *epic* seems,
Not from *poetic*, but from *monkish* dreams.
    The *dev'l*, who *prieſt* and *sorc'rer* muſt obey,
The *sorc'rer* us'd to raise, the *parson* lay;   30
When *Eachard* wav'd his pen, the *hiſt'ry* shows,
The *parson* conjur'd, and the *fiend* uprose.
A camp at diſtance, and the scene a wood,
Here enter'd *Noll*, and there old *Satan* ſtood.
No tail his rump, his foot no hoof reveal'd;   35
Like a wise cuckold with his horns conceal'd:
Not a gay serpent glitt'ring to the eye;
But more than serpent, or than harlot sly:
For *lawyer*-like, a *fiend* no wit can 'scape,
The *dæmon* ſtands confeſt in *proper shape*!   40
Now spreads his parchment, now is sign'd the scroll;
Thus *Noll* gains empire, and the *dev'l* has *Noll*.
    Wond'rous hiſtorian! thus account for evil,
And thus for its success—'tis all the devil:
Though ne'er *that* devil we saw, yet *one* we see,   45
One of an *author* sure, and—*thou* art *he*.
    But dusky phantoms, Muse, no more pursue!
Now clearer objeċts open—yet untrue.

23–6 Contrast *Britannia's Miseries*, ll. 13 n. and 125–8.
  31–42 Rev. Laurence Echard, *History of England* (1718), II, 712–13, tells a tale about Oliver Cromwell's selling his soul to the devil in return for victory at the Battle of Worcester.

Awful the genuine historian's name!
False ones—with what materials build they fame?   50
Fabricks of fame, by dirty means made good;
As nests of martins are compil'd of mud:
Peace be with *Curll*—with him I wave all strife,
Who pens each *felon*'s and each *actor*'s life;
Biography that cooks the devil's martyrs,   55
And lards with luscious rapes the cheats of *Charters*.
          Materials, which belief in *Gazettes* claim,
Loose-strung, run jingling into hist'ry's name.
Thick as *Egyptian* clouds of raining flies;
As thick as worms, where man corrupting lies;   60
As pests obscene, that haunt the ruin'd pile;
As monsters flound'ring in the muddy *Nile*;
Minutes, memoirs, views and reviews appear,
Where slander darkens each recorded year.
In a past reign is feign'd some am'rous league;   65
Some ring or letter now reveals th' intrigue;
Queens with their minions work unseemly things,
And boys grow dukes, when catamites to kings.
Does a prince die? what poisons they surmise?
No royal mortal sure by nature dies.   70
Is a prince born? what birth more base believ'd?
Or, what's more strange, his mother ne'er conceiv'd!
Thus slander popular o'er truth prevails,
And easy minds imbibe romantick tales.
Thus, 'stead of history, such authors raise   75
Mere, crude, wild *novels* of bad hints for *plays*.
          Some usurp names.—An *English garrateer*,

63-4 Cf. *The Authors of the Town*, ll. 49-50.
65-6 Cf. *The Authors of the Town*, ll. 55-6.
67-8 Cf. *The Authors of the Town*, ll. 61-2.
69-70 Cf. *The Authors of the Town*, ll. 51-2.

71-2 This is a reference to the legend that the so-called James III was a supposititious child who had been conveyed into the queen's bed in a warming pan. In his life of Marlborough (*General Dictionary*, VII, 451) Birch alludes to 'the Queen's pretended labour'.

77-8 In 1711 M. Mesnager negotiated for peace with the British government on behalf of Louis XIV. A volume entitled *Minutes of the Negotiations of Monsr. Mesnager*

From *minutes* forg'd, is monsieur *Menager*.*
    Some, while on good or ill success they stare,
Give conduct a complexion dark or fair.   *80*
Others, as little to enquiry prone,
Account for actions, though their springs unknown.
    One *statesman* vices has, and virtues too;
Hence will contested characters ensue.
View but the black he's fiend, the bright but scan, *85*
He's angel. View him all—he's still a man:
But such historians all accuse, acquit;
No virtue these, and those no vice admit;
For either in a friend no fault will know,
And neither own a virtue in a foe.   *90*
    Where *hear-say knowledge* sits on publick names,
And bold *conjecture* or extols or blames,
Spring *party libels*; from whose ashes dead,
A *monster*, misnam'd *hist'ry*, lifts its head.
Contending factions croud to hear its roar!   *95*
But, when once heard, it dies to noise no more.
From these no answer, no applause from those,
O'er half they simper, and o'er half they doze.
So when in senate, with egregious pate,
Perks up Sir *Billy* in some deep debate,   *100*
He hems, looks wise, tunes thin his lab'ring throat,
To prove black white, postpone or palm the vote;
In sly contempt, some, *hear him! hear him!* cry;
Some yawn, some sneer; none second, none reply.
    But dare such miscreants now rush abroad,   *105*

* *The* Minutes *of Monsieur* Menager, *a Book calculated to vilify the Administration in the four last Years of Q. Ann's Reign. The truth is, that this Libel was not written by Mr.* Menager, *neither was any such Book ever printed in the* French *Tongue; from which it is impudently said in the Title Page to be translated.* [RS]

was published in 1717, just before Harley's trial, and was found to be favourable to Harley. But Defoe was widely suspected of being the real author. James Sutherland, *Defoe* (1937), pp. 218–20 and John Robert Moore, *Daniel Defoe* (Chicago, 1958), p. 259.
84 characters] character *LM*, 41.
100 Sir *Billy*] sir —— *GM*, 41. Sir Billy is probably Sir William Yonge.
102 palm. Influence as by bribery or trickery.

By blanket, cane, pump, pillory unaw'd?
Dare they imp falshood thus and plume her wings,
From present charaɛters and recent things?
Yes what untruths? or truths in what disguise?
What *Boyers* and what *Oldmixons* arise?   110
What *faɛts* from all but *them* and *slander* screen'd?
Here meets a *council*, no where else conven'd.
There from *originals* come, thick as spawn,
Letters ne'er wrote, *memorials* never drawn;
To *secret conf'rence* never held they yoke,   115
Treaties ne'er plan'd, and *speeches* never spoke.
From, *Oldmixon*, thy brow, too well we know,
Like *sin* from *Satan*'s, far and wide they go.
        In vain may *St. John* safe in conscience sit,
In vain with truth confute, contemn with wit;   120
Confute, contemn amid seleɛted friends;
There sinks the juſtice, there the satire ends.
Here, though a *cent'ry* scarce such leaves unclose,
From mold and duſt the slander sacred grows.
Now none reply where all despise the page;   125
But will dumb scorn deceive no future age?
Then, should dull periods cloud not seeming faɛt,
Will no fine pen th' unanswer'd lye extraɛt?
Well-set in plan, and polish'd into ſtile,
Fair, and more fair, may finish'd fraud beguile;   130
By ev'ry language snatch'd, by time receiv'd,
In ev'ry clime, by ev'ry age believ'd.
How vain to virtue truſt the great their name,
When such their lot for infamy or fame?

A CHARACTER.

TEXTS: (1) *GM*, 41, 494.
    (2) *LM*, 41, 409.

According to Johnson, Philip Yorke presided over the court when RS
was tried for obscenity in *The Progress of a Divine*, and dismissed the

case 'with encomiums upon the purity and excellence of Mr Savage's writings' (*Account*, pp. 389–90). For contrast RS introduced a character of Francis Page, the judge who had pronounced sentence of death on him for murder in 1727.

This poem may have been written before William Fortescue became a justice of the common pleas in 1738, but if so it must have been revised afterwards (see l. 8 and n.). Johnson described this satire as part of 'An Epistle on Authors' (*Account*, p. 355 n. 3). Cf. *On False Historians*.

FAir *Truth*, in Courts where *Justice* should preside,
Alike the *Judge* and *Advocate* would guide;
And these would vie each dubious Point to clear,
To stop the Widow's and the Orphan's Tear;
Were all like *YORK*, of delicate Address,   5
Strength to discern, and Sweetness to express;
Learn'd, just, polite, born ev'ry Heart to gain;
Like *Cummins* mild, like *Fortescue* humane;
All eloquent of Truth, divinely known;
So deep, so clear, all Science is his own.   10
    Of Heart impure, and impotent of Head,
In Hist'ry, Rhet'ric, Ethicks, Law, unread;
How far unlike such *Worthies*, once a *Drudge*,
From flound'ring in *low Cases*, rose a *JUDGE*.
Form'd to make *Pleaders* laugh, his *Nonsense* thunders, 15
And, on *low Juries*, breathes contagious Blunders.
His *Brothers* blush, because no Blush he knows;
Nor e'er '*one uncorrupted Finger shows*'.
See, drunk with pow'r, the *Circuit Lord* exprest!
Full, in his Eye, his *Betters* stand confest;   20
Whose Wealth, Birth, Virtue, from a Tongue so loose,
'Scape not provincial, vile, buffoon Abuse.
Still to what Circuit is assign'd his Name,
There, swift before him, flies the Warner *Fame*.

* *The Hon*. William Fortescue *Esq; one of the* Justices *of his* Majesty's *Court of* Common Pleas. [RS]

18 The line is from a poem by Philip, Duke of Wharton, called 'On the Bishops and Judges'. *The New Foundling Hospital for Wit* (1786), I, 224: 'When *Page* one uncorrupted Finger shows.'

Contest stops short, Consent yields ev'ry Cause   25
To Cost, Delay, endures 'em, and withdraws.
But how 'scape *Pris'ners*? To their Trial chain'd,
All, all shall stand condemn'd, who stand arraign'd.
Dire *Guilt*, which else would Detestation cause,
Pre-judg'd with Insult, wond'rous Pity draws.   30
But 'scapes ev'n *Innocence* his harsh Harangue?
Alas!—ev'n *Innocence* itself must hang;
Must hang to please him, when of Spleen possest:
Must hang to bring forth an abortive Jest.

  Why liv'd he not ere *Star-chambers* had fail'd,   35
When Fine, Tax, Censure, all, but Law prevail'd;
Or Law, subservient to some murd'rous Will,
Became a Precedent to murder still?
Yet ev'n when Patriots did for Traytors bleed,
Was e'er the Job to such a Slave decreed;   40
Whose savage Mind wants sophist Art to draw,
O'er murder'd Virtue, specious Veils of Law?

  Why, *Student*, when the Bench your youth admits;
Where, though the worst, with the best rank'd he sits;
Where sound Opinions you attentive write,   45
As once a *Raymond*, now a *Lee* to cite,
Why pause you scornful when he dins the Court?
Note well his cruel Quirks and well report.
Let his own Words against himself point clear
Satire more sharp than Verse when most severe.   50

EPITAPH *On Mrs* JONES,

Grandmother to Mrs Bridget Jones, *of* Llanelly
in Carmarthenshire.

TEXTS: (1) *GM*, 41, 547.
 (2) *LM*, 41, 512.

IN Her, whose relicks mark this sacred earth,
 Shone all domestic and all social worth:

First, heav'n her hope with early offspring crown'd;
And thence a second race rose num'rous round.
Heav'n to industrious virtue blessing lent,   5
And all was competence, and all content.
    Though frugal care, in Wisdom's eye admir'd,
Knew to preserve what industry acquir'd;
Yet, at her board, with decent plenty blest,
The journeying stranger sat a welcome guest.   10
Prest on all sides, did trading neighbours fear
Ruin, which hung o'er exigence severe?
Farewel the friend, who spared th' assistant loan—
A neighbour's woe or welfare was her own.
Did piteous lazars oft attend her door?   15
She gave.—Farewel the parent of the poor:
Youth, age, and want, once chear'd, now sighing swell,
Bless her lov'd name, and weep a last farewell.

The Employment of BEAUTY.

A POEM

Addressed to Mrs BRIDGET JONES, a young Widow Lady of Llanelly, Carmarthenshire.

TEXTS: (1) *GM, 41, 324.
    (2) LM, 41, 302.

ONce *Beauty* wishing fond desire to move,
    Contriv'd to catch the heart of wand'ring *Love*.
Come purest atoms! *Beauty*, aid, implores;
For new soft texture leave etherial stores.
They come, they croud, they shining hues unfold,   5
Be theirs a form, which *Beauty*'s self shall mold!
To mold my charmer's form she all applied;
Whence *Cambria* boasts the birth of *Nature*'s pride.
    She calls the *Graces*—such is *Beauty*'s state,
Prompt at her call, th'obedient *Graces* wait.   10
First your fair feet they shape, and shape to please;

Each stands design'd for dignity and ease.
Firm, on these curious pedestals, depend
Two polish'd pillars; which, as fair, ascend;
From well-wrought knees, more fair, more large, they
       rise;   15
Seen by the *Muse*, though hid from *mortal* eyes.
More polish'd yet, your fabrick each sustains;
That purest temple where perfection reigns.
A small, sweet circle forms your faultless waist,
By *Beauty* shap'd, to be by *Love* embrac'd.   20
Beyond that less'ning waist, two orbs devise,
What swelling charms, in fair proportion, rise!
Fresh-peeping there, two blushing buds are found;
Each like a rose; which, lillies white surround.
There *feeling Sense*, let pitying sighs inspire;   25
'Till panting pity swell to warm desire:
Desire, though warm, is chast; each warmest kiss,
All rapture chast, when *Hymen* bids the bliss.
Rounding and soft, two taper arms descend;
Two snow-white hands, in taper fingers, end.   30
Lo! cunning *Beauty*, on each palm, designs
Love's fortune and your *own*, in mystic lines;
And lovely whiteness, either arm contains,
Diversified with azure-wand'ring veins;
The wand'ring veins conceal a gen'rous flood,   35
The purple treasure of cœlestial blood.
Rounding and white your neck, as curious, rears
O'er all a face, where *Beauty*'s self appears.
Her soft attendants smooth the spotless skin,
And, smoothly oval, turn the shapely chin;   40
The shapely chin, to *Beauty*'s rising face,
Shall, doubling gently, give a double grace.
And soon sweet-opening, rosy lips disclose
The well-rang'd teeth in lilly-whitening rows;
Here life is breath'd, and florid life assumes   45

---

15 more fair, more large] more large, more fair *LM*, 41.

A breath, whose fragrance vies with vernal blooms;
And two fair cheeks give modesty to raise
A beauteous blush at praise, though just the praise.
And nature now, from each kind ray, supplies
Soft clement smiles, and love-inspiring eyes;   *50*
New Graces, to those eyes, mild shades, allow;
Fringe their fair lids, and pencil either brow.
While *sense* of *Vision* lights up orbs so rare,
May none, but pleasing objects visit there!
Two little porches, (which, one sense empowers,   *55*
To draw rich scent from aromatic flow'rs.)
In structure neat, and deck'd with polish'd grace,
Shall equal first, then heighten *Beauty*'s face.
To *smelling sense*, Oh, may the flow'ry year,
Its first, last, choicest incense, offer here.   *60*
Transparent next, two curious crescents bound
The two-fold entrance of inspiring sound,
And, granting a new *power* of *sense* to *bear*,
New finer organs form each curious ear;
Form to imbibe what most the soul can move,   *65*
Music and Reason, Poesy and Love.
Next, on an open front, is pleasing wrought
A pensive sweetness, born of patient thought:
Above your lucid shoulders locks display'd,
Prone to descend, shall soften light with shade.   *70*
All, with a nameless air, and mien unite,
And, as you move, each movement is delight.
Tun'd is your melting tongue and equal mind,
At once by knowledge heighten'd and refin'd.

    The *Virtues* next to *Beauty*'s nod incline;   *75*
For, where they lend not light, she cannot shine:
Let these, the temp'rate *sense* of *taste*, reveal,
And give, while nature spreads the simple meal,
The palate pure, to relish health design'd,
From luxury as taintless as your mind.   *80*
The *Virtues*, Chastity and Truth, impart,
And mold to sweet benevolence your heart.

Thus *Beauty* finish'd—Thus she gains the sway,
And *Love* still follows where she leads the way.
From ev'ry gift of Heav'n, to charm is thine;   85
To love, to praise, and to adore, be mine.

VERSES *sent to Mrs* BRIDGET JONES, *with the* Wanderer, *a Poem; alluding to an Episode, where a young Man turns* Hermit, *for the Loss of his Wife* OLYMPIA.

TEXTS: (1) *GM, 41, 381.
(2) LM, 41, 358.

WHen with delight fond *Love* on *Beauty* dwelt;
    While this the *youth*, and that the *fair* exprest,
Faint was his joy compar'd to what I felt,
    When, in my angel BIDDY's presence, blest.

Tell her, my muse, in soft, sad, sighing breath,   5
    If she his piercing grief can pitying see,
Worse, than to him was his OLYMPIA's death,
    From her each moment's absence is to me.

VALENTINE's DAY,
A POEM *address'd to a young* Widow LADY.

TEXTS: (1) *GM, 42, 155–6.
(2) LM, 42, 146–7.

Chloe, to whom this poem is addressed, is Mrs Bridget Jones, to whom RS had addressed the two preceding ones. She had evidently rejected him as a proposed second husband, and he is writing now in some resentment, though not without hoping for a change of heart. Whether or not Chloe partially relented it is hard to say, but in his lines *To John Powell* he speaks of his still being Chloe's (l. 58).

Valentine's Day must have been written in the February of either 1741 or 1742. In it RS announces his intention of returning to England. By September 1742 he had certainly reached Bristol. Yet the other poems to Mrs Jones all belong to 1741.

ADieu ye rocks that witness'd once my flame;
Return'd my sighs and echo'd *Chloe*'s name!
Cambria farewell!—my *Chloe*'s charms no more
Invite my steps along *Llannelley*'s shore;
There no wild dens conceal voracious foes;   5
The beach no fierce, amphibious monster knows;
No Crockodile there flesh'd with prey appears,
And o'er that bleeding prey weeps cruel tears;
No false *Hyæna*, feigning human grief,
There murders him, whose goodness means relief: 10
Yet tides, conspiring with unfaithful ground,
(Though distant seen) with treach'rous arms, surround.
There quicksands, thick as beauty's snares, annoy,
Look fair to tempt, and, whom they tempt, destroy.
I watch'd the seas, I pac'd the sands with care,   15
Escap'd, but wildly rush'd on beauty's snare.
Ah!—better far, than by that snare o'erpower'd,
Had sands engulph'd me, or had seas devour'd.
    Far from that shore, where syren beauty dwells
And wraps sweet ruin in resistless spells;   20
From *Cambrian* plains; which *Chloe*'s lustre boast,
Me native *England* yields a safer coast.
Chloe farewell!—now, seas, with boist'rous pride,
Divide us, and will ever far divide;
Yet while each plant, which, vernal youth, resumes,   25
Feels the green blood ascend in future blooms;
While little feather'd songsters of the air
In woodlands tuneful woo and fondly pair,
The muse exults[,] to beauty tunes the lyre,
And willing Loves, the swelling notes inspire.   30
    Sure on this day, when hope attains success,
Bright *Venus* first did young *Adonis* bless.
Her charms not brighter *Chloe* sure than thine;
Though flush'd his youth, not more his warmth than mine.
Sequester'd far within a myrtle grove;   35

---

21 lustre] lustres *LM*, 42.

Whose blooming bosom courts retiring love;
Where a clear sun, the blue serene, displays,
And sheds, through vernal air, attemper'd rays;
Where flow'rs their aromatic incense bring,
And fragrant flourish in eternal spring;   40
There mate to mate each dove responsive cooes,
While this assents, as that enamour'd wooes.
There rills amusive, send from rocks around,
A solitary, pleasing, murm'ring sound;
Then form a limpid lake. The lake serene   45
Reflects the wonders of the blissful scene.
To love the birds attune their chirping throats,
And on each breeze immortal music floats.
There, seated on a rising turf is seen,
Graceful, in loose array, the *Cyprian* Queen;   50
All fresh and fair, all mild, as *Ocean* gave
The Goddess, rising from the azure wave,
Dishevel'd locks distill cœlestial dews,
And all her limbs, divine perfumes, diffuse.
Her voice so charms, the plumy, warb'ling throngs,   55
In list'ning wonder lost, suspend their songs.
Its sounds 'why loiters my *Adonis*?' cry,
'Why loiters my *Adonis*?' rocks reply.
'Oh, come away!' they thrice, repeating, say;
And *Echo* thrice repeats 'Oh, come away!'   60
Kind Zephyrs waft 'em to her lover's ears;
Who, instant at th' inchanting call, appears.
Her placid eye, where sparkling joy refines,
Benignant, with alluring lustre shines.
His locks, which, in loose ringlets, charm the view,   65
Float careless, lucid from their amber hue.
A myrtle wreath, her rosy fingers frame,
Which, from her hand, his polish'd temples claim;
His temples fair, a streaking beauty stains;
As smooth, white marble shines with azure veins.   70
He kneel'd. Her snowy hand, he tremb'ling seiz'd,
Just lifted to his lip, and gently squeez'd;

The meaning squeeze return'd, love caught its lore
And enter'd, at his palm, through every pore.
Then swell'd her downy breasts, till then enclos'd,   75
Fast-heaving, half conceal'd and half expos'd:
Soft she reclines. He, as they fall and rise,
Hangs, hov'ring o'er 'em, with enamour'd eyes,
And, warm'd, grows wanton—as he thus admir'd,
He pry'd, he touch'd, and, with the touch, was fir'd.   80
Half angry, yet half pleas'd, her frown beguiles
The boy to fear; but, at his fear, she smiles.
The youth less tim'rous and the fair less coy,
Supinely am'rous they reclining toy.
More am'rous still his sanguine meanings stole   85
In wistful glances, to her soft'ning soul;
In her fair eye her soft'ning soul he reads;
To freedom, freedom, boon to boon, succeeds.
With conscious blush, th' impassion'd charmer burns;
And, blush for blush, th' impassion'd youth returns.   90
They look, they languish, sigh with pleasing pain,
And wish and gaze, and gaze, and wish again.
'Twixt her white, parting bosom steals the boy,
And more than hope preludes tumultuous joy;
Through every vein the vig'rous transport ran,   95
Strung ev'ry nerve, and brac'd the boy to man.
Strugling, yet yielding, half o'erpower'd, she pants,
Seems to deny, and yet, denying, grants.
Quick, like the tendrils of a curling vine,
Fond limbs with limbs, in am'rous folds, entwine.   100
Lips press on lips, caressing and carest,
Now eye darts flame to eye, and breast to breast.
All she resigns, as dear desires incite,
And rapt he reach'd the brink of full delight.
Her waist compress'd in his exulting arms,   105
He storms, explores, and rifles all her charms;
Clasps in extatic bliss th' expiring fair,
And, thrilling, melting, nestling, riots there.
      How long the rapture lasts, how soon it fleets,

How oft it pauses, and how oft repeats;   110
What joys they both receive and both bestow,
Virgins may guess, but wives experienc'd know:
From joys, like these, (Ah, why deny'd to me?)
Sprung a fresh, blooming boy, my fair, from thee.
May he, a new *Adonis*, lift his crest,   115
In all the florid grace of youth confest!
First let him learn, to lisp your lover's name,
And, when he reads, here annual read my flame.
When beauty first shall wake his genial fire,
And the first, tingling sense excite desire;   120
When the dear object, of his peace possest,
Gains and still gains, on his unguarded breast:
Then may he say, as he this verse reviews,
So my bright mother charm'd the poet's muse.
His heart thus flutter'd oft 'twixt doubt and fear,   125
Lighten'd with hope, and sadden'd with despair.
Say, on some rival did she smile too kind?
Ah, read—what jealousy distracts his mind!
Smil'd she on him? He imag'd rays divine,
And gaz'd and gladden'd with a love like mine.   130
How dwelt her praise upon his raptur'd tongue?
Ah!—when she frown'd, what plaintive notes he sung?
And could she frown on him,—Ah, wherefore tell!
On him, whose only crime was loving well?
        Thus may thy son, his pangs with mine compare; 135
Then wish his mother had been kind as fair:
For him may Love, the myrtle wreath entwine;
Though the sad willow suits a woe like mine!
Ne'er may the filial hope, like me, complain!
Ah!—never sigh and bleed, like me, in vain!   140
        When death affords that peace which love denies,
Ah, no!—far other scenes my fate supplies;
When earth to earth my lifeless coarse is laid,
And o'er it hangs the yew or cypress shade:
When pale I flitt along the dreary coast,   145
An hapless lover's pining plaintive ghost;

Here annual on this dear returning day,
While feather'd choirs renew the melting lay;
May you, my fair, when you these ſtrains shall see,
Juſt spare one sigh, one tear to love and me,   *150*
Me, who, in absence or in death, adore
Those heavenly charms, I muſt behold no more.

---

148 While] when *LM*, 42.

To JOHN POWELL, *Esq; Barriſter of Law.*

TEXTS: (1) **GM*, 42, 490.
    (2) *LM*, 42, 454.

To the Author of the Gentleman's Magazine.

SIR,   Briſtol, Sept 10.

AS there are many, in England *and eſpecially in* Wales, *who bear*
the same name as the gentleman, who is the subjeɛ of the following
lines, it may not be improper to premise some particulars concerning   5
him to the publick. The chief reason, that induces me to this, is that
he is so truly amiable in the eyes of all, who have the honour of know-
ing him, that they will readily do the author the juſtice of acknow-
ledging that he has only aim'd to ſpeak of him as he is, without
embellishing, heightening, or attempting to heighten or embellish any   10
one part of so excellent a charaɛer.

    His eſtates lie in the counties of Brecon *and* Radnor. *He is*
the eldeſt son of the late Gabriel Powell, *Esq; of* Swansea *in*
the county of Glamorgan, *and brother to the truly worthy gentleman*
now of the same name and place; where is generally his residence.   15
He married the reliɛ of —— Herbert *Esq; of the* Fryars, *in the*
said county of Glamorgan.   *I am, Sir,*
                                            Yours &c. R.S.

I N me long absent, long with anguish fraught,
  In me, though silence long has deaden'd thought,

---

1 Gentleman's Magazine] LONDON MAGAZINE *LM*, 42.
2 *LM,* 42 *omits place and date.*
3 *who bear*] *that bear LM,* 42.   *9* *to speak*] *at ſpeaking LM,* 42.
16 *reliɛ of*] *Reliɛ of the late LM,* 42.

Yet mem'ry lives, and calls the muse's aid,
To snatch our friendship from oblivion's shade.
As soon the *Sun* shall cease the world to warm,   5
As soon *Llannelly's* fair* that world to charm,
As grateful sense of goodness, true like thine,
Shall e'er desert a breaſt so warm as mine.

      When imag'd *Cambria* ſtrikes my mem'ry's eye,
(*Cambria*, my darling scene!) I, sighing, cry   10
Where is my *Powell*? dear associate!—where?
To him I would unbosom ev'ry care;
To him, who early felt, from beauty, pain;
Gall'd in a plighted, faithless virgin's chain.
At length, from her ungen'rous fetters, freed,   15
Again he loves! he wooes! his hopes succeed!
But the gay bridegroom, ſtill by fortune croſt,
Is, inſtant, in the weeping wid'wer loſt.
Her, his sole joy! her from his bosom torn,
What feeling heart, but learns, like his, to mourn?   20
Can nature then, such sudden shocks, suſtain?
Nature thus ſtruck, all reason pleads in vain!
Though late, from reason yet he draws relief,
Dwells on her mem'ry; but dispels his grief.
Love, wealth and fame (tyrannic passions all!)   25
No more enflame him, and no more enthrall.
He seeks no more, in *Rufus'* hall, renown;
Nor envies pelf the jargon of the gown;
But pleas'd with competence, on rural plains,
His wisdom courts that ease, his worth obtains.   30
Would private jars, which sudden rise, encrease?
His candour smiles all discord into peace.
To party ſtorms is public weal resign'd?
Each ſteady, patriot virtue ſteers his mind.
Calm, on the beach, while madd'ning billows rave,   35

* *Mrs* Bridget Jones. [RS]

---

27 *Rufus' hall.* Westminster Hall, famous as a meeting place for lawyers, was
built by William Rufus.

He gains philosophy from ev'ry wave;
Science, from ev'ry object round, he draws;
From various nature and from nature's laws.
He lives o'er ev'ry past, historic age;
He calls forth ethicks from the fabled page.   40
Him evangelic truth, to thought, excites;
And him, by turns, each classic muse delights.
With wit well-natur'd; wit, that would disdain
A pleasure rising from another's pain;
Social to all, and most of bliss possest,   45
When most he renders all, around him, blest;
To unread squires illiterately gay;
Among the learn'd, as learned full as they;
With the polite, all, all-accomplish'd ease,
By nature form'd, without deceit, to please.   50
　　　Thus shines thy youth, and thus my friend, elate
In bliss as well as worth, is truly great.
Me still should ruthless fate, unjust, expose
Beneath those clouds, that rain unnumber'd woes;
Me, to some nobler sphere, should fortune raise,   55
To wealth conspicuous, and to laurel'd praise;
Unalter'd yet be love and friendship mine;
I still am *Chloe*'s, and I still am thine.

LONDON *and* BRISTOL *delineated.*

TEXTS: (1) *LONDON* and *BRISTOL* COMPAR'D. A SATIRE:
Written in NEWGATE, *Bristol*, BY THE LATE RICHARD SAVAGE, *Esq;*....
1744. (Published in December, 1743, by M. Cooper as noted in *GM*,
43, 672.)   [1744.]
　(2) *AN ACCOUNT OF THE LIFE OF Mr RICHARD
SAVAGE [by S. Johnson], 1744, pp. 168–73: 'LONDON *and*
BRISTOL *delineated.*'

RS wrote this poem whilst imprisoned in Bristol and sent it to Edward
Cave in London for publication (*Account*, pp. 424–6). Cave objected to
RS's wish to publish anonymously while determined to make his author-
ship of the poem widely known, and also to the word 'delineated' in

the title. Johnson explains that 'the author preferr'd [this title]...to that of *London and Bristol Compared*, which, when he began the piece, he intended to prefix to it'. Cave declined to publish the poem, and it was not published during RS's life. When, after RS's death, Johnson announced in the newspapers his intention of writing a biography of RS, he promised, among other things, a text of this poem (*General Evening Post*, 25 and 27 August 1743 (quoted in J. L. Clifford, *Young Sam Johnson* (1955), p. 262)). But he was anticipated by a rival. In December 1743, just as he had finished his work and was receiving payment for it, M. Cooper brought the poem out in a separate pamphlet with the earlier version of the title. Johnson makes no mention of this publication, though he could hardly have been ignorant of it. The two editions differ in more than their titles. There are thirteen variants, ten of them insignificant; the remaining three suggest that Johnson's text is probably the better of the two.

By 'delineate' RS understood 'to make the first draught of', as explained in Johnson's *Dictionary*. The word was not uncommon in his time in this sense. In 1712 the Rev. Wm. Guldwin published a poem entitled *Bristol Delineated*.

TWO Sea-port Cities mark *Britannia*'s Fame,
And these from Commerce different Honours claim.
What different Honours shall the Muses pay,
While one inspires and one untunes the Lay?
   Now silver *Isis* bright'ning flows along,   5
Echoing from *Oxford*'s Shore each classic Song;
Then weds with *Tame*; and these, O *London*, see
Swelling with naval Pride, the Pride of Thee!
Wide deep unsullied *Thames* meand'ring glides
And bears thy Wealth on mild majestic Tides.   10
Thy Ships, with gilded Palaces that vie,
In glitt'ring Pomp, strike wond'ring *China*'s Eye;
And thence returning bear, in splendid State,
To *Britain*'s Merchants, *India*'s eastern Freight.
India, her Treasures from her western Shores,   15
Due at thy Feet, a willing Tribute pours;
Thy warring Navies distant Nations awe,
And bid the World obey thy righteous Law.
Thus shine thy manly Sons of lib'ral Mind;

2 And these] They *1744*.

Thy Change deep-busied, yet as Courts refin'd; 20
Councils, like Senates that enforce Debate
With fluent Eloquence, and Reason's Weight.
Whose Patriot Virtue, lawless Pow'r controuls;
Their *British* emulating *Roman* Souls.
Of these the worthiest still selected stand, 25
Still lead the Senate, and still save the Land:
Social, not selfish, here, O Learning trace
Thy Friends, the Lovers of all human Race!
 In a dark Bottom sunk, O *Bristol* now,
With native Malice, lift thy low'ring Brow! 30
Then as some Hell-born Sprite, in mortal Guise,
Borrows the Shape of Goodness and belies,
All fair, all smug to yon proud Hall invite,
To feast all Strangers ape an Air Polite!
From *Cambria* drain'd, or *England*'s western Coast, 35
Not elegant yet costly Banquets boast!
Revere, or seem the Stranger to revere;
Praise, fawn, profess, be all Things but sincere;
Insidious now, our bosom Secrets steal,
And these with sly sarcastic Sneer reveal. 40
Present we meet thy sneaking treach'rous Smiles;
The harmless Absent still thy Sneer reviles;
Such as in Thee all Parts superior find;
The Sneer that marks the Fool and Knave combin'd.
When melting Pity wou'd afford Relief, 45
The ruthless Sneer that Insult adds to Grief.
What Friendship can'st thou boast? what Honours claim?
To Thee each Stranger owes an injur'd Name.
What Smiles thy Sons must in their Foes excite?
Thy Sons to whom all Discord is Delight; 50
From whom eternal mutual Railing flows;
Who in each other's Crimes, their own expose;
Thy Sons, though crafty, deaf to Wisdom's Call;

---

32 Borrows the Shape of Goodness] The Shape of Goodness borrows, *1744*.
39 Secrets] Secret *1744*.   40 these] then *1744*.

Despising all Men and despis'd by all.
Sons, while thy Clifs a ditch-like River laves,   55
Rude as thy Rocks, and muddy as thy Waves;
Of Thoughts as narrow as of Words immense;
As full of Turbulence as void of Sense:
Thee, Thee what senatorial Souls adorn?
Thy Natives sure wou'd prove a Senate's Scorn.   60
Do Strangers deign to serve Thee? what their Praise?
Their gen'rous Services thy Murmurs raise.
What Fiend malign, that o'er thy Air presides,
Around from Breaſt to Breaſt inherent glides,
And, as he glides, there scatters in a Trice   65
The lurking Seeds of ev'ry rank Device?
Let foreign Youths to thy Indentures run!
Each, each will prove, in thy adopted Son,
Proud, pert and dull—Though brilliant once from Schools,
Will scorn all Learning's as all Virtue's Rules;   70
And, though by Nature friendly, honeſt, brave,
Turn a sly, selfish, simp'ring, sharping Knave.
Boaſt petty-Courts, where 'ſtead of fluent Ease;
Of cited Precedents and learned Pleas;
'Stead of sage Council in the dubious Cause,   75
Attorneys chatt'ring wild, burlesque the Laws.
So shameless Quacks, who Doĉtor's Rights invade,
Of Jargon and of Poison form a Trade.
So canting Coblers, while from Tubs they teach,
Buffoon the Gospel they pretend to preach.   80
Boaſt petty Courts, whence Rules new Rigour draw;
Unknown to Nature's and to Statute Law;
Quirks that explain all saving Rights away,
To give th' Attorney and the Catch-poll Prey.
Is there where Law too rig'rous may descend?   85
Or Charity her kindly Hand extend?

55 Clifs] Clifts *1744.*
68 in thy adopted Son] thy true-adopted Son *1744.*
76 chatt'ring wild] chatter, and *1744.*
77 Doctor's Rights] Galen's Art *1744.*
81 whence Rules] whose Quirks *1744.*   86 Or] Does *1744.*

Thy Courts, that shut when Pity wou'd redress,
Spontaneous open to inflict Distress.
Try Misdemeanours!—all thy Wiles employ,
Not to chastise the Offender but destroy;   90
Bid the large lawless Fine his Fate foretell;
Bid it beyond his Crime and Fortune swell.
Cut off from Service due to kindred Blood
To private Welfare and to public Good,
Pitied by all, but thee, he sentenc'd lies;   95
Imprison'd languishes, imprison'd dies,

.   .   .   .

Boast swarming Vessels, whose *Plæbeian* State
Owes not to Merchants but Mechanics Freight.
Boast nought but Pedlar Fleets—In War's Alarms,
Unknown to Glory, as unknown to Arms.   100
Boast thy base **Tolsey*, and thy turn-spit Dogs;
Thy †*Hallier*'s Horses and thy human Hogs;
Upstarts and Mushrooms, proud, relentless Hearts;
Thou Blank of Sciences! Thou Dearth of Arts!
Such Foes as Learning once was doom'd to see;   105
Huns, *Goths*, and *Vandals* were but Types of Thee.
          Proceed, great *Bristol*, in all-righteous Ways,
And let one Justice heighten yet thy Praise;
Still spare the Catamite and swinge the Whore,
And be, whate'er *Gomorrah* was before.   110

* A Place where the Merchants used to meet to transact their Affairs before the
Exchange was erected. [RS]
    † Halliers are the Persons who drive or own the Sledges, which are here used
instead of Carts. [RS]

---

87 Courts] Chests *1744*.
96 dies,...] dies. *1744*.
99 Pedlar] peddling *1744*.
    101–2 The two footnotes appended to these lines, which do not occur in the
other text, may have been the work of Johnson rather than RS.
    103 Mushrooms] Muckworms *1744*.

APPENDIX

MISCELLANEOUS POEMS AND *TRANSLATIONS.*

TEXTS: (1) *MISCELLANEOUS POEMS AND *TRANSLATIONS.*
By several HANDS. *Publish'd by* RICHARD SAVAGE, *Son of the late Earl*
RIVERS.…MDCCXXVI. [*MP*, 1.] (No. 336 in A. E. Case's *Bibliography
of English Poetical Miscellanies* (Oxford, 1935). Published in February
1726.)
  (2) The same. (No. 336b in Case. Published in September 1726.)
[*MP*. 2.] This issue lacks the preface and part of the dedication.

For the complicated history of this volume, see *AB*, pp. 74–8, 94–5.

> *Multa Poëtarum veniet Manus, auxilio quæ*
> *Sit mihi—*   Hor.

[DEDICATION]

TO THE RIGHT HONOURABLE LADY *Mary Wortley Mountague.*

MADAM,

THAT I have the Ambition to address my Miscellany
to the Loveliest Patroness in the World, is a Presump- 5
tion, I confess, in *Me*, who have not the Honour to be known
to your Ladyship: But I have a Motive to it, still more
powerful than the flattering Hope of your condescending to
forgive me; I mean, the Goodness, Tenderness, and Sweetness of Disposition, so natural to your Ladyship. For, 10
since, in Nature, as well as in Painting, no Colours appear
so strong, or strike so forcibly, as the *contrasted*; Who better
qualified to distinguish how much *beyond Woman* your
Ladyship is adorn'd, and inspir'd, than One, who has been
unhappy from his Birth, by Absence of those *natural* 15
Qualities, from the Breast, He was born to depend on?
  Nature seems to have form'd my Mind, as inconsistently,
as Fortune has my Condition: She has given me a Heart that

Motto: Horace, *Satires*, 1, 4, 141–2.
10–21 For, since, in Nature…the Enemy of Flattery] *omitted in* MP, 2.

is as *proud* as my Father's; to a Rank in Life, almoſt as *low* as the Humanity of my Mother! But as Fortune is not more 20 my Enemy, than I am the Enemy of Flattery, I know not how I can forbear this Application to your Ladyship; because there is scarce a Possibility, that I shou'd say more than I believe, when I am speaking of your Excellence.

Since our Country has been honour'd by the Glory of 25 your *Wit*, as Elevated and Immortal as your *Soul*! It no longer remains a Doubt, whether your Sex have Strength of Mind, in Proportion to their Sweetness!—There is something in your *Verses*, as diſtinguish'd as your *Air*!—They are as ſtrong as Truth; as deep as Reason; as clear as Inno- 30 cence; and as smooth as Beauty!—They contain a nameless, and peculiar, Mixture, of Grace, and Force; which is at once so movingly serene, and so majeſtically lovely, that it is too amiable to appear any where, but in your *Eyes*, and your *Writings*. 35

Forgive me, Madam, if (while I feel the divine Influence of your *Spirit*, which no Words but Yours can *diſplay*, and no Form but Yours cou'd have enshrin'd) I presume to lay before you such unpardonable Compositions as my own: Those of my Friends will, I doubt not, prove worthy of 40 your Perusal; and, in some Measure, atone the Faults of His, who begs Permission to subscribe Himself,

> *With the utmoſt Devotion,*
> *MADAM,*
> *Your Ladyship's moſt Humble,* 45
> *and moſt Obedient Servant,*
> RICHARD SAVAGE.

---

22 to your Ladyship] *omitted in MP*, 2.

PREFACE*

Crudelis Mater magis, an Puer improbus Ille?
Improbus Ille Puer, crudelis tu quoque Mater.   Virg.

MY Readers, I am afraid, when they observe *Richard Savage* join'd so close, and so constantly, to *Son of the late Earl Rivers*, will impute to a ridiculous Vanity, what is the Effect of an unhappy Necessity, which my hard Fortune has thrown me under—I am to be pardon'd for adhering a ⁵ little tenaciously to my Father, because my Mother will allow me to be No-body; and has almost reduced me, among heavier Afflictions, to That uncommon kind of Want, which the *Indians* of *America* complain'd of at our first settling among them; when they came to beg *Names* of the *English*, ¹⁰ *because* (said They) *we are Poor Men of ourselves, and have none we can lay Claim to.*

The Good-Nature of Those, to whom I have not the Honour to be known, would forgive me the ludicrous Turn of this Beginning, if they knew but how little Reason I have ¹⁵ to be merry.—It was my Misfortune to be Son of the abovemention'd Earl, by the late Countess of *Macclesfield*, (now Widow of Colonel *Henry Bret*;) whose Divorce, on Occasion of the Amour which I was a Consequence of, has left something on Record, which I take to be very remarkable; and it ²⁰ is This: Certain of our Great Judges, in their *temporal* Decisions, act with a *spiritual* Regard to the *Levitical Divinity*; and in particular, to the *Ten Commandments*: Two of which seem, in my Case, to have visibly influenced their Opinions. —*Thou shalt not commit Adultery*, pointed fullest on my ²⁵ Mother: But, as to *The Lord's visiting the Sins of the Fathers on the Children*, it was consider'd as what cou'd regard *me* only: And, for that Reason, I suppose, it had been inconsistent with the Rules of Sanctity, to assign Provision out of

---

*The entire Preface was omitted in MP, 2. Motto: Virgil, *Eclogues*, VIII, 49–50.

1–3 The italicized words in these lines are quoted from RS's title-page. He repeated this description of himself in the heading to each of his poems in *MP*.

my Mother's return'd Estate, for Support of an Infant *30* Sinner.

Thus, while *legally* the Son of one Earl, and *naturally* of another, I am, *nominally*, No-body's Son at all: For the Lady, having given me *too much Father*, thought it but an equivalent Deduction, to leave me *no Mother*, by way of Ballance.—So *35* I came sported into the World, a kind of Shuttlecock, between Law and Nature:—If Law had not beaten me back, by the Stroke of an Act, on purpose, I had now been *above Wit*, by the Privilege of a Man of Quality: Nay, I might have preserved, into the Bargain, the Lives of *Duke* *40* *Hamilton* and *Lord Mohun*, whose Dispute arose from the Estate of That Earl *of Macclesfield*, whom (but for the mention'd Act) I must have *call'd Father*.—And, if Nature had not struck me off, with a stranger Blow than Law did, the other Earl, who was most *emphatically* my Father, cou'd *45* never have been told, I was *dead*, when He was about to enable me, by his *Will*, to have *liv'd*, to some purpose. An unaccountable Severity of a *Mother*! whom I was then not old enough to have deserv'd it from: And by which I am a single unhappy Instance, among That Nobleman's Natural *50* Children; and thrown, friendless, on the World, without Means of supporting *myself*; and without Authority to apply to Those, whose Duty I know it is to support me.

Thus, however ill qualified I am to *live by my Wits*, I have the best Plea in the World for attempting it; since it is *55* too apparent, that I was *Born to it*.—Having wearied my Judgment with fruitless Endeavours to be *happy*; I gave the Reins to my Fancy, that I might learn, at least, to be *Easy*.

But I cease awhile to speak of *myself*, that I may say something of my *Miscellany*—I was furnish'd, by the Verses of my *60* Friends, with *Wit* enough to deserve a Subscription; but I wanted another much more profitable Quality, which shou'd

---

40 Cf. *Another* [*Littany*], ll. 17–18. The Duke of Hamilton and Lord Mohun had married nieces of the Earl of Macclesfield, who left all his property to the latter. Hamilton instituted a suit in Chancery, in the course of which an insult was given. In the duel that followed, both principals were killed.

have imbolden'd me to solicite it: By means of which natural Defe&, (Another of my Wants, that, I *hope*, may be imputed to my Mother!) I had met with little Encouragement, but 65 for the Endeavours of some few Gentlemen, in my Behalf, who were generous enough to consider my Ill-fortune, as a Merit, that intitled me to their Notice.

Among These I am particularly indebted to the Author of the *Plain-Dealers*, who was pleas'd, in Two of his Papers, 70 (which I intreat his Pardon, for reprinting, before my Miscellany) to point out my unhappy Story to the World, with so touching a Humanity, and so good an Effe&, that many Persons of Quality, of all Ranks, and of both Sexes, distinguish'd themselves with the Promptness he had 75 hinted to the Noble-minded; and not staying till they were applied to, sent me the Honour of their Subscriptions, in the most liberal, and handsome Manner, for Encouragement of my Undertaking.

I ought here to acknowledge several Favours from Mr. 80 *Hill*, whose Writings are a shining Ornament of this Miscellany; but I wave detaining my Readers, and beg leave to refer 'em to a Copy of Verses call'd the *Friend* (page 59) which I have taken the Liberty to address to that Gentleman.

To return to the Lady, my Mother.—Had the celebrated 85 Mr. *Locke* been acquainted with her Example, It had certainly appear'd in his *Chapter* against *Innate Practical Principles*; because it wou'd have compleated his Instances of Enormities: Some of which, though not exa&ly in the Order that he mentions 'em, are as follows—*Have there not* 90 *been* (says he) *whole Nations, and those of the most civiliz'd People, amongst whom, the Exposing their Children, to perish by*

---

82 Wave. The usual spelling in the eighteenth century of *waive*.

83 page 59] page 126 MP.

86–8 The reference is to *An Essay Concerning Human Understanding* (1690), by John Locke. My references are to the ninth edition, 'with large Additions' (2 vols. 1726). Chapter iii, book i, is entitled: 'No Innate Practical Principles.'

90 ff. 'Have there not been whole Nations, and those of the most Civilized People, amongst whom, the exposing their Children, and leaving them in the Fields, to perish by Want or Wild Beasts, has been the Practice, as little condemned or scrupled as the begetting them?' (i, 34).

Want or wild Beasts, has been a Practice as little condemn'd, or scrupled, as the begetting them? Were I inclinable to grow serious, I cou'd easily prove that I have not been more 95 gently dealt with by Mrs. *Bret*; but if this is any way Foreign to my Case, I shall find a nearer Example in the whimsical One that ensues.

It is familiar (says the afore-cited Author) *among the* MENGRELIANS, *a People professing Christianity, to bury* 100 *their Children alive without Scruple*—There are indeed sundry Sects of *Christians*, and I have often wonder'd which cou'd be my *Mamma*'s; But now I find she piously professes, and practises *Christianity* after the manner of the *Mengrelians*; she industriously obscured me, when my Fortune depended 105 on my being known, and, in that Sense, she may be said to have buried me alive; and sure, like a *Mengrelian*, she must have committed the Action without Scruple, for she is a Woman of Spirit, and can see the Consequence without Remorse. *The Caribees* (continues my Author) *were wont to* 110 *castrate their Children, in order to fat and eat 'em*—Here indeed I can draw no Parallel; for to speak but Justice of the Lady, she never contributed ought to have me pamper'd, but always promoted my being starved: Nor did she, ev'n in my Infancy, betray Fondness enough to be suspected of a 115 Design to devour me; but, on the contrary, not enduring me ever to approach Her, offer'd a Bribe to have had me ship'd off in an odd Manner, to one of the Plantations—When I was about *Fifteen*, Her Affection began to awake, and had I but known my Interest, I had been handsomely provided for: 120 In short I was solicited to be bound Apprentice to a very honest and reputable Occupation—a *Shoemaker*; An Offer, which, I undutifully rejected. I was, in fine, unwilling to understand her in a literal Sense, and hoped, that like the Prophets of Old, she might have hinted her Mind in a kind 125

99 ff. 'It is familiar among the Mengrelians, a People professing Christianity, to bury their Children alive without Scruple' (1, 34).

110 ff. 'The *Caribees* were wont to Geld their Children, on purpose to Fat and Eat them' (1, 34).

of Parable, or proverbial way of speaking: as thus—that
one Time or other I might, on due Application, have the
Honour of *taking the Length of her Foot.*

Mr. *Locke* mentions *another Set of People, that dispatch their
Children, if a pretended Astrologer declares 'em to have unhappy* 130
Stars.—Perhaps my *Mamma* has procur'd some *cunning Man*
to calculate my Nativity; or having had some ominous Dream,
which preceeded my Birth, the dire Event may have appear'd
to her in the dark and dreary bottom of a *China* Cup, where
Coffee-stains are often consulted for Prophecies, and held as 135
infallible as were the Leaves of the ancient *Sybils.*—To be
partly serious: I am rather willing to wrong her Judgment,
by suspecting it to be tainted a little with the Tenets of
Superstition, than suppose she can be Mistress of a sear'd
Conscience, and act on no Principle at all.   140

---

129 *ff.* 'Do they not still, in some Countries, put them into the same Graves with
their Mothers, if they die in Child-birth; or despatch them, if a pretended Astrologer
declares them to have unhappy Stars?' (1, 34).

INDEX

Addison, Joseph (1672–1719); poet and essayist, 22, 49, 71, 119

Anne, Queen (1665–1714), 22

Argyle, John Campbell, Duke of (1680–1743); friend and neighbour of Pope; patron of Thomas Killigrew, 76

Atterbury, Francis (1662–1732); Bishop of Rochester and Dean of Westminster, 31, 35

Augusta, Princess, of Saxe Gotha (d. 1772); Princess of Wales, 223

Bacon, Francis (1561–1626); philosopher, 4, 107, 139, 178

Balderston, Katharine Canby, 114

Bangor, Bishop of, *see* Hoadly, Benjamin

Barrel, —; in 1717 Proctor for the Chapter of Rochester; member of the Committee of the Lower House of Convocation that censured the Bishop of Bangor, 32

Benson, Martin (1689–1752); chaplain to the Prince of Wales; became Bishop of Gloucester in 1735, 191

Betterton, Thomas (*c.* 1635–1710); actor, 41

Birch, Thomas (1705–66); 1732–43, Rector of Ulting in Essex; 1735, F.R.S.; assisted Edward Cave with *GM*; editor of the *General Dictionary*, 66, 170, 188, 212, 234, 239, 241

Bisse, Thomas (1675–1731); in 1716 Chancellor of Hereford; member of the Committee of the Lower House of Convocation that censured the Bishop of Bangor, 32

Bolingbroke, Henry St John, Viscount (1678–1751); Tory and Jacobite; 1715–23 in exile; after 1723 neighbour and friend of Pope, 22, 73, 239, 243

Boyer, Abel (1667–1729); author of the Whig periodical *The Political State* and other political and historical compilations, 243

Brett, Anne (Mrs Henry) (? 1668–1753); formerly Lady Macclesfield, 87–92, 93, 216, 265–9

Browne, Moses (1704–87); poet and fisherman; author of a poem in honour of RS entitled *The Fate of the Muse*, 73

Buchanan, George (1506–82); Scottish humanist, 4, 237

Bullock, Christopher (? 1690–1724); actor and dramatist; 1710–14 at Drury Lane, 1714–24 at Lincoln's Inn Fields, 40, 74

Burnet, Gilbert (1690–1726); 1715–26, Prebendary of Salisbury; son of Gilbert Burnet (1643–1715), Bishop of Salisbury, 38

Burton, Robert (1577–1640); miscellaneous writer, 114

Cadell, Thomas (d. *c.* 1791); Bristol bookseller; father of Johnson's London bookseller, 9

Cadière, Catherine; French girl, 195

Calamy, Edmund (1671–1732); dissenting minister and supporter of the divines ejected in 1662, 31

Cannon, Robert (1663–1722); Archdeacon of Norfolk; member of the Committee of the Lower House of Convocation that censured the Bishop of Bangor, 32

Carlisle, William Nicolson, Bishop of (1655–1727), 37, 38

Caroline, Queen (1683–1737); wife of George II, 92, 169–72, 179–81, 183–4, 205–8, 208–10, 218–19, 220, 234–7

Case, Arthur Ellicott, 263

Cave, Edward (1691–1754); printer and publisher of *GM*; used the pseudonym 'Sylvanus Urban', 8–9, 9, 80, 170, 212, 256–7

Charles V (1500–58); Holy Roman Emperor, 135

Charles VI (1685–1740); Holy Roman Emperor, 85

Charles XII (1682–1718); King of Sweden, 85

Charles Edward, Prince (1720–1788); the Young Pretender; son of James, the Old Pretender, and grandson of James II, 21

Charteris, Francis (1675–1732); famous card sharper and swindler, satirized by Pope and RS as 'Charters', 241

Chetwood, William Rufus (d. 1766); prompter at Drury Lane Theatre and, for a while, a bookseller, 40, 164

'Chloe', see Jones, Bridget (junior)

Churchill, Charles (1656–1714); brother of the Duke of Marlborough; took Mrs Oldfield into keeping after the death of Arthur Maynwaring, 164, 166, 168

Churchill, John, Duke of Marlborough (1650–1722); suspected of Jacobite sympathies, though he had deserted James II in order to support William of Orange; his career was over by 1711, 17, 74, 164, 185, 241

Cibber, Colley (1671–1757); actor and dramatist; became poet laureate in 1730, 168–9

Cibber, Theophilus (1703–58); actor and dramatist; son of Colley Cibber, 48

Cicero, Marcus Tullius ('Tully'); Roman orator, 4, 136

Clarke, Samuel (1675–1729); Queen Caroline's favourite divine; admirer of Newton; advocate of the use of reason and common sense in religion; member of the latitudinarian party, 70, 178, 191

Clifford, James Lowry, 257

'Clio', see Sansom, Martha Fowke

Cockburn (or Cockbourn), John (1652–1729); once a nonjuror; participated in the Bangorian Controversy on the high church side, 34

'Codex, Dr.', see Gibson, Edmund

Coke, Roger (fl. 1696); historical writer, 67

Cole, William (1714–82); one of Horace Walpole's antiquarian correspondents, 94

Collins, William (1721–59); poet, 19, 24

Compton, Sir Spencer (? 1673–1743); brother-in-law to the Duke of Dorset; Young's fourth satire was dedicated to him, 76

Comyns, Sir John (d. 1740); succeeded Sir Francis Page in 1726 as Baron of the Exchequer; in 1736 transferred to Common Pleas; and in 1738 became Lord Chief Baron of the Exchequer, 244

Concanen, Matthew (1701–49); poet and journalist; contributor to MP, 67, 73

Congreve, William (1670–1729); dramatist; in 1725 he had been unproductive for twenty-five years, 77, 79, 168

Cooke, Thomas (1703–56); poet, contributor to MP, 71

Cooper, Mary; bookseller, 8, 256–7

Cowper, Mary, Countess (1685–1724); 24

Cromwell, Oliver (1599–1658); Protector, 240

Cummins, see Comyns, John

Curll, Edmund (1675–1747); bookseller noted for scurrilous and scandalous publications, 70, 182, 192, 241

Davies, Richard (1675–1746); Proctor for the chapter of St Asaph; member of the Committee of the Lower House of Convocation that censured the Bishop of Bangor, 32

Dawson, Thomas; Proctor for the chapter of Sarum; member of the Committee of the Lower House of Convocation that censured the Bishop of Bangor, 32

Defoe, Daniel (1660–1731); journalist and novelist, 242

Dennis, John (1657–1734); critic and dramatist; at one time he had lived 'in great familiarity' with RS, 73, 182

Derwentwater, James Radcliffe, Earl of (1689–1716); a grandson of Charles I because his mother, Mary Tudor, was a natural daughter of Charles II; captured at the Battle of Preston, 16, 22–3, 24, 25

Dodington, George Bubb, Baron Melcombe (1691–1762); Whig political boss and Lord of the Treasury; perhaps the original of Pope's 'Bufo'; received dedications from Young, Thomson, Fielding, Whitehead, Bentley, etc., 82–3, 85

Dorset, Lionel Cranfield Sackville, Duke of (1688–1765); patron to Edward Young; brother-in-law to Sir Spencer Compton; according to

272

Dorset (*cont.*)

Account (p. 337) at one time friend and patron to RS, 76

Duck, Stephen (1705–56); poet; protégé of Queen Caroline, who made him keeper of her library (Merlin's Cave) at Richmond, 207

Dunton, John (1659–1733); projector, pamphleteer, and bookseller, 39

Dyer, John (1699–1757); poet and friend of RS; contributor to *MP*, 52–3, 55–6

Echard, Laurence (*c.* 1670–1730); historian, 67, 240

'Egerton, William'; possibly an alias of Edmund Curll (q.v.), 41

Eliot, Thomas Stearns, 2

Eusden, Laurence (1688–1730); poet laureate, 73, 170

Evans, Thomas (1742–84); bookseller; member of the syndicate that published Johnson's *Lives of the Poets*, 10, 189

Fénelon, François de Salignac de la Mothe (1651–1715); Bishop of Cambrai; famed as preacher, 190

Fenton, Elijah (1683–1730); schoolmaster and poet; assistant to Pope, 106

Fortescue, William (1678–1749); friend to Pope; became justice of Common Pleas in 1738; Pope alludes to his humanity in a letter, 26 March 1736 (*Correspondence*, IV, 6–8), 244

Foster, James (1697–1753); popular dissenting clergyman; friend of James Thomson and Bishop Rundle, 188–90, 191

Frederick Louis, Prince of Wales (1707–51); founded opposition court; supported by Bolingbroke, 5, 215, 219–20, 223, 233

Freind, Robert (1667–1751); Proctor for the chapter of Oxford and headmaster of Westminster School; member of the Committee of the Lower House of Convocation that censured the Bishop of Bangor, 32

Gascoigne, Richard (d. 1716); 'His Grandfather was kill'd in the Service of King *Charles* I, and his Father in the Service of the unfortunate King *James* II, at the Siege of Limerick'

(Robert Patton, *History of the Rebellion*, 2nd ed., 1717, p. 150), 24

Gay, John (1685–1732); poet and dramatist, 19, 20, 66–7, 74–5

Genest, John, 47, 48

George I (1660–1727), 16–26, 32, 82–7, 223

George II (1683–1760), 82–7, 88–9, 170, 172, 177, 181, 223, 234–7

Gibbs, James (1682–1754); architect of St Martin-in-the-Fields, the steeple of St Clement Danes, and other well-known buildings, 134

Gibson, Edmund (1669–1748); Bishop of London; known as 'Dr. Codex' on account of his monumental *Codex Juris Ecclesiastici*; he was Walpole's chief adviser on church policy between 1723 and 1736, 189, 191, 193, 196, 201, 202, 203, 204

Girard, J.-B.; jesuit, 195

Girling, Robert; spy, 15–16

Goldsmith, Oliver (1728–74); poet, dramatist, and miscellaneous writer, 134

Greene, Donald Johnson, 173

Gretton, R. H., 210

Guldwin, William; poet and priest, 257

Halifax, Charles Montagu, Earl of (1661–1715); patron to Pope, Congreve, Addison, Newton, Prior; one of the models for Pope's 'Bufo', 79

Hall, John (d. 1716); Jacobite; called 'Mad Jack Hall of Otterbourn', 16, 24

Halley, Edmund (1656–1742); astronomer, 101

Hamilton, James Douglas, Duke of (1658–1712), 266

Hancocke, John; pamphleteer, 69

Harley, Robert, Earl of Oxford (1661–1724); Tory statesman, 242

Harris, Thomas (d. 1820); proprietor and manager of Covent Garden Theatre, 10

Hart, George; bailiff of Burford, 210

Harte, Walter (1709–74); occasional poet; friend of Pope; later tutor to Mr Stanhope, natural son of the Earl of Chesterfield, 187–8

Haywood, Eliza (1690–1756); novelist and dramatist; friend and probably mistress of RS, 43–4, 50–1, 66, 73

Hendel, George Frederick (1685–1759); composer, 139

Henley, John (1692–1756); mountebank preacher; called 'The Orator', 201

Hertford, Frances Seymour, Countess of (1699–1754), 19

Hickes, George (1642–1715); nonjuror; titular Bishop of Thetford, 27

Hildyard, Samuel, see Hilliard, Samuel

Hill, Aaron (1685–1750); poet, translator, projector; joint author of the *Plain Dealer*; contributor to *MP*, 1, 3, 8, 40, 46, 47–8, 59–60, 60–3, 63, 74–5, 80, 87–8, 95, 106, 169–70, 215–18, 219–20, 267

Hill, Mrs Aaron (d. 1731), 63–4

Hilliard, Samuel; a Samuel Hilliard was prebendary of Lincoln (J. Nichols, *Literary Anecdotes*, 1812, I, 265), 34

Hoadly, Benjamin (1676–1761); from 1715 to 1721 Bishop of Bangor; leader of latitudinarian party and one of the chief Whig appointees to the bench; a voluminous controversialist, 27–40, 196

Hobbes, Thomas (1588–1679); philosopher, 188–9

Hogarth, William (1697–1764); artist, 4

Howard, Henrietta (1681–1767); later Countess of Suffolk; lady in waiting to Princess Caroline and patroness of Gay, 76

Howe (or How), John Grubham (1657–1722); poet and politician, 27

Howel[l], William (c. 1638–83); historian, 67, 69

Hughes, Helen Sard; 19

Jacob, Giles (1686–1744); compiler, 27

James Francis Edward, Prince (1688–1766); the 'Old Pretender'; called 'James III' and 'Chevalier de St George'; son of James II, 17–19, 22–5, 241

Johnson, Samuel (1709–84); essayist, editor, and poet (NOTE. The following references include citations of his *Account*), 1, 2, 4, 5, 7, 8, 9, 10, 19, 26, 114, 164, 170, 174, 183, 187, 191, 220, 238, 239, 243–4, 256–7, 260

Joliffe, John (d. 1758); nephew of Sir William Joliffe, one of the directors of the Bank of England; a landed gentleman, belonging to an ancient family, 81–2

Jones, Bridget (senior) (d. 1741); grandmother of the Mrs Bridget Jones to whom RS wrote three poems, 245–6

Jones, Bridget (junior) (1713–1780); 'Chloe'; a famous beauty belonging to one of the best Welsh families, living in Llanelly, near Swansea; her first husband, Thomas, died in January 1740, 245, 246–9, 249, 249–54, 255, 256

Keene, Theophilus (?1680–1718); actor-manager: 1704, Drury Lane; 1714, Lincoln's Inn Fields, 40–1

Kenmure, William Gordon, Viscount (d. 1716); Commander-in-Chief of the Scottish Jacobites in the '15, 23

Kennett, White (1660–1728); Dean of Peterborough, 37

Knight, Mrs John (d. 1756); sister of Pope's friend, Secretary Craggs; her husband was J.P. and M.P., 187–8

Law, William (1686–1761); skilled controversialist; author of *The Serious Call*, 34

Lee, William (1688–1754); in 1737, Lord Chief Justice, 245

Leeuwenhoek, Anthony van (1632–1723); Dutch microscopist, 77

Locke, John (1632–1704); philosopher; 4, 107, 178, 267–9

Longinus, Cassius (c. 213–73); Greek philosopher and critic, 181

Macclesfield, Charles Gerard, Earl of (1659–98); claimed by RS as his legal father, 266

Macclesfield, Lady, see Brett, Anne

Mackartney, Lieutenant-General George (?1660–1730); second in the duel between the Duke of Hamilton and Lord Mohun; he was accused of having treacherously stabbed the wounded Duke, was brought to trial only in June 1716, and, though found guilty, was let off with a branding, 16, 26

McKillop, Alan Dugald, 8, 95, 102, 105, 134, 220

Mallet, David (?1705–65); poet, contributor to *MP*, 102, 106

Mar, John Erskine, Earl of (1675–1732); leader of the '15; escaped with the Pretender to France, 22, 33

Marlborough, Duke of, see Churchill, John

Maynwaring, Arthur (1668–1712); influential Whig journalist; Mrs Oldfield was his mistress for eight or nine years, 164

Mesnager, Nicolas (1658–1714); French diplomat; 1711–12, he was in London engaged in secret negotiations leading to the Treaty of Utrecht, 241–2

Mitchell, Joseph (1684–1738); minor poet and dramatist, 73

Mohun, Charles, Lord (? 1675–1712); heir to Lord Macclesfield, 266

Montagu, Lady Mary Wortley (1689–1726); letter writer, 63, 70, 139, 263–4

Moore, Cecil Albert, 5, 220, 233

Moore, John Robert, 242

Morland, George (1763–1804); painter, 4

Moss, Robert (1666–1729); Dean of Ely; member of the Committee of the Lower House of Convocation that censured the Bishop of Bangor, 31–2

Mountague, see Montagu, Lady Mary Wortley

Newton, Sir Isaac (1642–1727); physicist, 4, 101, 139, 147, 179

Nichols, John (1745–1826); printer and antiquary, 9

Nicolson, Marjorie Hope, 101, 110

North, Francis, Baron Guilford (1704–90); succeeded in 1734 to title of Lord North, which he held in addition to that of Baron Guilford, 170

Oglethorpe, James Edward (1696–1785); he took out a charter for a colony in Georgia in which slavery was to be forbidden; on several occasions he gave RS financial help, 233

Oldfield, Anne (1683–1730); actress; benefactress to RS, 41–3, 139, 164–9

Oldmixon, John (1673–1742); miscellaneous writer; author of Critical History of England (1724), 67, 243

Orange, Anne, Princess of (1709–59); eldest daughter of George II, 183–7

Orange, William, Prince of (d. 1751); hereditary stadholder of the Netherlands; in 1734 married Anne, eldest daughter of George II, 183–7

Ormonde, James Butler, Duke of (1665–1745); Jacobite general in the '15; fled to France with the Pretender and was attainted, 22

Oxburgh, Henry (d. 1716); Jacobite; executed at Tyburn after the '15; his head affixed to Temple Bar, 24

Page, Sir Francis (c. 1661–1741); one of the Justices of the King's Bench; presided over RS's trial for murder in 1727, 244–5

Paul, William (1678–1716); Jacobite chaplain in the '15, 16, 24

Peter the Great, Tsar of Russia (1672–1725), 105

Philips, Ambrose (? 1675–1749); poet and dramatist, 3, 45, 72

Philips, John; perhaps a pseudonym for George Sewell (1690–1726), 32–3

Pope, Alexander (1688–1744); poet, 1, 3, 28, 71, 72, 74–5, 75, 77, 83, 107–8, 147, 164, 188, 210–11, 215; his Dunciad cited, 20, 73

Powell, John (1705–69); prominent barrister of Swansea with distinguished family connections, 254–6

Raymond, Robert (1673–1733); Lord Chief Justice, 245

Rivers, Richard Savage, Earl (c. 1660–1712); alleged natural father of RS, 46, 263, 265

Rochford, Bessy [Savage], Countess of (1699–1746); natural daughter of Earl Rivers and hence half-sister of RS if his claims are valid; married the Earl of Rochford in 1714, 46–7

Rochford, Frederick Nassau-de-Zulestein, Earl of (1683–1738); married Bessy Savage, natural daughter of Earl Rivers, in 1714, 46

Roscius, Quintus (c. 126–62 B.C.); Roman comic actor, 41

Rowe, Elizabeth Singer (1674–1737); poetess; friend of Thomson's patroness, the Countess of Hertford, 136

Rufinus; Byzantine poet, 237

Ruhe, Edward Lehman, 66

Rundle, Thomas (c. 1688–1743); in 1734 nominated to see of Gloucester; his appointment opposed by Gibson, Bishop of London, on grounds of deism; in 1735 made Bishop of Derry instead; friend and patron of Thomson, 191, 202, 204

Rutland, Bridget, Duchess of (d. 1734), 64–6